DISCOURSES OF BREXI

"Addressing a wide range of data and methods, *Discourses of Brexit* decodes the political, social and discursive strategies that shaped the 'No' vote on the British EU referendum . . . a valuable contribution to both political science and discourse studies."

Salomi Boukala, *Panteion University of Social & Political Sciences, Greece*

"We have been told that 'Brexit means Brexit'. This book finds that it means rather more than that. Contributors explore the many things Brexit has been made to mean across genres and media. [. . .] It will be of interest and use to political scientists, media scholars and many others concerned with the future of political debate in Britain."

Alan Finlayson, *University of East Anglia, UK*

Discourses of Brexit provides a kaleidoscope of insights into how discourse influenced the outcome of the EU referendum and what discourses have sprung up as a result of it. Working with a wide variety of data, from political speeches to Twitter, and a wide range of methods, *Discourses of Brexit* presents the most thorough examination of the discourses around the British EU referendum and related events. It provides a comprehensive understanding of the discursive treatment of Brexit, while also providing detailed investigations of how Brexit has been negotiated in different contexts. *Discourses of Brexit* is key reading for all students and researchers in language and politics, discourse analysis and related areas, as well as anyone interested in developing their understanding of the referendum.

Veronika Koller is Reader in Discourse Studies at Lancaster University, UK.

Susanne Kopf is a Research and Teaching Assistant at WU Vienna University of Economics and Business, Austria.

Marlene Miglbauer is Senior Lecturer in English Language, Linguistics and E-Learning at the University of Teacher Education Burgenland, Austria.

DISCOURSES OF BREXIT

Edited by Veronika Koller, Susanne Kopf and Marlene Miglbauer

LONDON AND NEW YORK

First published 2019
by Routledge
2 Park Square, Milton Park, Abingdon, Oxon OX14 4RN

and by Routledge
52 Vanderbilt Avenue, New York, NY 10017

Routledge is an imprint of the Taylor & Francis Group, an informa business

British Library Cataloguing-in-Publication Data
A catalogue record for this book is available from the British Library

Library of Congress Cataloging-in-Publication Data
A catalog record has been requested for this book

ISBN: 978-1-138-48554-9 (hbk)
ISBN: 978-1-138-48555-6 (pbk)
ISBN: 978-1-351-04186-7 (ebk)

Typeset in Bembo
by Swales & Willis Ltd, Exeter, Devon, UK

Printed and bound in Great Britain by
TJ International Ltd, Padstow, Cornwall

Veronika Koller dedicates this book to her son, Ayo, British child of immigrant parents.

Susanne Kopf dedicates this book to her parents.

Marlene Miglbauer dedicates this book to Raphael.

CONTENTS

TABLES

FIGURES

ACKNOWLEDGEMENTS

The editors would like to thank Piotr Cap, Greg Myers and Stephanie Schnurr for reviewing the editors' contributions to this volume. We would also like to thank Gerlinde Mautner for her helpful comments on many of the chapters.

CONTRIBUTORS

Samuel Bennett is Assistant Professor at Adam Mickiewicz University, Poland. His research centres around discursive constructions of migrant integration, community, (non-)belonging and exclusion, and populist politics. He is the author of *Constructions of Migrant Integration in British Public Discourse* (2018) and serves on the board of a migrant integration NGO in Poland.

Email: sbennett@wa.amu.edu.pl

Catherine Bouko is Assistant Professor in Multilingual Communication/French at Ghent University, Belgium. Her research interests are citizenship, identity and ideology in the digital world. She is developing a multilingual and multimodal approach to social media content, with her main research methods drawing on semiotics, pragmatics and discourse analysis.

Email: catherine.bouko@ugent.be

Piotr Cap is Professor of Linguistics at the University of Łódź, Poland. His interests are in pragmatics, critical discourse studies and political linguistics. His books include *Proximization* (2013) and *The Language of Fear* (2017). He is managing editor of the *International Review of Pragmatics*.

Email: piotr.cap@uni.lodz.pl

Massimiliano Demata is Associate Professor for English Language at the University of Turin, Italy. He is the author of *Representations of War and Terrorism* (2008) and his current research focuses on populism, social media and multimodality in American politics.

Email: massimiliano.demata@unito.it

1

INTRODUCTION

Context, history and previous research

Veronika Koller, Susanne Kopf and Marlene Miglbauer

At the time of writing this introduction (January 2019), Brexit continues to be an omnipresent and inescapable news item across the United Kingdom (UK) and mainland Europe. Curiously though, how and even if Britain will leave the European Union is still unclear. With the spectre of Brexit looming, regular government business in the UK has seemingly ground to a halt, and pundits and people alike are left to wonder what Europe – and the European Union (EU) – will look like after 29 March 2019. At this moment of uncertainty and paralysis, we invite readers to turn back and seek to understand how we got to this point.

The present volume is the first comprehensive exploration of discourses surrounding the UK's departure from the EU and as such a step towards understanding the reasons for, and processes of, Brexit. It covers multiple facets of the phenomenon and provides a kaleidoscopic view on aspects of Brexit. First, our contributors draw on data ranging from traditional news media to official governmental communications and parliamentary debates to social media platforms. Thus, we gain an insight into how a plethora of voices in various contexts and multiple public spheres have made sense of Brexit and Brexit-related matters. Second, and as the chronological organisation of this volume already indicates, the studies presented here examine pre-referendum data on Brexit reaching as far back as 2012. The individual chapters present insights from both Leave and Remain campaigns during the run-up to the EU referendum in 2016 and also cover its immediate and extended aftermath, from the UK government's decision to trigger Article 50 of the Treaty on European Union[1] to a time when the exit negotiations were well underway. Third, the wide array of methodological approaches used serves a triangulatory purpose and once more exemplifies this book's multifaceted perspective. Contributing scholars draw on traditionally quantitative methods, such as corpus linguistic analyses, as well as fine-grained qualitative analysis, for example multimodal analysis. What is more, contributors to this edited volume live and work across Europe and beyond. Thus, this edited volume allows a pan-European perspective to studying Brexit, which is further enriched by a more distant view of the phenomenon (Zappavigna, Chapter 4 this volume). Finally, we cannot but note the remarkable coincidence that amidst this diversity of researchers, it is three Austrians (with links to the UK) who have the privilege of editing this volume on the discourses of Brexit.

The first step towards making sense of Brexit and the discourses surrounding this phenomenon is to examine the political-historical context of Brexit. In the following section, we will address the recent rise of right-wing populism and how Brexit can be viewed as a manifestation of this populist trend.

Political and historical context: Brexit as a manifestation of right-wing populism

The British EU referendum that took place on 23 June 2016 can be regarded as the culmination of the uneasy and complex relationship Britain has had with the European Union since becoming a member in 1973. In fact, Britain's relationship with Europe in general has been rather complex even since the end of World War Two (Ramiro Troitiño et al., 2018). Tellingly, and importantly for recent developments, the terms 'Europe' and 'European Union' have frequently been conflated in the British media, by politicians and thus by citizens (Hardt-Mautner, 1995, p. 183; McCormick, 2013, p. vi).

Britain's request to join the European Economic Community (EEC) – the predecessor to the EU – was vetoed twice by France in the 1960s. After having finally joined the EEC in 1973, only two years later, the first referendum on Britain's membership was held. Although two-thirds of voters decided to stay within the Common Market, Britain's stance on being a member had become difficult and Euroscepticism would become part of the British political landscape from the 1980s onwards (Spiering, 2004; Gifford, 2017). In particular, former Prime Minister Margaret Thatcher played a decisive role in both establishing a sceptical standpoint towards the EU and reaching agreements with the EU that still benefit Britain, such as the UK rebate (Daddow, 2013).

The 2016 referendum result surprised the British political establishment as the polls had forecast a majority for staying in the EU. There are a myriad of reasons why a majority of the electorate voted to end British EU membership (Gietel-Basten, 2016; Goodwin & Heath, 2016; Clarke et al., 2017). Delving deeper into voters' reasons and motivations would go beyond this introduction (but see Miglbauer & Koller, Chapter 6 this volume). Interestingly, the supporters of Brexit were not confined to political parties but both large parties in the UK had so-called Remainers and Brexiteers in their ranks (see Wenzl, Chapter 3 this volume). Next to the fertile ground of Euroscepticism (Vasilopoulou, 2016), there are two aspects that played a crucial role for the success of the Leave campaign: the refugee crises of 2015/2016 and campaigners' tendency to draw on right-wing populist ideas and rhetoric.

Lamond, I. R., & Reid, C. (2017). *The 2015 UK general election and the 2016 EU referendum: Towards a democracy of the spectacle*. Basingstoke: Palgrave Macmillan.

Larsen, H. (1997). British discourses on Europe: Sovereignty of parliament, instrumentality and the non-mythical Europe. In K. E. Jørgensen (Ed.), *Reflective approaches to European governance* (pp. 109–127). Basingstoke: Palgrave Macmillan.

Lilleker, D. G. (2016). Mixed feelings: How citizens expressed their attitudes towards the EU. In D. Jackson, E. Thorsen, & D. Wring (Eds), *EU referendum analysis 2016: Media, voters and the campaign* (p. 106). Poole: The Centre for the Study of Journalism, Culture and Community, Bournemouth University. Available at www.referendumanalysis.eu, accessed 6 December 2018.

McCormick, J. (2013). *Why Europe matters*. Basingstoke: Palgrave Macmillan.

Mullen, A., & Burkitt, B. (2005). Spinning Europe: Pro-European Union propaganda campaigns in Britain, 1962–1975. *Political Quarterly, 76*(1), 100–113.

Mudde, C. (2004). The populist zeitgeist. *Government and Opposition, 39*(4), 541–563.

Potts, A., & Ylänne, V. (2018). 'Forget the stroppy, whingeing young who blame us wrinklies for Brexit!' A corpus-based discourse analysis of media representation of voter age and identity following the EU referendum. Paper presented at the 7th Conference on Critical Approaches to Discourse Analysis Across Disciplines, 4–6 July, Aalborg/Denmark.

Ramiro Troitiño, D., Kerikmäe, T., & Chochia, A. (Eds) (2018). *Brexit: History, reasoning and perspective*. Cham: Springer International.

Saunders, R. (2016). A tale of two referendums: 1975 and 2016. *Political Quarterly, 87*(3), 318–322.

Simaki, V., Paradis, C., Skeppstedt, M., Sahlgren, M., Kucher, K., & Kerren. A. (2017). Annotating speaker stance in discourse: The Brexit blog corpus. *Corpus Linguistics and Linguistic Theory*. https://doi.org/10.1515/cllt-2016-0060

Spiering, M. (2004). British euroscepticism. *European Studies, 20*(1), 127–149.

Trevisan, F. (2016). The view from across the pond: Brexit on American media. In D. Jackson, E. Thorsen, & D. Wring (Eds), *EU referendum analysis 2016: Media, voters and the campaign* (p. 44). Poole: The Centre for the Study of Journalism, Culture and Community, Bournemouth University. Available at www.referendumanalysis.eu, accessed 6 December 2018.

Vasilopoulou, S. (2016). UK Euroscepticism and the Brexit referendum. *Political Quarterly, 87*(2), 219–227. https://doi.org/10.1111/1467-923X.12258

Wodak, R. (2003). Populist discourses: The rhetoric of exclusion in written genres. *Document Design, 4*(2), 132–148. https://doi.org/10.1075/dd.4.2.04wod

Wodak, R. (2015). *The politics of fear: What right-wing populist discourses mean*. London: Sage.

Wodak, R. (2016). 'We have the character of an island nation': A discourse-historical analysis of David Cameron's 'Bloomberg speech' on the European Union. *European University Institute Working Paper Series RSCAS 2016/36*. Available at http://cadmus.eui.eu/bitstream/handle/1814/42804/RSCAS_2016_36.pdf?sequence=1&isAllowed=y, accessed 6 December 2018.

person or the knowledge that they expound [Vaara, 2014]), role model authority (opinion leaders) and the authority of tradition. The second type of legitimation is *moral evaluation*, in which a process or event is constructed with reference to value systems, while the third is *rationalisation*, that is, whether a proposal will work or whether it is effective (van Leeuwen, 2008, p. 106). The final type is *mythopoesis*. These are moral, or cautionary, tales that warn against the consequences of not conforming to social norms; they are future projections of negative scenarios that serve to (de-)legitimise a course of action (Vaara, 2014). Mythopoetic legitimation is a particularly potent strategy in the discursive construction of crises – such as Brexit – which seek to foretell the future as negative and often set up the speaker as the hero/saviour.[1] Similarly, for Dunmire (2005, p. 484) "political evocations of the future tap into – indeed, prey upon – the public's general anxiety about the inherent ambiguity and indeterminacy of the future in order to influence social perceptions, cognitions and actions". Within the context of Brexit, anxiety would, at first glance, favour Remain and, logically, the Leave camp would have to delegitimise the status quo. However, in cognitive terms, change (Leave) is profiled against the status quo (Remain) and as such focuses attention and is easier to communicate through, for example, crisis frames (cf. Bennett, forthcoming a).

At the micro-discursive level, legitimating strategies are "built into the vocabulary" as part of a "system of linguistic objectification" (Berger & Luckmann, 1966, p. 112): via nominalisation, processes and actions are represented as if they were objects, which has the effect of reifying the actions. By taking on "the roles, functions and characteristics of nouns" (Dunmire, 2005, p. 481) they are given agent roles. The (de)legitimisation is achieved through how these newly agentified objects are referred to. For example, nominational strategies are used to construct in-groups and out-groups, while predicational strategies are employed to ascribe "evaluative attributions" (Reisigl & Wodak, 2001, p. 45) to them. Another element is deontic modality (e.g. realised by the modal verbs 'should', 'must', 'needs to'), which in the analysis below can point to normative evaluations (Koller, 2012, p. 25). Based on this theoretical approach, in this chapter I orient myself to three research questions (following Sowinska, 2013, p. 796):

1 What values are referred to in the analysed texts?
2 How are these values construed in linguistic terms?
3 How are these construals "conducive to the actions the speaker wishes to legitimize" (ibid.)?

European (Union) values and the UK

EU values

Nowhere have values as key markers of collective identity been more evident and important than in the European project since 1945. Nordin (2014, p. 119) argues that institutions are held together via shared beliefs, along with "socially agreed norms and principles", part of which we can understand as collectively shared, normative values. Communicative acts by and within EU institutions transform values into material action and in doing so, EU actors also interpret and (de)activate these values as they see fit (Lucarelli, 2008, p. 29). Throughout its existence the European Union (and its precursors) has foregrounded two stable and interconnected values: that of a common (violent) history and a desire for a (peaceful) future that is ensured through unity and common goals. These values are used to discursively legitimise the EU's foundation, continued existence and expanding role and scope. In this way, the EU can be seen as a supra-national institutional actor that self-represents as an (imagined) collective sharing a common temporal trajectory, as well as a teleological one in that it develops towards full integration. This can be seen as far back as in the preamble to the Treaty Establishing the European Coal and Steel Community (1951, p. 11), which stated that the ECSC would create an economic community as the cornerstone for a broader and deeper community among peoples long divided by bloody conflicts and create the institutional basis for giving direction to their future, now common destiny.

While the EU started out as a project of economic integration, which would lead to shared interests in the name of peace (Kielar, 2010), other values developed over time as integration deepened. The core cluster of what we know today as 'European' values has maybe most succinctly been described by Triandafyllidou et al. (2009, p. 195) as the "1968 values" of democracy, freedom, and human rights. At the time, these key common values were used to positively identify Western Europe in comparison to the Eastern bloc countries (Kielar, 2010) and so this was "not just an intellectual exercise, but also realpolitik" (Zielonka, 2013, p. 40). After the fall of the Iron Curtain and the subsequent 'big bang' enlargement of 2004/2007, the EU's set of values, as markers of a socio-politico-economic collective identity, were not so much backgrounded as recontextualised in light of new members joining. They were also added to in the form of a new frame of unity, and, as Wodak and Weiss (2005, p. 121) note, a focus on diversity expressed a new ideology of "one culture determined by many cultures".

It can thus, I believe, be convincingly argued that the continued internal coherence of the EU relies on the "positive affirmation of a set of values" (Lucarelli, 2008, p. 32) in an attempt to avoid the mistakes of history. In doing so, Europe's history of war and conflict becomes a temporal Other, what Lucarelli (ibid.) terms Europe's 'real' other. Following Cap's (2010; Chapter 5 this volume) proximisation theory of legitimation, the EU – as a deictic centre – places itself along the historical axis (i.e. it is not separated from its history as such), but narrates history in a way that represents the institution as a peacebuilder against the historical backdrop of war and bloodshed. From this perspective it is possible to conceive of the EU's set of values as an attempt to distance itself as much as possible from what is discursively constructed as its greatest threat, i.e. a return to the past.

context of ongoing negotiations. Again there is an intertextual reference to treaties, but the values – here formulated as 'principles' – are additionally lexicalised and emphasised with the idiomatic 'in particular', which modifies the subsequent specific noun phrases.

The Brexit TV debate

As can be expected, the legitimation of action through values in UK Brexit discourse was done very differently than in the texts by EU institutional actors. EU values were criticised, other values were reinterpreted, and alternative values were spoken of that were constructed as more important to Britain than EU ones.

While EU actors deployed their collective values in speeches on Brexit, reference to these same values were, perhaps understandably, less easily detected in the words of Leave speakers during the BBC TV debate. Moreover, when they were present, they were not only coded in less obvious lexical choices, but were also attacked.

(7) What we've got now is an institution that has utterly outgrown its historic roots, which were noble, has now become so cumbersome (Gisela Stuart, Labour-Leave).

(8) I'm told, 'you can't do this, you can't do this', because of the EU. There are five presidents of the EU. Can anyone name them? And did anyone vote for them? You don't vote for them, because you are not allowed to vote for them, and you can't kick them out either [applause]. And the problem is, the problem is that in the EU there are 10,000 officials, nearly twice the number of people in this room by the way, who earn more than the UK Prime Minister. And you're paying for them. And that gravy train is continuing (Andrea Leadsom, Conservative-Leave).

Over the years, one major critique of the EU from Eurosceptics has been the drive towards ever-closer union and deeper integration, which has often been couched in terms of an 'overly bureaucratic' 'European super-state'. In example (7), Stuart constructs the EU as being guilty of overreaching its original remit. As a whole, the sentence is a (temporally) contrastive one that depicts the EU as having wrongly moved away from its original *raison d'être*. Her critique is mitigated by the middle clause, where the adjective 'noble' places positive value on the original reasons for the EU's existence. However, this positive value becomes frozen in time by the use of the past tense and as such, the EU is no longer noble. In addition, the impact of this mitigation is bookended and diminished by the intensification strategies of 'utterly outgrown' in the opening clause and 'so cumbersome' in the closing cause.

In example (8), Leadsom criticises the EU on three fronts: having too much power, showing a democratic deficit and engaging in inefficient working practices and financial management. The first sentence is an example of heteroglossia

(Bakhtin, 1981), in this case specifically ventriloquation, which "occurs when a speaker speaks through the voice of another for the purpose of social or interactional positioning" (Samuelson, 2009, p. 52). Leadsom's 'I am told "you can't . . ."' is the fallacious basis for the strawman argument she builds in the later sentences.[4] She employs rhetorical questions, which are performative speech acts that set up an evaluation or conclusion that is shared by the target audience. After the applause Leadsom interrupts her narrative with a comment on the situational context in 'nearly twice the number of people in this room by the way'. In doing so she shifts from being a narrator presenting facts to being an interlocutor (Reyes-Rodriguez, 2008). The aim here is to provide a visceral comparison. Lastly, she addresses the audience directly by using the second-person pronoun, which personalises the claim. Overall, there is little cohesion in her claims. The first sentence does not thematically link to the second and the claim of undemocratic systems is, logically at least, unconnected to the criticism of the EU being a 'gravy train'. However, when taken as a small part of a much larger set of criticisms against the EU, the claims gain coherence for those in the audience predisposed to, and primed for, anti-European arguments.

While examples (7) and (8) do not explicitly mention European values, example (9) is one of the few instances where a key EU value is directly challenged.

(9) That picture and pictures exactly the same appeared in the media well before in the early part of this year, highlighting what is completely wrong with the Schengen system, what is completely wrong with the EU fundamental tenet of freedom of movement of people (Diane James, UKIP-Leave).

The immediate context of the passage was the suggestion by a debate participant that James should apologise for UKIP's infamous 'breaking point' poster (see Cap, Chapter 5 this volume).[5] Rather than apologise, James instead used the poster as a delegitimising strategy against the EU value of freedom of movement. So, although the poster had been taken down a few days earlier, its persuasive power within the Brexit debate was prolonged.

While Leave supporters criticised EU values, Remain participants in the debate did sometimes use them explicitly as legitimating arguments for continued membership:

(10) The wonderful thing is that people can come from different traditions, come from different communities, but they see themselves as common citizens of the EU (Frances O'Grady, Trade Union Congress-Remain).

(11) I'm passionate about the fact that we are sat around a table with 27 countries, 11 of which a quarter a century ago were on the other side of the iron curtain, 6 of which had nuclear weapons on their soil pointed right here. Today they are our friends and our neighbours. We put that at risk at our peril (Tim Farron, Liberal Democrats-Remain).

president-schulz-2014-2016/en/press-room/speech_at_the_european_council_by_martin_schulz__president_of_the_european_parliament_.html, accessed 15 March 2018.

Sowinska, A. (2013). A critical discourse approach to the analysis of values in political discourse: the example of freedom in President Bush's State of the Union addresses (2001–2008). *Discourse & Society, 24*(6), 792–809. https://doi.org/10.1177/0957926513486214

Treaty establishing the European coal and steel community [*Vertrag über die Gründung der Europäischen Gemeinschaft für Kohle und Stahl*] (1951). Available at https://eur-lex.europa.eu/legal-content/DE/TXT/PDF/?uri=CELEX:11951K/TXT&from=EN, accessed 29 July 2018.

Triandafyllidou, A., Wodak, R., & Krzyżanowski, M. (Eds) (2009). *The European public sphere and the media: Europe in crisis*. Basingstoke: Palgrave Macmillan.

Tusk, D. (2016a, 2 February). Letter by President Donald Tusk to the members of the European Council on his proposal for a new settlement for the United Kingdom within the European Union. Available at www.consilium.europa.eu/en/press/press-releases/2016/02/02/letter-tusk-proposal-new-settlement-uk, accessed 15 March 2018.

Tusk, D. (2016b, 16 February). Remarks by President Donald Tusk after his meeting in Prague with Prime Minister Bohuslav Sobotka. Available at www.consilium.europa.eu/en/press/press-releases/2016/02/16/tusk-meeting-sobotka-prague, accessed 15 March 2018.

Tusk, D. (2016c, 14 March). Remarks by President Donald Tusk following his meeting in Helsinki with Prime Minister of Finland Juha Sipilä. Available at www.consilium.europa.eu/en/press/press-releases/2018/03/14/remarks-by-president-donald-tusk-after-his-meeting-with-prime-minister-of-finland-juha-sipila, accessed 15 March 2018.

Tusk, D. (2016d, 17 May). Remarks by President Donald Tusk following his meeting in Copenhagen with Danish Prime Minister Lars Løkke Rasmussen. Available at www.consilium.europa.eu/en/press/press-releases/2016/05/17/tusk-meeting-denmark-prime-minister-rasmussen-copenhagen, accessed 15 March 2018.

Vaara, E. (2014). Struggles over legitimacy in the Eurozone crisis: Discursive legitimation strategies and their ideological underpinnings. *Discourse & Society, 25*(4), 500–518. https://doi.org/10.1177/0957926514536962

Van Dijk, T. (1998). *Ideology: A multidisciplinary approach*. London: Sage.

van Leeuwen, T. (2008). *Discourse and practice: New tools for critical discourse analysis*. Oxford: Oxford University Press.

Wodak, R., & Weiss, G. (2005). Analysing European Union discourses: Theories and applications. In R. Wodak & P. Chilton (Eds), *A new agenda in (critical) discourse analysis* (pp. 121–135). Amsterdam: Benjamins.

Zielonka, J. (2013). Europe's new civilizing missions: The EU's normative power discourse. *Journal of Political Ideologies, 18*(1), 35–55. https://doi.org/10.1080/13569317.2013.750172

3

'THIS IS ABOUT THE KIND OF BRITAIN WE ARE'

National identities as constructed in parliamentary debates about EU membership

Nora Wenzl

Introduction

The UK's decision to leave the European Union has caused a stir in both British and international politics. While there were two clear sides to the debate – Remain and Leave – the Conservative party was officially neutral, allowing MPs to support either campaign. Considering that British political discourses have frequently portrayed the EU in terms of a pragmatic union, rather than one based on common values or a common European identity (Bourne, 2016), it is unsurprising that topics pertaining to business, economics and trade dominated the debate. Closer examination of the arguments brought forth by both sides, however, reveals that discourses on the European Union are permeated by the topic of national identity.

Drawing on the discourse-historical approach (DHA) to critical discourse studies (CDS) (Reisigl & Wodak, 2001) this chapter illustrates how Conservative politicians strategically construct visions of British national identity while arguing for or against continuing membership in the EU.[1] The particular focus of this chapter lies on a corpus-assisted critical discourse study of concordance lines of 'we are', as these linguistic constructions allow an insight into discursive constructions of the collective self. In the following, I briefly outline the conceptual framework of the DHA, before providing an overview of the realisation of national identity constructions in discourse. The analysis presented then addresses pertinent patterns of identity constructions of the Remain and Leave sides within the Conservative Party. My findings suggest that, while both sides of the debate construct vastly different images of the EU, the picture of British identity that is presented does not vary as much as one might expect. In particular, Conservative politicians on the Remain side essentially undercut their own argumentation by presenting a vision of Britishness that is separate from, and different to, other EU member states and the EU as a whole.

Through the use of passive voice, the 'we'-group is put into a powerless position where they are receiving information and instructions but have no voice themselves. Additionally, constructions such as 'we are being told that' or 'we are asked to believe that' call into question what follows. These sentences thus carry the connotation that those telling and asking might not be speaking the truth. As is frequent in passive constructions, however, the agents themselves remain obscure. First, this strategy of vagueness has the advantage that speakers can voice concerns the public might believe to be true, without having to explicitly cite a source. Example (15), for instance, taps into the common Eurosceptic fear of losing British sovereignty (Spiering, 2015) but leaves open who exactly is trying to convince the public that this fear is unjustified.

(15) *We are told* that we have a lot of influence in the EU.

Second, in the context of parliamentary discourse, where it is forbidden to directly accuse another MP of a lie, these constructions are a safe way for a speaker to imply that the public are being lied to by the Remain side or the Prime Minister, without explicitly saying it. In example (16), for instance, the speaker not only suggests that the renegotiations did not bring any improvement for the UK regarding its EU membership; they also insinuate that 'the Minister and Prime Minister' are actively attempting to fool the public into believing an untruth by redressing a failure as a triumph. By suggesting that this plan is not working, government representatives are presented as foolish while the 'we'-group that the speaker claims to be part of is discursively empowered. Moreover, another association that, according to Spiering (2015), has some tradition in Eurosceptic thinking is hinted at here; namely the celebration of British 'common sense' that sees through the lies told by elites, as shown in example (16).

(16) As a result of my great triumph in these renegotiations, we can now vote to stay in the EU. If the Minister and the Prime Minister think that *we are all going to be fooled* by such nonsense, they are sadly mistaken.

Additionally, passive constructions are employed to convey an image of the United Kingdom as impotent in the face of the EU. Example (17) illustrates this usage with the EU metaphorically pictured as a vehicle that forces the government and citizens of the United Kingdom into policies they do not want, while the renegotiated terms of membership are depicted as merely 'emergency brakes'. The imagery employed here evokes a picture of the EU's plan for ever-closer union as an almost catastrophic event that Britain will not be able to escape as long as it remains a member.

(17) As *we are driven* in the EU vehicle towards ever-closer union and political union, how does it help to try to fit a couple of emergency brakes that lie within the control of the EU, not us?

The impression of a powerless 'we'-group is not only conveyed by the use of passive constructions, but also becomes evident when examining the attributes that 'we' is associated with. Words such as 'constitutionally unable', 'impotent', 'not free', 'locked into', 'reliant', 'subject to' and 'susceptible', as well as 'trapped', carry strong negative connotations of being trapped and convey an image of a Britain that is at the mercy of the EU and unable to take action. It must be noted, however, that these attributes are used mainly in relation to matters of policy and bureaucracy, as in example (18).

(18) *We are now subject to* so many legal restrictions and obligations as a result of an extremely voluminous consolidated treaty and thousands of directives.

The plural pronoun in this case can be understood on several levels, from referring only to those involved in the legislative process – those who have to make laws conforming to EU regulations – to all UK citizens, whose rights and duties are, among other things, regulated by EU law. Understood in this latter sense, example (18) implies that every British citizen is restricted in his or her everyday actions by EU regulations. While it cannot be denied that everybody is affected by these laws, the use of the first-person plural pronoun here withholds the fact that a large number of EU directives in fact only impact certain groups or legal entities, as well as the fact that certain EU laws do not restrict but benefit British citizens. However, in many cases, the use of 'we' in connection with the aforementioned attributes erases these distinctions and implies that the EU is a burden to everyone by overestimating the impact it has on citizens' day-to-day lives. With regard to discussions about EU legislation, it is noticeable that advantages of the system of EU regulations are rarely mentioned. On several occasions, the EU is thus vilified and presented as a radical Other, whose values are incompatible with British ones.

Of course, the image of being unfree while a member of the EU is a traditional element of Euroscepticism (Spiering, 2015). A special predilection for freedom and sovereignty is thought to be a natural part of the British character – and it is this image of the British self that is being evoked and addressed with this language of entrapment (see also Buckledee, 2018, p. 79). Example (19) illustrates how the EU is spoken about almost as if it were a prison, leaving the UK unfree to make its own decisions. The EU represents a radical Other that is controlling, forcing the country into trade agreements it did not choose and curtailing the government's power to influence the country.

(19) *We are locked into* EU trade agreements, rather than our own bilateral agreements with places such as China, Mexico, Brazil, India, South Africa and Canada.

(20) We in this country are different from our European partners in many ways. That does not mean that we are in any sense better, but *we are different*. We have a very different concept of sovereignty that is deeply entrenched in our history.

Example (20) is particularly interesting, since it shows a more nuanced perception of the EU as a non-radical Other that is different, but not the enemy. Additionally, the same supposedly essential characteristics of Britishness – singularity and sovereignty – that are also called upon in Remain arguments are evoked here as reasons for the incompatibility of the UK with other EU member states.

British entitlement

A sense of British singularity is also conveyed by the fact that the United Kingdom is only rarely constructed in terms of its memberships in the EU and other groups. There are only a handful of instances where 'we' can be interpreted as encompassing the UK and other European member states. Instead, the UK's involvement in other organisations such as the OECD or NATO is stressed. An effort is thus made to highlight the UK's global connections apart from the Union in an attempt to argue that EU membership is not as important for the country as Remain supporters maintain it to be. A sense of national pride and British self-confidence is conveyed, as in example (21), by defining the UK in terms of its market power and international connections. Interestingly, instances of 'we are the fifth largest economy in the world' can also be found in the Remain corpus. However, those in favour of continuing EU membership use this fact to illustrate the importance of the EU for the British market, whereas those arguing to leave list it as one of the reasons why the UK does not need the Union. Additionally, the possibility of regaining WTO membership in the future is frequently evoked to show that membership, instead of benefiting the country, is effectively holding it back.

(21) I am confident about Britain's future. *We are the fifth largest economy* in the world. *We are a member* of many prominent international organisations. Our influence in the world would increase if we were to take back our seat at the World Trade Organisation.

There is also a sense of British entitlement to the Leave arguments that is not present in the examined Remain concordances. Referring to the British trade deficit, the United Kingdom is both explicitly referred to as the 'customer' of other European Union countries, and implicitly characterised as a country that should be in a strong negotiating position. Example (22) is interesting in this respect, as the speaker additionally mentions Germany, a country with a trade surplus. Instead of the EU, Germany is the Other to the UK here and a dissatisfaction with that country's relative power within the EU is voiced.

(22) We would like to hear more questioning of our deficit and a reminder that *we are the customers* more than the producers; it is the other way round for the Germans. It is unusual for the customers to be in a weak position and the producers in a strong position.

Moreover, the idea that the EU is not doing enough for the United Kingdom as a net contributor is hinted at in example (22) and explicitly voiced several times elsewhere. This creates an image of the UK as being part of a system that is unfair and unprofitable. In fact, membership is constructed as being detrimental to the UK's economic well-being.

Conclusion

The examination of concordance lines for 'we are' has shown that Conservative politicians on both sides of the debate use the pronoun 'we' to strategically align themselves with different groups, most notably employing the pronoun to stand for the entire nation. Thereby, they construct images of Britishness while making their case for or against membership.

In the Remain subcorpus, speakers construct a British identity that relies implicitly on elements of British exceptionalism, stressing the country's greatness and expressing pride in its long history of democracy. They thereby assume the stable existence of an 'essential' Britishness that includes a natural love for liberty and democracy. Furthermore, Britain is constructed as being a major player, not only on the world stage but also within the EU. This is achieved by highlighting global connections and group memberships, as well as by the predominant use of active voice. Although MPs assert that the UK is 'better off in', EU membership is often associated with duties imposed on the country and its relationship with the EU is framed as a merely pragmatic one. Thus, while arguing for membership, pro-European MPs undermine their reasoning with latent Euroscepticism and the linguistic highlighting of British singularity.

Supporters of leaving the EU, on the other hand, construct a more explicitly negative picture of the EU as both a radical and non-radical Other. The version of British identity they present is somewhat contradictory in nature, since the UK is constructed both as powerless in the face of the overreaching EU and as a powerful global player. The frequent use of passive constructions, as well as the language of entrapment used, construct Britain as being caught in a prison-like EU, unable to make independent decisions. The British public, in turn, is construed as voiceless while higher powers – the EU, the Prime Minister, Remain supporters – are attempting to persuade them of half-truths. MPs, however, question these alleged lies on behalf of the general public and draw on the association of Britishness with 'common sense' to declare that the electorate is able to see through the lies they are being told by the Remain side. The EU is described as an unjust system in which the UK is a customer who is treated unfairly. Just like the Remain side, MPs advocating to leave the EU highlight British singularity and the country's difference from other European countries – in contrast to pro-European MPs, however, speakers wishing to leave the EU construct the Union as a hindrance, not a vehicle, for British greatness.

While the picture of the Other is far more negative in the Leave corpus, the construction of the British self is not as different across the two groups as one might expect it to be. Both sides of the debate highlight the importance of British sovereignty and call upon the Whig interpretation of history by stressing the country's long history of democracy. Speakers on both sides frequently construct the UK as being separate from, and different to, other European countries and only infrequently align themselves linguistically with the EU. While the strategy of distancing oneself from the EU makes sense for those advocating to leave the Union, it is a somewhat surprising – and certainly ineffective – strategy for the Remain side. While there are manifold reasons for why the vote for Brexit came about, my findings suggest that the failure of the Remain side to unequivocally embrace the EU and highlight the advantages of membership may have contributed to the outcome. Remain arguments examined in the corpus are laced with latent Euroscepticism and frequently draw on images of British identity that are at odds with the country being a member of the EU. By drawing on ideas of British exceptionalism instead of construing a British identity that is compatible with membership in a supranational organisation such as the EU, MPs arguing for Remain effectively weakened and even undermined their own arguments.

Notes

1 Note that the corpus' specific focus is on Conservative discourses. As the Conservative Party is strongest in England and most Conservative MPs are therefore from that country, the vision of British identity presented is one that is deeply rooted in English identity, although it is presented as universally British.
2 For a similar distinction, see Darics and Koller (2018, p. 217) on in-groups, out-groups and "associated groups".
3 The notion of a radical Other is linked to van Dijk's concept of the "ideological square" (2006, p. 734), which states that ideological discourse, and political discourse in particular, often aims to emphasise positive aspects of the in-group and negative aspects of the out-group, while downplaying negative aspects of the in-group and positive aspects of the out-group. In comparison with van Dijk's model, the usefulness of distinguishing between friendly, non-radical and radical Others becomes evident, as this distinction allows for the identification of a friendly Other, that is, in fact, an out-group portrayed in very positive terms.
4 Working with Hansard transcripts comes with certain caveats resulting from the fact that the language used is slightly altered by transcribers in order to correct and formalise it and make spoken discourse appropriate to the written channel (Slembrouck, 1992; Mollin, 2007). Since the present study, however, is not concerned with pragmatic aspects of parliamentary discourse, the alterations made to the transcript were deemed to be of little consequence to the findings.
5 The italics in all the examples in this chapter are mine.

References

Anderson, B. R. O. (2006). *Imagined communities: Reflections on the origin and spread of nationalism* (Revised ed.). London: Verso.

Anthony, L. (2017). AntConc. Tokyo, Waseda University. Available at www.laurenceanthony.net/software, accessed 24 February 2017.

Baker, P. (2010). *Using corpora in discourse analysis*. London: Continuum.

Baker, P., Gabrielatos, C., KhosraviNik, M., Krzyżanowski, M., McEnery, T., & Wodak, R. (2008). A useful methodological synergy? Combining critical discourse analysis and corpus linguistics to examine discourses of refugees and asylum seekers in the UK press. *Discourse & Society, 19*(3), 273–306. https://doi.org/10.1177/0957926508088962

Billig, M. S. (1995). *Banal nationalism*. London: Sage.

Bourne, R. (2016). Why did the British Brexit? What are the implications for classical liberals? *Economic Affairs, 36*(3), 356–363. https://doi.org/10.1111/ecaf.12205

Buckledee, S. (2018). *The language of Brexit: How Britain talked its way out of the European Union*. London: Bloomsbury.

Bull, P., & Fetzer, A. (2006). Who are we and who are you? The strategic use of forms of address in political interviews. *Text & Talk, 26*(1), 3–37. https://doi.org/10.1515/TEXT.2006.002

Daddow, O. J. (2004). *Britain and Europe since 1945: Historiographical perspectives on integration*. Manchester: Manchester University Press.

Darics, E., & Koller, V. (2018). *Language in business, language at work*. London: Macmillan Higher Education.

Fairclough, N., & Wodak, R. (1997). Critical discourse analysis. In T. A. van Dijk (Ed.), *Discourse studies: A multidisciplinary introduction* (vol. 2, pp. 258–284). London: Sage.

Gibbins, J. (2014). *Britain, Europe and national identity: Self and other in international relations*. Basingstoke: Palgrave Macmillan.

Hall, S. (Ed.) (1996). *Modernity: An introduction to modern societies*. Malden, MA: Blackwell.

Hall, S., & Du Gay, P. (Eds). (1996). *Questions of cultural identity*. London: Sage.

Hansard Online. (2018). Available at https://hansard.parliament.uk, accessed 13 July 2017.

Hardt-Mautner, G. (1995). Only connect: Critical discourse analysis and corpus linguistics. *Unit for Computer Research on the English Language Technical Papers, 6*. Available at http://stig.lancs.ac.uk/papers/techpaper/vol6.pdf, accessed 4 April 2016.

Krzyżanowski, M. (2010). *The discursive construction of European identities: A multi-level approach to discourse and identity in the transforming European Union*. Frankfurt am Main: Lang.

Mole, R. C. M. (Ed.) (2007). *Discursive constructions of identity in European politics: Language and globalization*. Basingstoke: Palgrave Macmillan.

Mollin, S. (2007). The Hansard hazard: Gauging the accuracy of British parliamentary transcripts. *Corpora, 2*(2), 187–210. https://doi.org/10.3366/cor.2007.2.2.187

Mulderrig, J. (2012). The hegemony of inclusion: A corpus-based critical discourse analysis of deixis in education policy. *Discourse & Society, 23*(6), 701–728. https://doi.org/10.1177/0957926512455377

O'Halloran, K. (2011). Critical discourse analysis. In J. Simpson (Ed.), *The Routledge handbook of applied linguistics* (pp. 445–459). London: Routledge.

Partington, A. (2010). Modern diachronic corpus-assisted discourse studies. *Corpora, 5*(2), 83–108. https://doi.org/10.3366/cor.2010.0101

Piao, S. (2002). Multilingual corpus toolkit. Available at https://sites.google.com/site/scottpiaosite/software/mlct, accessed 14 March 2017.

Reisigl, M., & Wodak, R. (2001). *Discourse and discrimination: Rhetorics of racism and antisemitism*. London: Routledge.

Slembrouck, S. (1992). The parliamentary Hansard 'verbatim' report: The written construction of spoken discourse. *Language and Literature, 1*(2), 101–119. https://doi.org/10.1177/096394709200100202

Spiering, M. (2015). *A cultural history of British Euroscepticism*. Basingstoke: Palgrave Macmillan.

van Dijk, T. A. (2006). Politics, ideology, and discourse. In K. Brown (Ed.), *Encyclopedia of language & linguistics* (pp. 728–740). New York: Elsevier.

Ward, P. (2004). *Britishness since 1870.* London: Routledge.

Wodak, R. (2006). What CDA is about: A summary of its history, important concepts and its developments. In R. Wodak & M. Meyer (Eds), *Methods of critical discourse analysis* (2nd edn, pp. 1–14). London: Sage.

Wodak, R. (2016). 'We have the character of an island nation': A discourse-historical analysis of David Cameron's 'Bloomberg speech' on the European Union. European University Institute working paper series RSCAS 2016/36. http://cadmus.eui.eu/bitstream/handle/1814/42804/RSCAS_2016_36.pdf?sequence=1&isAllowed=y, accessed 22 August 2016.

Wodak, R., de Cillia, R., Reisigl, M., & Liebhart, K. (2009). *The discursive construction of national identity.* 2nd ed. Edinburgh: Edinburgh University Press.

Zhang, M., & Mihelj, S. (2012). Hong Kong identity and the press–politics dynamics: A corpus-assisted discourse study. *Asian Journal of Communication, 22*(5), 506–527. https://doi.org/10.1080/01292986.2012.701315

4

AMBIENT AFFILIATION AND #BREXIT

Negotiating values about experts through censure and ridicule

Michele Zappavigna

Introduction

Brexit[1] has been described as "the leading edge of an ongoing anti-expert revolution" (Fuller, 2017, p. 575). Controversy regarding the role of experts has spawned debate in countless Twitter interactions where social media users negotiate values about the status of experts in society. Discourses devaluing the legitimacy of expertise refract "questions of both class (antipathy to ruling elites, the very architects of austerity) and nation (expertise symbolised 'elsewhere'; international institutions, EU bureaucrats and those seeking to protect global free trade)" (Clarke & Newman, 2017, p. 110). In the aftermath of both the Brexit decision and the 2016 US Presidential election, commentators have begun worrying about whether we are entering a 'post-truth' era in which facts and experts are undermined in favour of emotional reactions to events. Some have claimed that the public have become more tolerant of politicians who lie or ignore expert knowledge (e.g. scientific consensus about climate change) due to what has been termed an emergent 'post-truth' ethos where a lack of interest in facts "has become a political stance" (Higgins, 2016). What is at stake is the extent to which truth, and the expert knowledge that is associated with determining truth, is valued and how challenges to truth become a "mechanism for asserting political dominance" (McIntyre, 2018, p. xiv). Which views achieve dominance depends in part on how they are taken up in online public discourses, particularly on social media platforms.

Within social media environments, the nature of the ambient 'bonding' that occurs will impact which kinds of views are able to achieve prominence and also which views are considered to have veracity within a certain group or community of users. We know from research into gossip that criticising someone can be a highly aligning activity (Eggins & Slade, 1997/2005; Dunbar, 2004; Bosson et al., 2006), and that it is closely related to the establishment of in-group/out-group boundaries (Tajfel, 1970; Gagnon & Bourhis, 1996; Wert & Salovey,

2004; Jaworski & Coupland, 2005). Terms such as 'media bubbles', 'silos' and 'echo chambers' (Jasny et al., 2015; Berghel, 2017) have been used to describe how particular social media communities tend to exclude outside viewpoints that are seen as incommensurable, and this kind of characterisation may also explain how experts tend to be seen as part of an 'elite' out-group (Speed & Mannion, 2017). For instance, political hashtag communities often adopt homogenous hashtagging practices and link to similar media, rarely straying outside the dominant viewpoint of their political discourse community (Bouma et al., 2017).

In tandem with these practices eroding the status of experts are ongoing discourses seeking to destabilise the status of 'facts', as well as counter-discourses ridiculing both of these tendencies (Zappavigna, 2017). For example, frequent hashtags, visible in agnate discourses at the time of the Brexit debate, include #FakeNews and #AlternativeFacts. These references co-occur with a debate in the United States about the relative significance of facts and opinions. The proliferation of these tags may be viewed as symptomatic of an ongoing decline in public trust of expert judgement, fuelled by social media platforms where displays of public affect are prominent (Keane & Razir, 2014). This perhaps contributes to an increasing gap that has already been identified between expert advice and public attitudes more generally (Spicer, 2016).

To date there have been few language-focused studies of Brexit discourses that have addressed discourses about expertise in particular. For example, there has been some preliminary work on the role of metaphor in influencing whether facts are determined by the public to be plausible (Musolff, 2017; Đurović & Silaški, 2018). Most linguistic work on Brexit, however, has been concerned with particular issues such as immigration and the discursive construction of fear and othering (Cap, 2016; Chapter 5 this volume). Alternatively, researchers have been interested in political language, such as the evaluative language used in the Remain campaign (Buckledee, 2018), or on the linguistic formation of stance more generally, for example in blogging (Simaki et al., 2017). This chapter approaches discourse about experts from the perspective of affiliation, considering how microbloggers, users of platforms such as Twitter that afford publishing of character-constrained social media posts, align with (or de-align from) particular political values about expertise.

Background: 'had enough of experts'

An important contextual moment in the ongoing discourse about experts that occurred before the Brexit referendum was UK politician Michael Gove's statement during a Sky News interview with Faisal Islam in June 2016, in which he claimed that people had 'had enough of experts' (shown in italics below)[2]:

Michael Gove: The people who are arguing that we should get out are concerned to ensure that the working people of this country at last get a fair deal. I think the people of this country *have had enough of experts* with organisations from acronyms saying, saying that . . .

Interviewer: The people of this country *have had enough of experts*, what do you mean by that?
Michael Gove: with the, with the help from organisations with acronyms saying that they know what is best and getting it consistently wrong because these people . . .
Interviewer: The people of this country *have had enough of experts*?
Michael Gove: because these people are the same ones who have got consistently wrong what's [been] happening.

Gove's phrasing 'had enough of experts' was heavily quoted on social media platforms. Its prevalence was seen in a previous corpus-based study by the author of the types of voices involved in Brexit discourse about experts (Zappavigna, 2017). The corpus in this present study was created by querying the Twitter API for posts containing one or more of the words 'expert', 'experts' and 'expertise' together with the hashtag '#brexit' from 2 July 2016 to 23 October 2017, resulting in a dataset of 35,020 tweets. The most common 3-gram in this corpus was 'had enough of', found in posts referencing Gove's original phrasing 'had enough of experts', for example:

(1) @guardian #Brexit Why should we worry? Britain has had enough of experts.
(2) #MichaelGove #idiotnation @Bertie_Waster Well there were no facts in the #Brexit campaign because 'we've all had enough of experts'.
(3) @BorisJohnson it'll all be fine eh? @michaelgove so the public have had enough of experts?
(4) @User we've all had enough of experts telling us facts. #brexit
(5) @User1 @User2 @FT he's just an expert and the #Brexit campaign taught us 'we've had enough of experts' Too late now.
(6) @User1 it's post #brexit now Pete we've had enough of experts! #r4today

The 'had enough of experts' phrasing appeared to crystallise the anti-intellectual sentiment of the Leave campaign before the referendum and its tendency to pathologise 'elites' and 'so-called experts'. Gove's statement spawned a phrasal template meme, with social media users producing large volumes of posts referencing the phrase via various forms of quotation. Many of these posts humorously mocked the 'had enough of experts' viewpoint (Zappavigna, 2017), for example:

(7) So Gove has *had enough of experts*. I'd love to be his Doctor, "Mr Gove this is Dave, he's a builder, he'll be doing your prostate exam today".
(8) *Had enough of experts*, next time I go to hospital I will insist on having my operation performed by a chef. He's good with a knife after all.

The phrase was also often used interactively as a retort in exchanges debating political points about Brexit; for example, in the following extract from a longer exchange:

(9) User A: The beauty of the crushing defeat of the left is they still do not see the real reasons. I love EU.
(10) User B: You sound like an expert. People have *had enough of experts*.

This chapter seeks to build on Zappavigna's (2017) study of quoted voices in order to understand how the values that these voices reference are interactively negotiated in the process of affiliation.

Dataset

Since the aim of this study was to explore how values regarding experts were negotiated, instances of user interaction needed to be sampled. Given the prevalence of the 'had enough of' 3-gram in the corpus, described in the previous section, this seemed like an important discursive site. The frequency of the phrase further prompted a search of Gove's Twitter stream for the word 'expert' to determine whether he had produced more discourse about the status of experts and whether members of the public had interacted with him regarding his views. The search returned the following three posts, two of which are directed at Jo Maugham QC, a British barrister (see also Figure 4.1):

Post 1

An expert writes . . .

Jo Maugham QC @JolyonMaugham:

Labour can't make headway – even when the Government is in utter meltdown. It really must re-evaluate its strategy and leadership. [URL]

Post 2

An expert in English language teaching replies [URL]

[Deleted tweet by unknown user]

Post 3

A distinguished expert in tax law provides a winning self-portrait

Jo Maugham QC @JolyonMaugham:

Replying to @user1 @user2

It's not that you guys are so consistently wrong. It's that you're so consistently staggeringly mediocre.

Amusingly, all of these posts were instances where Gove cited people as experts (in what appeared a genuine rather than sarcastic manner). In each post the 'expert' was referenced in a projecting clause:

An expert writes

An expert . . . replies

A distinguished expert . . . provides . . .

Each post multimodally embedded the 'expert' user's post as a form of quotation via the resource of 'meta-vocalisation' (Zappavigna, 2017, p. 329), where a quoted source is instantiated via modal affordances specific to a social media platform e.g. via an @mention, retweet or hashtag (Figure 4.1). For example, the first tweet in Figure 4.1 embeds a post by Jo Maugham QC that, in turn, embeds another post presenting figures from a poll about Brexit: "Do you think that Theresa May has done a good job or a bad job at handling Britain's exit from the European Union?" All replies to these three posts by Gove were collected resulting in a specialised dataset of 138 replies (117 replies to Post 1, 9 replies to Post 2, and 12 replies to Post 3). Unsurprisingly, as we will see, the replies in this set mostly ridicule Gove and his apparent hypocrisy.

Rather than representing simple dialogue, these conversational interactions are perhaps best thought of as 'multilogues' since they often involve multiple

FIGURE 4.1 All uses of 'expert' in Gove's Twitter stream[3]

participants and overlapping exchanges, rather than orderly dialogic exchanges (Zappavigna & Martin, 2017). These can be approached from either a synoptic perspective, in which Gove's initial post is seen as the nucleus to which all replies are related (Figure 4.2), or from a dynamic perspective, in which a user may enter the 'conversation' at any point and at any time (right-hand side Figure 4.3).

An example of the kind of interaction that Gove's post engendered is the conversation-like fragment in Figure 4.4. The initiating post in this exchange is

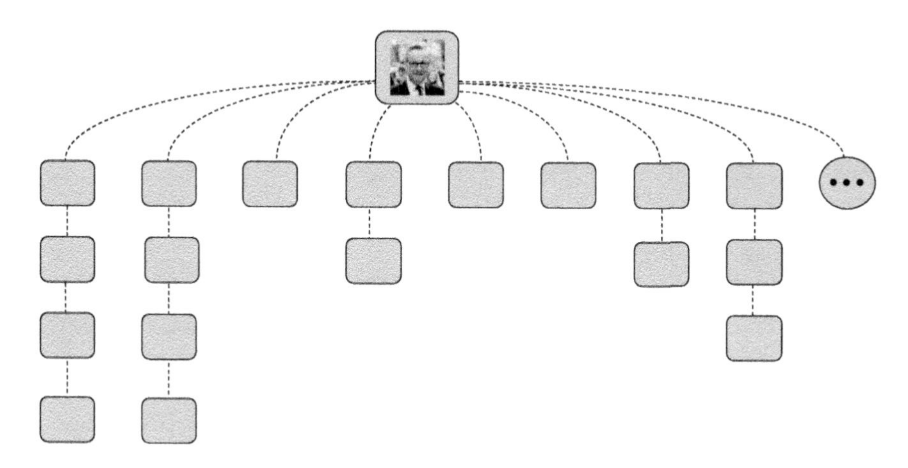

FIGURE 4.2 A synoptic perspective on Gove's Twitter exchanges[4]

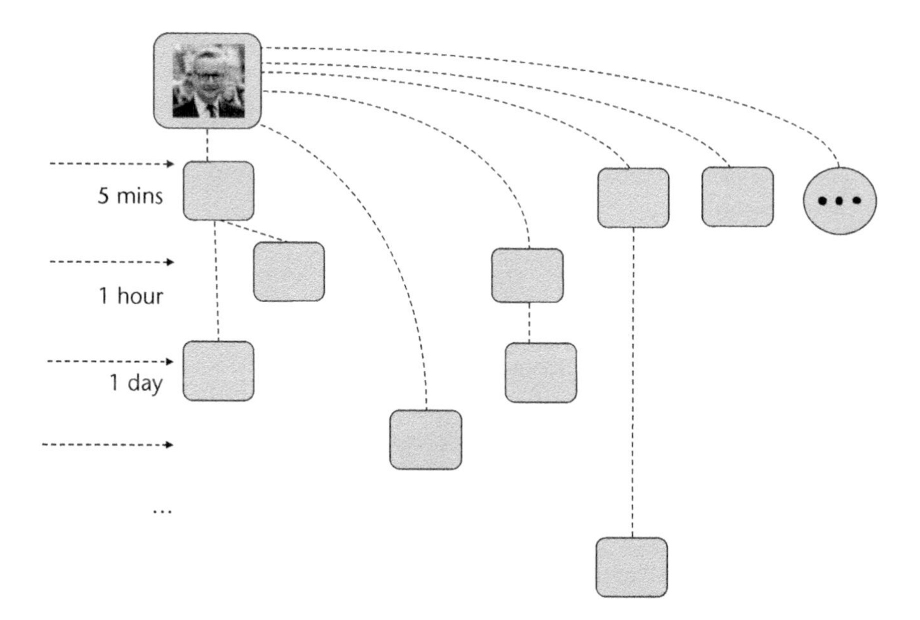

FIGURE 4.3 A dynamic perspective on Gove's Twitter exchanges

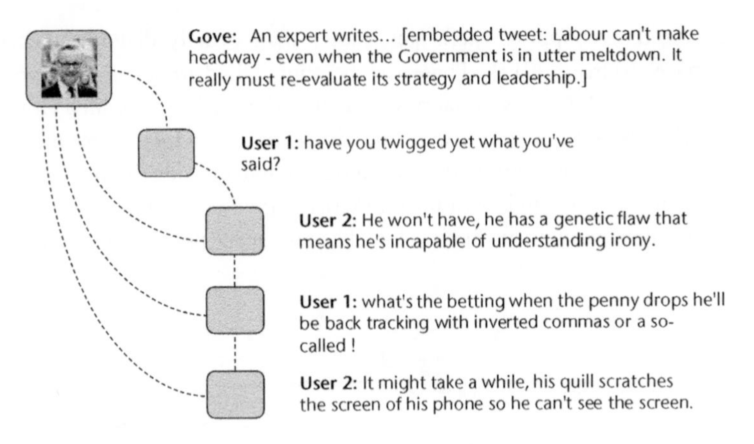

Gove: An expert writes... [embedded tweet: Labour can't make headway - even when the Government is in utter meltdown. It really must re-evaluate its strategy and leadership.]
User 1: have you twigged yet what you've said?
User 2: He won't have, he has a genetic flaw that means he's incapable of understanding irony.
User 1: what's the betting when the penny drops he'll be back tracking with inverted commas or a so-called !
User 2: It might take a while, his quill scratches the screen of his phone so he can't see the screen.

FIGURE 4.4 An example of a conversation-like fragment

Gove's tweet, which is directly replied to by User 1. The next user then replies to User 2 and their reply is also presented by Twitter as including Gove, thus seeming to inherit the address in the previous exchange even though the post appears to be talking about Gove rather than to him (though @mentions have been noted to have the dual function of acting as a reference and as a vocative [Zappavigna, 2012, p. 34]). Without directly inspecting the output of the Twitter API, and consulting only how the tweet appears to the user via the Twitter web interface, it is ambiguous whether or not the original user (in this case Gove) has been manually addressed by the user, or has been automatically added to the thread by the system. This is part of the way that the affordances of the platform are linked with the dynamics of the interaction and with what is and is not possible in terms of structure. Theoretically the interaction is never complete as another user may enter and reply to any of the posts at any point in the unfolding exchange.

The subsequent sections explore affiliation (social bonding) in the 139 replies to Gove's expert tweets.

Method

The replies to Gove's expert tweets were analysed using the framework for exploring affiliation that will be explained below, together with a system network for considering the dialogic dimension of affiliation (Figure 4.5). However, in order to understand the main unit of analysis used in modelling affiliation, it is first necessary to explain the concept of 'coupling'. This is the fundamental concept used to explore how values are instantiated in discourse as the fusion of experience with evaluation (i.e. ideation with attitude), and as such, 'coupling' is the key 'ingredient' needed to understand how people align or de-align around values in their interactions.

Construing values as couplings

Clearly expressing support for, or criticising, particular values is central to political discourse. Therefore, in order to understand the role these values play in social bonding, we need to understand how they are realised in discourse. According to a social semiotic perspective, values are visible in discourse as combinations or 'couplings'[5] of meanings involved in the creation of attitudinal stances. At the most abstract level, coupling refers to coordinated discursive choices occurring across semiotic dimensions (Martin, 2008, p. 39). This means that there is a recurrent coordination of linguistic variables across a text, for instance selections in interpersonal and experiential meanings, as associations of ideation and attitude (e.g. the co-selection of negative evaluation and experts in the 'had enough of experts' tweets mentioned earlier). In essence this concerns a "relation of '*with*': variable *x* comes with variable *y*" (Zhao, 2011, p. 144). This co-selection may occur across any dimension of language, and also across modalities (e.g. gesturing co-occurring with speech).

One of the most studied forms of coupling is ideation-attitude coupling, theorised to have a key role in how values are 'tabled', i.e. how they are offered interactively as potential bonds in discourse (Zappavigna, 2018). This form of coupling has been explored across communicative domains such as casual conversation (Knight, 2008, 2010a, 2010b, 2013), academic discourse (Hao & Humphrey, 2009; Hood, 2010), business writing (Szenes, 2016), legal proceedings (Zappavigna et al., 2008; Martin et al., 2013) and social media discourse (Zappavigna & Martin, 2017; Zappavigna, 2018).

The method used to annotate the attitude component of the couplings explored in this chapter is derived from the appraisal framework (Martin & White, 2005). This framework has been used in a number of social media studies, including studies of affiliation (Zappavigna, 2011, 2012, 2014a, 2014b, 2014c, 2015; Martin et al., 2013; Page et al., 2014), solidarity building (Drasovean & Tagg, 2015), identity construction (Vásquez, 2014), narrative (Page, 2012) and social tagging (Chiluwa & Ifukor, 2015; Zappavigna, 2015). Appraisal postulates three discursive regions of attitudinal meaning: affect (expressing emotion, e.g. 'love', 'disgust', 'fear', etc.), judgement (assessing behaviour, e.g. 'evil', 'ethical', 'trustworthy', etc.) and appreciation (estimating value, e.g. 'beautiful', 'treasured', 'noteworthy', etc.) (Figure 4.5). Each system may be approached at ever-increasing levels of delicacy depending on the analytical task at hand, although it has to be acknowledged that some appraisal subcategories can be fuzzy and ambiguous. Nevertheless, affect, for example, may be specified as dis/inclination, for instance:

(11) If at least one or two expert types could say something vaguely reassuring that would be great. Bit *scared* right now. #Brexit #EUref

It may be also be categorised as un/happiness, for instance:

(12) It's more about the EU laws that generates money but I am no expert either just *sad* about. #Brexit

In addition affect may be realised as in/security:

(13) Every fuckers an expert on politics today. #Brexit #*Worried*

Finally, affect may be specified as dis/satisfaction:

(14) #Brexit: "We've *had enough* of experts" – UK MP Michael Gove. America then says "We've *had enough* of expert politicians." #ElectionNight

The more delicate categorisations of judgement and appreciation are indicated on the network in Figure 4.5 as a series of probe questions that can assist in establishing the meaning to be annotated.

Appraisal also acknowledges that much evaluative meaning is not realised directly in evaluative lexis but may be implied in various ways through 'invoked'

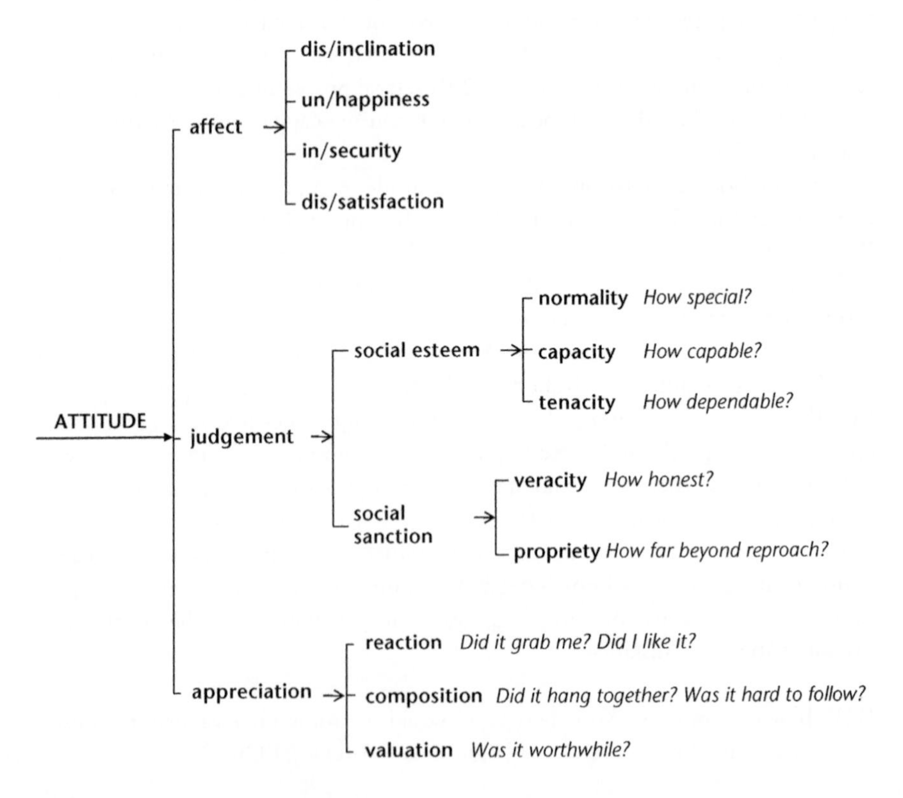

FIGURE 4.5 The system of attitude

Source: Based on Martin and White (2005).

appraisal (Hood & Martin, 2005). The framework distinguishes between three systems of invoked evaluation:

- *Provoke*, where attitude is invoked by lexical metaphor,[6] for example the post below negatively evaluates the capacity of 'experts' via the fortune teller metaphor:

(15) The Bank of England and other *experts are not fortune tellers* – they can't predict the future with a high degree of accuracy. Complaining that it's bad, but not as bad as they said it would be, doesn't mean that #Brexit is good. It's a calamity and it must be stopped.

- *Flag*, where attitude is signalled by intensification or counter-expectancy; for example the upscaled graduation 'too much' in the following post negatively evaluates the amount of communication from experts in a quote:

(16) I recall the pro-Brexit types telling us 'we've heard *too much* from experts'.

- *Afford*, where attitude is activated by ideational tokens that trigger particular cultural values, for example 'investment banker' in the post below is not explicitly evaluative but triggers negative associations (e.g. corporate greed) that reinforces the negative inscribed judgement of 'vested interest' in the final clause:

(17) Also I'm pretty sure her *investment banker* husband has capital interest in EU markets. She has a vested interest in messing up Brexit.

Accounting for invoked meaning is particularly important for interpreting Brexit discourse due to the way that political discourse tends to involve calling upon different kinds of cultural meanings that are negatively or positively evaluated depending on the particular political orientation being construed. It is also important due to the role that humour and innuendo tend to play in political tweeting.

Gove's 'had enough of experts' phrase can be annotated as an ideation-attitude coupling, using square brackets to indicate the scope of the coupling and forward slash to signify the fusion of ideation and attitude:

[ideation: experts (trigger)/attitude: token of affect (negative satisfaction)]

There were some variations of the same coupling pattern with different ideational triggers, for example some posts inserted Gove himself:

(18) People in this country have *had enough of Michael Gove*. #ToryLeadership #Brexit #Gove2016

(19) To paraphrase, "I think the people of this country have *had enough of Michael Gove* . . ." The Experts #Brexit #MichaelGove #Tory #TheresaMay

[ideation: Michael Gove (trigger)/attitude: token of affect (negative satisfaction)]

Modifying the original coupling in this way functions as a form of humorous ridicule. Negotiating couplings interactively is the discursive mechanism for forging (or breaking) social bonds, a concept to which we now turn.

Bonding by negotiating couplings

Social semiotic research into affiliation (the forging of social connections) is largely based on Knight's (2008, 2010a, 2010b, 2013) research into bonding in casual conversation. This work explored how social bonds are realised interactively in dialogic communication. It focused on how interpersonal meanings function in conversational humour between friends chatting about their everyday experiences. In contrast to face-to-face conversation, social media exchanges incorporate dimensions of both interactive dialogue and ambient 'multilogue', as described earlier. This also means that the bonding that is possible in social media communication can incorporate both dialogic affiliation, where participants negotiate couplings in particular exchanges, and communing affiliation, where participants 'commune around' a coupling without necessarily engaging in a direct encounter with another user (for instance by engaging in a hashtagging practice) (Zappavigna & Martin 2017, p. 4; Zappavigna 2018, p. 201). In other words, affiliation can occur both when people interact directly (dialogic affiliation) and when people commune around something but do not interact directly (communing affiliation).

This chapter is focused on the dialogic dimension of affiliation in microblogging. Figure 4.6 is a system network for the different choices a language user may make when interactively negotiating a coupling. The most essential choice is between whether to respond to a coupling that has been tabled in an initiating move or to disengage and ignore it entirely.

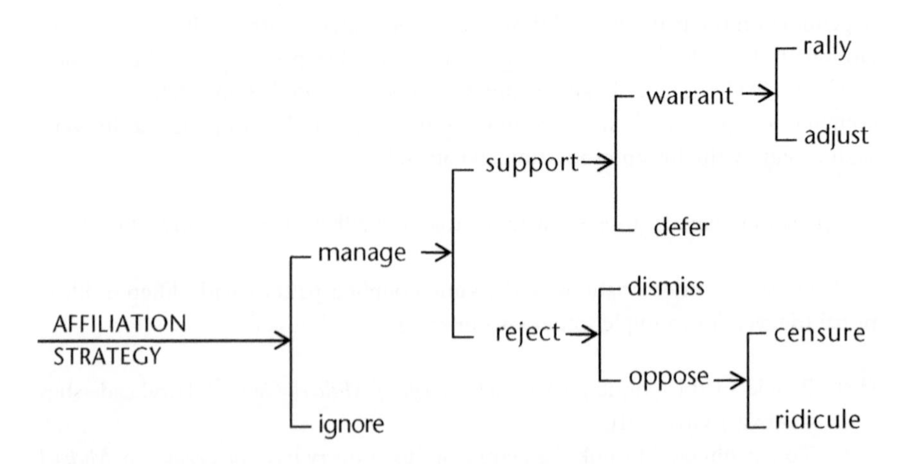

FIGURE 4.6 Affiliation strategies for negotiating couplings

If a responding move is made, it may manage the coupling in various ways. The first choice is between supporting or rejecting the coupling. Support can be realised by warranting the coupling. For example, in the following tweet User 1 tables three couplings as annotated below, the final one of which judges Gove in terms of negative capacity:

(20) User 1: Michael Gove says he is 'radically skeptical' and doesn't value 'expert opinion' – what an idiot! #Brexit #UKIP

[ideation: Gove/attitude: positive capacity]

[ideation: expert opinion/attitude: negative valuation]

[ideation: Gove/attitude: negative capacity]

This final coupling is then replayed in User 2's response as a supporting move rallying around the same coupling of Gove with negative capacity. After this, another coupling is used in a different supporting choice (adjusting): this coupling selects a different attitude from the same system (propriety rather than capacity), hence it is coded as an adjusting choice rather than a rallying choice:

(21) User 2: he's an idiot. How could he? @username

support: warrant: rally

[ideation: Gove/attitude: negative capacity]

support: warrant: adjust

[ideation: Gove's behaviour: attitude negative propriety (afforded)]

Alternatively, a coupling may be deferred if it creates what Knight (2010b) refers to as a 'wrinkle' with another bond that the interactants already share. By 'wrinkle', Knight is referring to a coupling that interrupts the bonding process, creating social tension because it realises "a *potential* bond that cannot be shared by the conversational participants and which contrasts in a laughable way with an *implicated* bond that they share together" (Knight, 2010a, p. 208). In face-to-face interaction, deferral of a bond is typically achieved, according to Knight, by 'laughing off' the coupling. It, however, is not a choice that appears to be regularly made within the Brexit discourse about experts on Twitter. An example from a more personal domain (similar to the 'diet talk' example used in Knight's research) is the following interaction where users appear to be laughing off an overeating bond:

(22) User 1: I think I ate way too much haha.

[ideation: User's eating/attitude: negative judgement (flagged)]

(23) User 2: Lol me too I had Mexcian for lunch lol!!!

support: defer

[ideation: User's 2's behaviour/ attitude: negative judgement (flagged)]

In the above, the negative judgement is invoked by being 'flagged' via the graduation ('*way too* much'), in other words, invoking a meaning of eating beyond reasonable limits. This kind of discourse can be very difficult to interpret without sufficient knowledge of the context of the interaction and the existing bonds that interactants share.

Returning to the system network, the clear alternative to supporting a tabled coupling is rejecting it. This may be achieved simply by dismissing it in a way that does not engage with the coupling at all, for instance using an eyeroll emoji or an expression such as 'yawn' or 'whatever' that closes down the interaction. For example there was one reply to Gove that consisted simply of a frowning eye-roll emoji:

(24) 

If, on the other hand, the interactant chooses to engage with the tabled coupling, they may actively reject it by opposing it through either censure or ridicule. These are the two dominant patterns in the responses to Gove's 'an expert writes/ replies/provides' tweets, which we will now explore in detail.

Analysis: affiliation through censure and ridicule

The choice between censure and ridicule is essentially a choice between criticising a stance or imitating it, although imitation is likely not the only means of realising ridicule. Censure involves critiquing a position, typically through some form of negative attitude, often negative judgement. On the other hand, ridicule mocks a persona or stance, usually by some form of imitation incorporating a replaying or reconstrual of a tabled coupling. Rhetorical strategies that are typically associated with ridicule, such as irony, mockery and sarcasm, are notoriously difficult to analyse, since the meanings at stake often rely on implicating rather than explicating interpersonal meanings. These strategies also tend to draw on the semiotic dexterity of language to simultaneously construe incongruous or contradictory meanings without losing, and indeed often fuelling, communicative power. Teasing, insulting, taunting and forms of jocular mockery have been the subject of much attention in linguistics (Haugh, 2010), informed by work on the bonding role of joking more generally (Boxer & Cortés-Conde, 1997; Norrick, 2003). It has been suggested that 'biting' forms of joking, such as sarcasm and mockery "can express both aggression and solidarity – aggression in the message, attacking others for their foibles and errors, and solidarity in the metamessage, including others in a playful relationship with increased involvement" (Norrick, 1994, p. 423). Martin (2000, p. 164) has suggested that sarcasm might be thought of as involving "discordant couplings – either between appraisal selections and what is being appraised, or among the appraisal variables themselves".

Returning to the network of affiliation strategies, censure is the choice to oppose a tabled coupling by challenging it attitudinally. This was frequently observed in replies to Gove's 'An expert writes' tweet (Figure 4.1). Gove's tweet tables a coupling that positively appreciates the verbiage of the embedded tweet through presenting the other user as an 'expert'. Depending on one's political stance, positive capacity is usually infused in the subject position of an expert. In other words, experts have been historically associated with positive intellectual capacity and social authority, but this association now appears to be dependent on whether positively evaluating experts conforms to the particular political worldview held by a microblogger.

(25) *Gove*: An *expert*[7] writes . . . [[embedded tweet]]

[ideation: quoted tweet/attitude: positive appreciation]

Of course it does not take long for the apparent hypocrisy of this projecting clause to be noted by ambient observers who censure Gove by negatively appreciating his discourse:

(26) User 1: have you twigged yet what you've said?

manage: reject: oppose: censure

[ideation: Gove's tweet/attitude: negative appreciation (afforded)]

This censure opens up a semiotic space for another user to offer their support for this negative assessment. User 2 provides a modified coupling that shifts the negative appreciation of Gove's verbiage to negative judgement of Gove's capacity:

(27) User 2: He won't have, he has a *genetic flaw* that means he's *incapable* of understanding irony.

manage: support: warrant: adjust

[ideation: Gove/attitude: negative capacity]

[ideation: Gove/attitude: negative capacity]

The initial respondent then rallies around this adjusted coupling:

(28) User 1: What's the betting when the penny drops he'll be back tracking with inverted commas or a so-called!

manage: support: warrant: rally

[ideation: Gove's communicative behaviour/attitude: negative capacity (afforded)]

Many of the censuring replies criticise Gove's framing of Maugham's tweet, for example:

(29) User 7: That's a very selective endorsement of Maugham's tweets Michael.

manage: reject: oppose: censure

[ideation: Gove's endorsement/attitude: negative appreciation (afforded)]

Some replies instead target a coupling inside the embedded tweet, pointing out that it is incommensurate with Gove's generally pro-government stance. These posts challenge Gove by appearing, on first pass, to support him but by, in fact, invoking a sarcastic tone to realise a form of censure:

(30) User 5: Glad to see that you are *honest* enough to agree that the 'Government is in utter meltdown' though. 2/2.

manage: support: warrant: rally

[ideation: User/attitude: positive affect]

[ideation: Gove/attitude: positive veracity]

[ideation: government/attitude: negative capacity (afforded)]

Due to the affordances of Twitter, which enables theoretically infinite replies, any move is always available for a potential reply. For instance the post above received the following censuring reply questioning the veracity of User 5's post:

(31) User 6: Where does he say that User 5?

manage: reject: oppose: censure

[ideation: User 5's post/ attitude: negative veracity (afforded)]

In the above, while no attitude is inscribed, the interrogative implies or affords negative judgement (veracity), appearing to question the truthfulness of User 5's claim.

A very frequent pattern in the replies was ridicule rather than explicit censure. This is in keeping with the patterning of the 'had enough of experts' discourse explored by Zappavigna (2017) and briefly introduced in the background to this chapter. For example, there were many posts that sarcastically invert Gove's apparent stance on experts in the manner of the following:

(32) User 7: Oh how you *love* experts.

manage: reject: oppose: ridicule

[ideation: experts/attitude: positive affect]

The modal affordances of Twitter mean that these kinds of ridiculing replies are not restricted to verbiage and can also be realised as images or videos. For example, one reply employed embedded video of a snippet of Gove's Sky News interview (at the point where he makes the 'had enough of experts' comment) as a responding move. Rather than ridicule employing imitation, this is ridicule where a recorded voice (rather than a quoted voice) is replayed as a form of mockery aimed at highlighting hypocrisy.

An example where a responding move is realised as an image was a cartoon together with the hashtag #StopBrexit. This visual reply appears to mock a generalised voice acting as an exemplar of the anti-expert viewpoint. The cartoon represented an exchange between two people, with Person 1 holding a newspaper featuring an image of three judges on the front page and the headline 'enemies of the people'[8]:

(33) Person 1: Bloody experts – economists, lawyers, academics – are *ruining* our country! It's time we were governed by *ignoramuses* . . .

[ideation: experts/attitude: negative propriety]

[ideation: government/attitude: negative capacity]

(34) Person 2: I think we are . . .

support: warrant: rally

[ideation: government/attitude: negative capacity]

All of the couplings sampled in this section appear to act in the service of a 'legitimate expert' bond, where what is at stake is the legitimacy of the expert voice as a source of information and influence. In terms of the affiliation strategies employed to negotiate these couplings, 40 per cent of the replies to Gove's posts employed censure and 60 per cent employed ridicule.[9] While it is difficult to quantify, almost all of the censure had humorous undertones, for example the following post, which questions Gove's capacity:

(35) Indeed. Unlike you, Michael, he actually is an expert. Whereas you merely disparage the superior intellectual abilities of others.

The above post may be interpreted as somewhat humorous since it is using Gove's own choice of words as a jibe. This is different, however, to the humour engendered through ridicule (the more common choice in the replies), where Gove's phrase in the Sky News interview is deliberately imitated in order to mock him:

(36) He is one expert we have definitely all had enough of.
(37) I thought you'd had enough of experts, Michael?
(38) Aren't we fed up with experts?

This tendency toward humour as a response to the online discourse of politicians has also been documented in work on responses to tweets by Donald Trump around the same time as the Brexit discourse reported on here (Zappavigna, 2018). Tweets about Brexit and Trump have demonstrated some discursive 'cross-pollination' due to the temporal adjacency, but also due to the similar questioning of the status of so-called expert 'elites' in both arenas of public discourse (Zappavigna, 2017, 2018), for instance many posts featured both hashtags:

(39) #brexit: #trump:

"I think we've all had enough of experts, don't you?"

Welcome to the post-factual age of the idiot. Protect yourselves.

Discourse about Trump displays a similar concern over the social status of experts and sources of legitimacy. Rather than debate about particular policies or issues, what is being negotiated is attitude about experts, which is perhaps the diversionary rhetorical motive of calling into question the nature of expertise in the first place.

Conclusion

This chapter has explored censure and ridicule as affiliation strategies in replies to tweets by Michael Gove, where he quotes 'experts' despite having previously been virally lampooned on social media for his use of the phrase 'had enough of experts' during a Sky News interview. It has detailed a framework for exploring how values are interactively negotiated in dialogic affiliation and applied to this set of replies. The analysis found that ridicule was the preferred option in the replies, which is unsurprising since users were drawing a connection between Gove's 'had enough of experts' phrase and his choice to use the 'expert' label in an attempt to legitimate his own political views. Thus the ridicule was aimed at exposing apparent hypocrisy.

In accord with previous research on the aligning function of criticism via gossip, humorous or witty negative evaluation appears to augment affiliation, and this may be the reason for the frequency of humour in the texts analysed. In cases where the humour involves a bond that the participants cannot share, it creates what Knight (2010b, p. 46) refers to as a semiotic 'wrinkle' that allows meanings that are too controversial to be laughed off. When the humour involves a bond that is targeted in direct opposition to something ('laughing at' rather than 'laughing off') it assists the interactants in their rallying around negative attitude, as we saw in the case of posts 'laughing at' Gove's apparent hypocrisy in his use of the term 'expert'.

Pro and anti-expert Brexit discourse might be thought of as indicative of the tendency of political support to be polarised, with each side rallying around the values that characterise their 'team' (and perhaps stifling discussion of actual issues). Adopting the perspective on coupling presented in this chapter, we might see these teams or communities as 'coupling chambers', where an initial coupling in a phrase such as 'had enough of experts' is re-instantiated many times over. It remains to be seen whether 'post-truth' is the optimal term for accounting for the kind of coupling patterns prevalent in the #Brexit era, where ideation is being used as a prop for sharing attitude (e.g. by introducing labels such as 'elites') and sharing attitude appears to be taking prominence over debating policy.

Notes

1 Brexit functions as a "complex nominal" (Fontaine, 2017) that condenses various contextual meanings about Britain leaving the European Union.
2 The italics in the numbered examples in this chapter are ours.
3 The content of the embedded tweet in the second post had been deleted from Twitter at the time of writing. This is part of the affordances of the semiotic mode and presents a challenge to analysts since exchanges between users may be viewed as ongoing processes, with ongoing meaning potential that need not be resolved in a particular time frame.
4 This representation is based on the 'Treeverse' visualisation (https://github.com/paulgb/Treeverse/blob/master/README.md#readme). The ellipsis "..." is used to indicate that the diagram is abridged (since space and cognitive constraints prevent representing the full set of replies).
5 Martin (2000, p. 164) first introduced the notion of coupling to explain humour "as involving discordant couplings – either between appraisal selections and what is being appraised, or among the appraisal variables themselves".
6 Systemic functional linguistics differentiates lexical metaphor, realised via lexis, from grammatical metaphor, realised via grammatical choices (see Taverniers, 2006).
7 Instances of inscribed attitude are shown in italics in the examples throughout this section.
8 The cartoon incorporates the front page of the *Daily Mail* on 4 November 2016.
9 Note that I have coded posts that are replies of support to an initial post containing ridicule as ridicule themselves, since in the context of the entire exchange they are contributing to the mockery of Gove's original post.

References

Berghel, H. (2017). Lies, damn lies, and fake news. *Computer, 50*(2), 80–85. doi:10.1109/MC.2017.56

Bosson, J. K., Johnson, A. B., Niederhoffer, K., & Swann, W. B. (2006). Interpersonal chemistry through negativity: Bonding by sharing negative attitudes about others. *Personal Relationships, 13*(2), 135–150. doi:10.1111/j.1475-6811.2006.00109.x

Bouma, J., de Groot, M., Adriaanse, M. L., Polak, S., & Zorz, S. (2017). Bottom-up filter bubble mapping based on Trump and Clinton supporters' tweets. Available at https://wiki.digitalmethods.net/Dmi/WinterSchool2017BeyondTheBubbleInside (accessed 12 August 2018).

Boxer, D., & Cortés-Conde, F. (1997). From bonding to biting: Conversational joking and identity display. *Journal of Pragmatics, 27*(3), 275–294. http://dx.doi.org/10.1016/S0378-2166(96)00031-8

Buckledee, S. (2018). *The language of Brexit: How Britain talked its way out of the European Union*. London: Bloomsbury.

Cap, P. (2016). *The language of fear: Communicating threat in public discourse*. New York: Springer.

Chiluwa, I., & Ifukor, P. (2015). 'War against our children': Stance and evaluation in #BringBackOurGirls campaign discourse on Twitter and Facebook. *Discourse & Society, 26*(3), 267–296. doi:10.1177/0957926514564735

Clarke, J., & Newman, J. (2017). 'People in this country have had enough of experts': Brexit and the paradoxes of populism. *Critical Policy Studies, 11*(1), 101–116. doi:10.1080/19460171.2017.1282376

Drasovean, A., & Tagg, C. (2015). Evaluative language and its solidarity-building role on TED.com: An appraisal and corpus analysis. *Language@Internet, 12*.

Dunbar, R. I. (2004). Gossip in evolutionary perspective. *Review of General Psychology, 8*(2), 100–110. http://dx.doi.org/10.1037/1089-2680.8.2.100

Đurović, T., & Silaški, N. (2018). The end of a long and fraught marriage: Metaphorical images structuring the Brexit discourse. *Metaphor and the Social World, 8*(1), 25–39. https://doi.org/10.1075/msw.17010.dur

Eggins, S., & Slade, D. (1997/2005). *Analysing casual conversation*. London: Equinox.

Fontaine, L. (2017). The early semantics of the neologism BREXIT: A lexicogrammatical approach. *Functional Linguistics, 4*(6), 1–15. doi:10.1186/s40554-017-0040-x

Fuller, S. (2017). Brexit as the unlikely leading edge of the anti-expert revolution. *European Management Journal, 35*(5), 575–580. https://doi.org/10.1016/j.emj.2017.09.002

Gagnon, A., & Bourhis, R. Y. (1996). Discrimination in the minimal group paradigm: Social identity or self-interest? *Personality and Social Psychology Bulletin, 22*(12), 1289–1301. doi:10.1177/01461672962212009

Hao, J., & Humphrey, S. (2009). The role of 'coupling' in biological experimental reports. *Linguistics & the Human Sciences, 5*(2), 169–194. doi:10.1558/lhs.v5i2.169

Haugh, M. (2010). Jocular mockery, (dis)affiliation, and face. *Journal of Pragmatics, 42*(8), 2106–2119. http://dx.doi.org/10.1016/j.pragma.2009.12.018

Higgins, K. (2016). Post-truth: a guide for the perplexed. *Nature*. Available at www.nature.com/news/post-truth-a-guide-for-the-perplexed-1.21054, accessed 13 August 2018.

Hood, S. (2010). *Appraising research: Evaluation in academic writing*. Basingstoke: Palgrave Macmillan.

Hood, S., & Martin, J. (2005). Invoking attitude: The play of graduation in appraising discourse. In R. Hasan, C. M. I. M. Matthiessen, & J. Webster (Eds), *Continuing discourse on language: A functional perspective* (pp. 739–764). London: Equinox.

Jasny, L., Waggle, J., & Fisher, D. R. (2015). An empirical examination of echo chambers in US climate policy networks. *Nature Climate Change, 5*, 782–785. doi:10.1038/nclimate2666

Jaworski, A., & Coupland, J. (2005). Othering in gossip: 'You go out you have a laugh and you can pull yeah okay but like . . .' *Language in Society, 34*(5), 667–694. doi:10.1017/S0047404505050256

Keane, B., & Razir, H. (2014). *A short history of stupid: The decline of reason and why public debate makes us want to scream*. Crows Nest, Australia: Allen & Unwin.

Knight, N. K. (2008). 'Still cool . . . and American too!': An SFL analysis of deferred bonds in internet messaging humour. *Systemic Functional Linguistics in Use: Odense Working Papers in Language and Communication, 29*, 481–502.

Knight, N. K. (2010a). *Laughing our bonds off: Conversational humour in relation to affiliation*. Unpublished PhD thesis. Sydney: University of Sydney.

Knight, N. K. (2010b). Wrinkling complexity: Concepts of identity and affiliation in humour. In M. Bednarek & J. R. Martin (Eds), *New discourse on language: Functional perspectives on multimodality, identity, and affiliation* (pp. 35–58). London: Continuum.

Knight, N. K. (2013). Evaluating experience in funny ways: How friends bond through conversational humour. *Text & Talk, 33*(4–5), 553–574. https://doi.org/10.1515/text-2013-0025

Martin, J. R. (2000). Beyond exchange: Appraisal systems in English. In S. Hunston & G. Thompson (Eds), *Evaluation in text: Authorial stance and the construction of discourse* (pp. 142–175). Oxford: Oxford University Press.

Martin, J. R. (2008). Tenderness: Realisation and instantiation in a Botswanan town. *Odense Working Papers in Language and Communication, 29*, 30–58.

Martin, J. R., & White, P. R. R. (2005). *The language of evaluation: Appraisal in English*. New York: Palgrave Macmillan.

Martin, J. R., Zappavigna, M., Dwyer, P., & Cléirigh, C. (2013). Users in uses of language: Embodied identity in Youth Justice Conferencing. *Text & Talk, 33*(4–5), 467–496. https://doi.org/10.1515/text-2013-0022

McIntyre, L. (2018). *Post-truth*. Cambridge, MA: The MIT Press.

Musolff, A. (2017). Truths, lies and figurative scenarios. *Journal of Language and Politics, 16*(5), 641–657. https://doi.org/10.1075/jlp.16033.mus

Norrick, N. R. (1994). Involvement and joking in conversation. *Journal of Pragmatics, 22*(3), 409–430. doi:http://dx.doi.org/10.1016/0378-2166(94)90117-1

Norrick, N. R. (2003). Issues in conversational joking. *Journal of Pragmatics, 35*(9), 1333–1359. doi:http://dx.doi.org/10.1016/S0378-2166(02)00180-7

Page, R. (2012). The linguistics of self-branding and micro-celebrity in Twitter: The role of hashtags. *Discourse & Communication, 6*(2), 181–201. https://doi.org/10.1177/1750481312437441

Page, R., Barton, D., Unger, J. W., & Zappavigna, M. (2014). *Researching language and social media: A student guide*. London: Routledge.

Simaki, V., Paradis, C., Skeppstedt, M., Sahlgren, M., Kucher, K., & Kerren, A. (2017). Annotating speaker stance in discourse: The Brexit blog corpus. *Corpus Linguistics and Linguistic Theory*, 1–34. https://doi.org/10.1515/cllt-2016-0060

Speed, E., & Mannion, R. (2017). The rise of post-truth populism in pluralist liberal democracies: Challenges for health policy. *International Journal of Health Policy and Management, 6*(5), 249–251. doi:10.15171/IJHPM.2017.19

Spicer, A. (2016). Why do you make stupid decisions when the experts tell you otherwise? *The Conversation*. Available at http://theconversation.com/why-do-you-make-stupid-decisions-when-the-experts-tell-you-otherwise-60020, accessed 13 January 2018.

Szenes, E. (2016). *The linguistic construction of business reasoning: Towards a language-based model of decision-making in undergraduate business*. Unpublished PhD thesis. Sydney: University of Sydney.

Tajfel, H. (1970). Experiments in intergroup discrimination. *Scientific American, 223*(5), 96–102.

Taverniers, M. (2006). Grammatical metaphor and lexical metaphor: Different perspectives on semantic variation. *Neophilologus, 90*(2), 321–332. doi:10.1007/s11061-005-0531-y

Vásquez, C. (2014). 'Usually not one to complain but . . .': Constructing identities in user-generated online reviews. In P. Seargeant & C. Tagg (Eds), *The language of social media: Identity and community on the internet* (pp. 65–90). Basingstoke: Palgrave Macmillan.

Wert, S. R., & Salovey, P. (2004). A social comparison account of gossip. *Review of General Psychology, 8*(2), 122–137. http://dx.doi.org/10.1037/1089-2680.8.2.122

Zappavigna, M. (2011). Ambient affiliation: A linguistic perspective on Twitter. *New Media & Society, 13*(5), 788–806. doi:10.1177/1461444810385097

Zappavigna, M. (2012). *Discourse of Twitter and social media*. London: Continuum.

Zappavigna, M. (2014a). Ambient affiliation in microblogging: Bonding around the quotidian. *Media International Australia, 151*(1), 97–103. https://doi.org/10.1177/1329878X1415100113

Zappavigna, M. (2014b). Enacting identity in microblogging through ambient affiliation. *Discourse & Communication, 8*(2), 209–228. doi:10.1177/1750481313510816

Zappavigna, M. (2014c). Enjoy your snags Australia . . . oh and the voting thing too #ausvotes #auspol: Iconisation and affiliation in electoral microblogging. *Global Media Journal: Australian Edition, 89*(2), 1–18.

Zappavigna, M. (2015). Searchable talk: The linguistic functions of hashtags. *Social Semiotics, 25*(3), 274–291. doi:10.1080/10350330.2014.996948

Zappavigna, M. (2017). 'Had enough of experts': Intersubjectivity and quotation in social media. In E. Friginal (Ed.), *Studies in corpus-based sociolinguistics* (pp. 321–343). London: Routledge.

Zappavigna, M. (2018). *Searchable talk: Hashtags and social media metadiscourse*. London: Bloomsbury.

Zappavigna, M., Dwyer, P., & Martin, J. (2008). Syndromes of meaning: Exploring patterned coupling in a NSW Youth Justice Conference. In A. Mahboob & N. K. Knight (Eds), *Questioning linguistics* (pp. 103–117). Newcastle-upon-Tyne: Cambridge Scholars Publishing.

Zappavigna, M., & Martin, J. R. (2017). #Communing affiliation: Social tagging as a resource for aligning around values in social media. *Discourse, Context & Media, 22*, 4–12. https://doi.org/10.1016/j.dcm.2017.08.001

Zhao, S. (2011). *Learning through multimedia interaction: The construal of primary social science knowledge in web-based digital learning materials*. Unpublished PhD thesis. Sydney: University of Sydney.

5

'BRITAIN IS FULL TO BURSTING POINT!'

Immigration themes in the Brexit discourse of the UK Independence Party

Piotr Cap

Introduction

The beginning of summer 2016 saw a momentous event in the history of modern Europe: the UK's referendum on EU membership. On 23 June 2016, after a long and heated campaign, 52 per cent of British voters cast their votes in favour of leaving the Union. Voting for Brexit, they put an end to the 43 years of the UK's membership in first the European Economic Community (EEC) and later the European Union (EU). The promise to hold the referendum was first announced by the then British Prime Minister David Cameron in January 2013, subject to the condition that the Conservative party win the next general election in 2015. Cameron's announcement was thus the starting point of a nationwide 'proto-referendum' debate, which lasted for the following three years, involving a variety of themes, attitudes and arguments among the supporters as well as opponents of Brexit. A theme that was particularly salient, and often marking the dividing line between the two sides, was *immigration* – discussed in the context of 'big' national issues such as sovereignty, democracy and economic prosperity. Looking back, there are reasons to believe that immigration (and mainly *anti*-immigration) topics and narratives pervading the Brexit debate have been influential for the evolution of attitudes surrounding the EU membership referendum and, consequently, its results.[1] Specifically, the anti-immigration discourse in 2013–2016 was instrumental in instilling a sense of public uncertainty and ever-growing anxiety, inspiring isolationist stances and explicitly xenophobic attitudes, which found their outlet on the day of the referendum. The leading role in perpetuating such attitudes is often attributed (e.g. Goodwin & Heath, 2016; Tournier-Sol, 2017) to the members and supporters of the oppositional United Kingdom Independence Party (UKIP), which made immigration a central issue of the Brexit campaign.

In this chapter, I explore the main characteristics of the UKIP anti-immigration discourse, as exemplified in the rhetoric of public addresses (including parliamentary speeches, press conference statements, as well as television and newspaper interviews and comments) by the former UKIP leader Nigel Farage between February 2013 and June 2016, i.e. throughout the entire period of the proto-referendum debate. Working with a corpus of 88 addresses in total, I identify discursive strategies whereby the influx of Middle East and North African refugees, as well as economic migrants from Eastern EU member states, is construed as a growing threat to the well-being, security and identity of the British people and Britain as a nation. This construal subsumes the adversarial position of Brussels as the warrant of free economic movement of all EU citizens, and as the staunch promoter of the movement of non-EU migrants between EU countries. As can be seen from Farage's rhetoric, defining the EU as an antagonistic entity helps UKIP strengthen their Brexit rationale (see also Miglbauer & Koller, Chapter 6 this volume). The main cognitive, discursive and linguistic-pragmatic strategies used to realise this goal are proximisation, deictic othering and conceptual metaphor. Before investigating these strategies, I start by placing the question of immigration in the broader context of the proto-referendum debate and its focus on the critical issues of Britain's political and economic sovereignty and independence. The awareness of that global context goes a long way toward understanding the relevance and effectiveness of Nigel Farage's rhetoric.

The proto-referendum debate: from sovereignty to immigration

It only takes a quick glance at British public discourse of 2013–2016, in its state-political, parliamentary as well as journalistic manifestations, to see that issues of immigration and anti-immigration are hardly ever addressed in isolation from the general theme of Britain's sovereignty and democracy. This theme is dominated by those who proclaim dissatisfaction with what they see as negative consequences of EU membership for the UK's political and socio-economic freedoms. While UKIP and Nigel Farage play the leading role here, it is interesting to note that, initially, isolationist values are expressed in many of the 2013 media appearances by top politicians of the ruling Conservative Party, including the then Prime Minister David Cameron. The most telling example is Cameron's speech at Bloomberg on 23 January 2013, in which he addresses questions of sovereignty and democracy, making an explicit link between British identity and foreign policy[2]:

(1) I know that the United Kingdom is sometimes seen as an argumentative and rather strong-minded member of the family of European nations. And it's true that our geography has shaped our psychology. We have the character of an island nation – independent, forthright, passionate in defence of our sovereignty. We can no more change this British sensibility than we can

drain the English Channel. And because of this sensibility, we come to the European Union with a frame of mind that is more practical than emotional. For us, the European Union is a means to an end – prosperity, stability, the anchor of freedom and democracy both within Europe and beyond her shores – not an end in itself (Cameron, 2013).

Later in the speech, Cameron goes on to note that "there is a gap between the EU and its citizens which [. . .] represents a lack of democratic accountability and consent that is felt particularly acutely in Britain" and affirms that "there is a growing frustration that the EU is seen as something that is done to people rather than acting on their behalf" (Cameron, 2013).

These excerpts show Cameron advocating not only British pragmatism ('a frame of mind that is more practical than emotional'), but also British exceptionalism, and enacting a strong political distinction by reference to an 'independent' and 'forthright' country that is an 'island nation'. The latter reference is a form of intertextuality, in that it is a programmatic deictic catchphrase, bringing to mind Winston Churchill's wartime speeches.[3] Cameron rejects the notion of a "single European demos" (a single European self; Cameron, 2013) and prioritises national parliaments, thereby privileging the 'national self' and rejecting a shared sense of European identity. Doing so, he confirms Marcussen et al.'s (1999, p. 628) observation that "classical Anglo-Saxon notions of political order emphasise parliamentary democracy and external sovereignty" and that "there is not much room for 'Europe' or 'Europeanness'" in British political space". This in turn implies that any act performed in the interest of 'Europe' is potentially anti-British and can be considered a threat (Todd, 2015).

As noted by Todd (2015), Cameron's Bloomberg speech sets the terms for the debate over the rest of 2013 and virtually the entire period preceding the referendum. Conservative backbenchers take his arguments further still, often arguing for a defence of British sovereignty through reference to history and especially the Second World War. For example, Richard Shepherd (Conservative) asserts:

(2) This vote, what we decide and what people in the future decide will determine the character and strength of our national constitutional history, which is being threatened. Why should we defer in such an adventure, when this is the most remarkable and ancient of all the democratic communities within Western Europe? Why? (Hansard, 2013–2014, p. 1201).

William Cash (Conservative) makes an intertextual reference to Churchill, stating:

(3) People have fought and died. The only reason we live in the United Kingdom in peace and prosperity is because, in the Second and First World Wars, we stood up for that freedom and democracy. Churchill galvanised the British people to stand up for the very principles that are now at stake (Hansard, 2013–2014, p. 1210).

Finally, Gordon Henderson (Conservative) argues that:

(4) It is inconceivable that only 30 years after the end of the Second World War, the British people would have willingly embarked on a programme to hand over swathes of their hard-won sovereignty to another state, and let us be clear: that is what the European Union aspires to be (Hansard, 2013–2014, p. 1232).

The references to the Second World War and Churchill serve to consolidate the national self (see also Wenzl, Chapter 3 this volume). They stress the centrality of the moment and prescribe the future course of action. The historical flashbacks activate reasoning by analogy: what makes current policies legitimate is, above all, their consistency with long accepted principles and solutions (Musolff, 2004, 2016). The past is thus invoked as a lesson to heed when going into an uncertain future. As Daddow (2006, p. 320) notes:

> This is the kind of commonsense history everyone knows even if they are not historians [. . .] the kind that tells [British people] all [they] need to know about Europe from Britain's martial past; its encounters with the Spanish Armada, at the battle of Trafalgar, with Napoleon at Waterloo, after the let-down of Munich in 1938 and against Hitler's Germany during the Second World War.

Indeed, the majority of voices in the 2013–2016 proto-referendum debate tend to see Great Britain as, in Shepherd's words, "the most ancient and remarkable of democratic communities" (Hansard, 2013–2014, p. 1201). Continental Europe is in turn framed as a threat to the "[British] national constitutional history" and to the principles of freedom and democracy for which "Churchill galvanised the British people to stand up" (Cap, 2017, p. 36). This conceptual arrangement provides a firm ideological groundwork for all policy issues, including the critical issue of immigration. UKIP's and Nigel Farage's rhetoric is constructed to be consistent, at least initially, with that groundwork, and indeed fits its main premises very well. From the very start, Farage builds his hard-Eurosceptic case on identity-related claims:

(5) The fact is we just don't belong in the European Union. Britain is different. Our geography puts us apart. Our history puts us apart. Our institutions produced by that history put us apart. We think differently. We behave differently [. . .] The roots go back seven, eight, nine hundred years with the Common Law. Civil rights. Habeas corpus. The presumption of innocence. The right to a trial by jury. On the continent confession is the mother of all evidence (Farage, 2013).

Farage's argument in example (5) initiates a number of strategies that are going to appear throughout most of his 2013–2016 discourse, getting increasingly salient and radical as the referendum date draws near. Specifically, he sets up a lasting Us vs Them distinction, which involves consistent deictic 'othering' of the adversarial Them party, based on allegedly insurmountable historical and ideological differences. He appeals to the weight of 'seven, eight, nine hundred years' of history, during which Britain has been 'different [from continental Europe]'. He also uses ethical dimensions of identity to differentiate a British tradition of presumption of innocence and jury trial from a continental system based on confession. In the same speech Farage goes on to affirm that "[British people] know that only by leaving the Union [they] can regain control of [their] borders, [their] parliament, democracy and [their] ability to trade freely with the fastest-growing economies in the world". Implying lack of control of the '[UK] borders', he sets up a direct link to the immigration theme, framing it as an issue of extreme urgency and consequentiality. Like Cameron and the Conservative MPs quoted above, he employs identity and cultural differentiation (Todd, 2015) to serve his political cause of increasing UKIP's electoral strength and achieving a British exit from the EU. The text in example (5) is thus an example of how Farage's rhetoric builds on the general aura of Euroscepticism observable right at the outset of the proto-referendum debate. The later discourse becomes gradually more distinctive; it makes the central arguments far more salient, thus unveiling specific rhetorical patterns and linguistic-pragmatic strategies used to make the case for Brexit. Most of these strategies are readily analysable within proximisation theory, which, as I show below, offers a feasible analytical handle on both conceptual and linguistic aspects of threat-based rhetoric.

Proximisation: theory and analysis

The enactment of the Us vs Them conceptual distinction, which lies at the core of the argument in example (5) and becomes a trademark of Farage's later speeches, provides for some effective rhetorical strategies involving fear appeals and coercion. One such strategy is *proximisation*, which builds on the positioning of the Us and Them groups in the opposite (central vs remote) domains of the discourse space (DS) – a socio-cognitive space activated by speaker's discourse (van Dijk, 1998; Chilton, 2004, 2005, 2010; Gavins, 2007). In its broadest sense, proximisation consists of presenting the remote Them – physically and temporally distant entities, events, states of affairs and adversarial hence 'distant' ideologies (van Dijk, 2017) – as increasingly threatening to the speaker and her addressee (the central Us). It thus involves a conceptualisation of *movement* (Werth, 1999) of the remote Them entities in the direction of the Us entities.[4] Notwithstanding its cognitive, mostly deictic underpinnings (cf. Levelt, 1989; Levinson, 2003), proximisation possesses some clear pragmatic goals. Projecting the Them entities as encroaching upon the Us group (both physical and ideological), the speaker aims to legitimise actions and policies that he or she proposes to neutralise the growing impact of the negative, 'foreign', 'alien', 'antagonistic' entities (Figure 5.1).

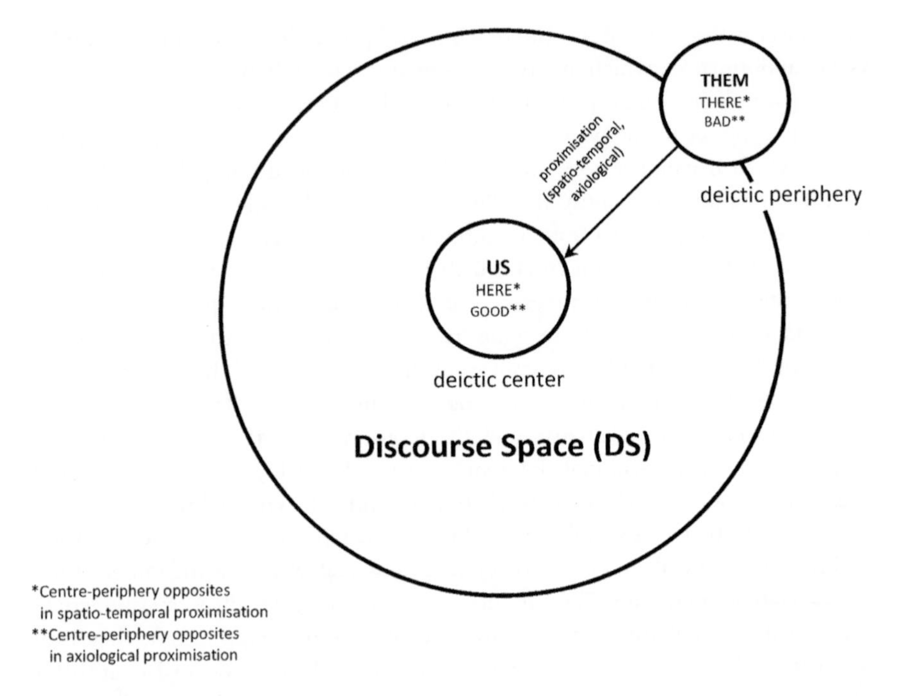

FIGURE 5.1 Proximisation in discourse space (DS)

The concept of proximisation was first applied in studies of coercion patterns in the US anti-terrorist rhetoric following 9/11 (Cap, 2006, 2008, 2010). Since then it has been used within different discourse domains, though most commonly in analyses of state political discourses: crisis construction and war rhetoric (Chovanec, 2010), anti-immigration discourse (Hart, 2010, 2014), political party representation (Cienki et al., 2010; Kaal, 2012), construction of national memory (Filardo Llamas, 2010, 2013), and design of foreign policy documents (Dunmire, 2011). These studies have refined the concept of proximisation, which can now be defined in more formal terms. In this chapter, I refer to proximisation as a forced construal operation meant to evoke closeness of an external threat, to solicit legitimisation of preventive means (Cap, 2013, 2017). As has been noted, the source of the threat is DS-remote entities, Them, which are conceptualised to be crossing the space to invade the Us entities, i.e. the speaker and his addressee. The threat is of a spatio-temporal as well as an ideological nature; thus, there are three main types of proximisation. First, 'spatial proximisation' is a forced construal of Them entities encroaching *physically* upon the Us entities. The spatial aspect of proximisation can be seen as primary, as the remaining types involve conceptualisations in metaphorically spatial terms. 'Temporal proximisation' is a forced conceptualisation of the envisaged conflict as not only imminent, but also momentous, historic and therefore requiring an immediate response and unique preventive measures. Spatial and temporal proximisation involve fear appeals and typically use various kinds of analogies to conflate the developing threat with an actual disastrous event in the past – so as to endorse the current scenario.[5] In turn, 'axiological proximisation' involves construal of a gathering ideological clash between the 'home values' of the DS central entities (Us) and the alien and antagonistic Them values. It is worth noting that the Them values are not just abstract entities; they possess a potential to materialise and impact the Us group. Finally, apart from the fear-based, coercive axiological proximisation, there is also a subtype that is, so to say, 'positive' – involving the Us entities and values. This 'positive-type' axiological proximisation consists of invoking commendable historical attitudes and behaviours as motivation for current action, a strategy we have already seen in example (4) above.

While early voices in the EU membership debate, viz. example (5), merely invoke the Us vs Them distinction, establishing some basic polarities and hardly performing proximisation as such, the pace of the debate and the growing radicalisation of attitudes quickly led to a new kind of discourse, in which the antagonism between the supporters and opponents of Brexit gets more acute. In this new discourse, immigration turns into the central and most frequent theme addressed by the UKIP party to make their case for the Leave vote. Accordingly, proximisation becomes the main conceptual tool and rhetorical strategy to picture the so-called influx of immigrants in terms of a developing 'Them-invasion'. This can be seen from the following examples (6–9), which reveal the growing radicalism of Farage's discourse in the 2014–2016 period. Analytically, they fall into two pairs, examples (6–7) and (8–9), illustrating two phases of UKIP's Brexit rhetoric, respectively. In the first phase (examples 6–7 below), Farage's fear appeals can be described as relatively moderate:

(6) In the last ten years opinion polls have shown substantial majorities in favour of cutting immigration to a rate at which it can be comfortably absorbed. Yet instead of listening to those who elected them, the government takes orders from the European Union and is throwing open our borders to more than 30 million Bulgarians and Romanians who may be coming to settle here [. . .] What do we call it if not yet another sovereignty-sapping power grab from EU elites? And with our sovereignty and identity at stake, the time to act is now. I mean, the time has come to defy Brussels and declare that our country is full up (Farage, 2014a).

(7) Truth is, in scores of our cities and market towns, this country in a short space of time is becoming unrecognisable. What I am saying is we now have nearly 10 per cent of our schools in this country where English is not the primary language of the homes those children come from. And further, Migration Watch estimates that over 250,000 people from Bulgaria, the EU's poorest country, may be arriving over the next five years. Under EU rules, we are powerless to deny them entry or benefits after restrictions were lifted in January [2014]. If we don't reclaim our powers from Brussels, we risk losing control not only of our country's borders, our identity, but also the welfare state (Farage, 2014b).

In examples (6–7), the status of Them is ascribed to mostly economic migrants from new members of the EU such as Bulgaria and Romania. In ideological terms, Them applies also to 'Brussels', as the promoter of free flow of people and the freedom of employment within the EU. This designation makes examples (6) and (7) relatively moderate in their fear-inducing and coercive appeal – although a possibility is left for threat levels to rise in the future (discourse) ('If we don't reclaim our powers from Brussels'). Such an arrangement involves a balanced use of different proximisation strategies. While spatial proximisation is used to construe the ongoing arrival of migrants from the new member states in physical terms, axiological proximisation is applied to construe some long-term consequences of immigration. These are conceptualised in largely socio-ideological terms, as a threat to sovereignty and national identity ('our sovereignty and identity at stake', 'we risk losing control not only of our country's borders, our identity'). The axiological aspect of proximisation in the two texts covers not only migrants, but also the 'EU elites' in Brussels, who are held responsible for enforcing 'sovereignty-sapping' policies against some of the countries' national interests. The argument in example (7) makes explicit one of such interests, namely the 'welfare state'. This phrase marks, incidentally, an important theme of UKIP's and Farage's anti-immigration discourse, which can be described as 'welfare chauvinism'. The term 'welfare chauvinism' was coined by Andersen and Bjørklund (1990) to account for the perspective that state support should be restricted to national citizens and not provided to 'others'.

At the pragmalinguistic and lexical levels, the proximisation strategies in examples (6) and (7) involve a variety of tools. First of all, much of the narration makes use of progressive tense forms. This pertains to both spatial and axiological proximisation. The progressive aspect increases the appeal of the projected physical impact ('30 million Bulgarians and Romanians [. . .] may be coming to settle here', '250,000 people [. . .] may be arriving over the next five years'), and also strengthens the identity-related claims and threats ('this country in a short space of time is becoming unrecognisable'). It has been noted (Dunmire, 2011; Cap, 2013) that the use of the progressive helps construe a – here negative – scenario by conflating the present and the future; it describes a current developing event that presages an ominous future. Such a scenario, involving temporal proximisation, derives extra strength from the strategic vagueness it carries, especially when specific modalities are used in support. As can be seen from examples (6) and (7), the encroachment threat has feeble temporal underpinnings and the apparent impossibility to determine the very moment or critical culmination of impact ('may be coming', 'may be arriving') only makes that threat bigger and harder to contain. At the same time, the conflation of the present and the (ominous) future results in centralising the present time frame as *the* moment to act preventively, thus revealing its coercive force.

As the proximisation strategies in examples (6) and (7) involve temporal projections and anticipations of the future, they are accompanied by rhetorical ploys whose goal is to earn credibility for the envisaged scenarios. Thus, the argument in example (7) makes use of 'source-tagging', a judgement attribution strategy whereby an authorial voice is invoked to communicate sensitive or controversial information (Mann & Thompson, 1988). By referring to research of the respectable think tank Migration Watch, Farage seeks to lend credibility to his threatening vision of mass migration from the new members of the EU, legitimising the urgent need for preventive measures. The criticality of the moment is graphically expressed in the last phrase in example (6) ('our country is full up'), which employs a conceptual metaphor to strengthen its pragmatic appeal (see the next section).

The other pair of examples (8–9 below) illustrates the second phase of Nigel Farage's Brexit rhetoric (2015–2016), in which the threat levels rise considerably:

(8) Mr Cameron and his ministers have chosen to duck questions about the scale of a new wave of immigration from Syria and other countries of the Middle East and North Africa. Today, the *Sun* reveals the shocking figure that nearly one in five of all rape or murder suspects is a non-EU migrant. [. . .] A report published today shows that, because of a loophole in the immigration rules, more than 20,000 migrants from outside the EU come to live here every year. It doesn't take a genius to work out that the two figures might be connected (Farage, 2015).

(9) We refuse to sacrifice our freedom and security for political correctness. We must call things by their true names. Rather than shedding tears like Federica Mogherini or organizing marches that solve nothing, the state should ensure the safety of its citizens [. . .] To those who are happy to welcome immigrants at our doors, I have a suggestion: go and see the refugee camps in Turkey. See the gangs and the riots. See the young Muslim criminals. See the anger, violence, and terror. It is there and is ready for export. This kind of evil might not have reached us yet, but it is well in sight. And there is noone in Brussels who can protect us when it comes (Farage, 2016b).

In this second phase, the status of Them is ascribed primarily to non-EU migrants and in particular Muslim immigrant groups from the Middle East and North Africa. This redirection of focus allows for a swift radicalisation of UKIP's isolationist rhetoric, which has ever since built upon the aura of fear triggered by concurrent terrorist attacks and other criminal acts involving Islamic perpetrators. Hence, a terrorist threat underlies the argument in example (9), where Farage indirectly refers to the July 2016 attack in Nice, in order to criticise the EU's passivity and lack of response ('Rather than shedding tears like Federica Mogherini [EU Foreign Minister] or organizing marches that solve nothing, the state should ensure the safety of its citizens').[6] At the same time, the everyday safety of the British people is called into question in comments such as example (8), the threat being linked again to a growing Muslim migration into UK ('a new wave of immigration from Syria and other countries of the Middle East and North Africa').

Finally, the strongest fear appeal is made in the narrative that develops in the second part of example (9) (from 'To those who are happy' until the end of the excerpt). This narrative exhibits a peculiar discursive structure, involving a causative connection between two consecutive segments, which can be described as 'abstract/ideological' and 'material/physical', respectively. The first segment ('refugee camps in Turkey [. . .] gangs and the riots [. . .] young Muslim criminals [. . .] anger, violence, and terror. It is there and is ready for export') provides socio-psychological context and conditions for a possible Them threat. The second segment ('This kind of evil might not have reached us yet, but it is well in sight') transforms the status of that threat, from a 'remote possibility' to an 'actual occurrence' within the Us space ('is well in sight'). Such a dynamic construal therefore involves both axiological and spatio-temporal proximisation. While the former forces the conceptualisation of a relatively distant vision based upon a specific contextual (ideological) arrangement, the latter turns that threatening vision into a material threat and nearly inevitable impact ('when it comes'). To smoothen this conceptual shift by lexical and grammatical means, a modality change is used – a possibility-setting *might*-phrase ('might not have reached us yet') leads to a more 'realistic' *be*-phrase ('is well in sight').

The analysed corpus (88 addresses in total) includes 47 such complex narratives, in which specific lexico-grammatical items, such as noun and verb phrases, occur in a linear order to construe, within the space of one, two or maximally three sentences, a subtle conceptual transformation of initially remote, largely abstract danger, into a concrete threat involving tangible, material consequences.[7] Interestingly, out of these 47 sequences, as many as 39 occur in the speeches and

TABLE 5.1 Monthly numbers of discourse sequences construing the 'remote possibility' to 'actual occurrence' conceptual transitions

Month	*Number*
January 2015	1
February 2015	0
March 2015	1
April 2015	0
May 2015	0
June 2015	1
July 2015	2
August 2015	2
September 2015	1
October 2015	2
November 2015	3
December 2015	2
January 2016	3
February 2016	4
March 2016	5
April 2016	5
May 2016	7
Total from January 2015 to May 2016	**39**

comments made after 1 January 2015. What is more, their number increases in the months preceding the referendum (see Table 5.1). That shows, perhaps most vividly, that Nigel Farage's rhetoric is indeed radicalising as the referendum date draws nearer. As has been noted, this development goes hand in hand with the gradual re-conceptualisation of the Them party: in the 2015 and 2016 texts, only one in four embodiments of Them is EU migrants, the remainder being immigrants and refugees from Muslim countries in the Middle East and North Africa. In these texts, the use of various proximisation strategies, and their interplays such as in example (9), contributes greatly to instilling an aura of fear, thus fueling isolationist attitudes.

Metaphorisation

A substantial part of Nigel Farage's anti-immigration discourse in the proto-referendum debate reveals extensive metaphorisation, which often adds extra strength to the appeal of threat patterns enacted by proximisation shifts. From a theoretical point of view this is hardly surprising, since metaphor and proximisation are fundamentally connected at the cognitive level of the discourse space (recall Figure 5.1). Specifically, the deictic centre, a 'home camp' of Us entities, is frequently conceptualised in/through discourse as a *container*, thus othering the non-members, which are conceptualised as Them entities. As a result, metaphorisation of the Us entities as elements in the container provides for some excellent rhetorical benefits, especially in fear-generating and coercive discourses. In particular, threats to the container and its Us elements can be symbolically derived from a limited volume of the container that 'fills up' quickly with Them entities in the process of proximisation.

Given these benefits, it is understandable that the conceptual metaphor of container has a long tradition in British (anti-)immigration discourse, recruiting the container schema to conceptualise the country (Charteris-Black, 2005; Hart, 2010). Charteris-Black (2005) presents evidence that metaphors construing UK as a container are a stable feature of the British discourse on immigration, reflecting and reinforcing an underlying cognitive arrangement, i.e. the perception of Britain as an island. In an attempt to explain where exactly the rhetorical powers of the container metaphor lie and how they get activated, Hart (2010, 2014) argues that the container schema emerges from ubiquitous and reoccurring experiences with the state of containment:

> Our encounter with containment and boundedness is one of the most pervasive features of our bodily experience [. . .]. From the beginning, we experience constant physical containment in our surroundings [. . .] We move in and out of rooms, clothes, vehicles, and numerous kinds of bounded spaces. We manipulate objects, placing them in containers (cups, boxes, cans, bags, etc.). In each of these cases there are [. . .] typical schemata for physical containment.
>
> *(Hart, 2010, p. 160)*

Thus, the container schema consists of three structural elements: an interior and an exterior defined by a boundary. The interior also includes a *centre-periphery* structure, and the container possesses, as has been noted, volume, which is to say a *full-empty* structure (Charteris-Black, 2005; Hart, 2010, 2014). As Hart (2010) argues, this arrangement holds some important implications for political discourse. First, it follows from the nature of the container schema that something is either in or out of the container; second, the experience of containment typically involves protection from, or resistance to, external forces. Altogether, the conventional character of metaphors based on the container schema increases credibility and pragmatic appeal of the discourses and texts where they occur.

In the corpus of Farage's 2013–2016 speeches the container metaphor involves multiple lexical items and phrases, such as 'wave [of immigration]', 'absorb', 'throw open', 'borders', 'full up' and 'burst', most of which could be seen surfacing randomly in examples (5–9) above. In combination, these items construe a metaphor scenario (Musolff, 2016) that justifies a restrictive immigration policy to contain what is conceptualised as a growing social threat. The scenario comprises a structured set of inferences, such as the following:

- The country – Britain – has a limited capacity.
- Continued immigration could cause the country (the 'container') to 'burst',
- Immigration will continue as, 'under orders from the EU', the government are 'throwing open [the country's] borders'.
- The country is thus under a real and growing threat.
- The only way to offset the threat is to force the government to ignore the 'orders' and maintain a tough immigration policy.

The final inference (to force the government to ignore the 'orders') is a direct instruction for the Brexit vote. The entire chain of inferences draws, as was noted, upon the conventionality of the container metaphor, which facilitates a swift processing of the conveyed insight. Farage's discourse also includes other reception facilitators, grounded in some further features of the container schema. As observed by Chilton (2004, p. 88), the container schema entails *exclusivity* such that members have to be either *in* or *out*. It further entails 'protection by means of exclusion', as opposed to any other means available to human societies. This makes it easier to accept and adapt to the reality pictured in the container metaphor on account of their territorial instinct and in-group allegiance (Jowett & O'Donnell, 1992). Since, under the container schema, the entity construed as 'container' is presupposed to cover a given territory and those inside the container are presupposed to own the territory it covers, the container metaphor reinforces the general aura of stability and permanence associated with that entity (Chilton, 2004, 2014; Musolff 2016, pp. 25–38). This is yet another reason why metaphors conceptualising countries in terms of bounded entities are extremely frequent in political discourse, and immigration discourse in particular, which Farage's rhetoric illustrates very well. Similar to proximisation strategies, conceptual metaphors involving the container schema rise in number and density toward the end of the proto-referendum debate:

(10) [D]ay in and day out we face waves of asylum seekers from Calais and Cherbourg [. . .] illegal entrants are already at our gates and we must stand firm because Britain is full to bursting point [. . .] and the flow shows no signs of slowing. There are reports that say we're better off with mass immigration. But to me, there is an issue here called the quality of life and I think that matters more than money. 'Cause, I am getting a bit tired of my kids coming home from school being taught about every other religion in the world, celebrating every other religious holiday but not actually being taught about Christianity. 'Cause, I would remind you, of the eight people who committed those atrocities in Paris a mere three months ago,[8] five of them had got into Europe posing as refugees (Farage, 2016a).

Made at the end of February 2016, the address in example (10) can be seen as directly instrumental in shaping attitudes on the eve of the referendum. The argument includes some explicit fear appeals, involving both ideological and physical threats. This duality is reflected in the two final sentences of the text, which construe, respectively, a cultural/religious identity threat, and an ominous material threat of terrorist attacks similar to the Paris attacks of November 2015. The job of preparing such a hard-hitting ending is notably left to metaphors, which develop an appealing argument that outlines a (favourable) context for the gathering threat. Thus, the first part of the text includes numerous lexical items and phrases depicting the (calibre of) the Them immigration impact ('waves of asylum seekers', 'flow [with] no signs of slowing'), as well as the already critical condition of the Us home camp ('illegal entrants are already at our gates and we must stand firm because Britain is full to bursting point'). As has been noted in the previous section, many of these container items are also, technically, markers of proximisation (especially spatial proximisation). The interplay of conceptual metaphor and proximisation can be further noticed in the use of a historical flashback to generate analogy (Musolff, 2004, 2016): the memory of the 'atrocities in Paris' is invoked and temporally proximised as a lesson to heed in the future. It is worth noting that, altogether, Farage's 2013–2016 discourse features a moderate number of such analogies, yet their occurrences increase markedly in the years 2015–2016. This corroborates the finding about the ever-growing explicitness of Farage's rhetoric in the course of the referendum debate.

Conclusion

The examples in the previous two sections are among the most representative in the corpus, thus painting a fair picture of UKIP and Nigel Farage's (anti-)immigration discourse in the four years preceding the referendum. In general, this discourse can be characterised as conceptually bipolar, recognising the Us/Them distinction and enacting this distinction with regard to ideological and policy issues. In the course of the proto-referendum debate, it expresses, first, some relatively moderate positions (as in the argument in the years 2013–2014), and later, a more radical stance (in the years 2015–2016). The ongoing radicalisation of Farage's rhetoric throughout the debate is both caused by, and reflected in, the change of discursive focus, which is gradually redirected from EU immigration to largely Middle East and North African immigration. This change can be seen as a natural consequence of simultaneous events (such as the Paris terrorist strikes and the 2015 refugee crisis), as well as an attempt to earn some extra popular support in the last months before the referendum vote. Altogether, Farage's discourse draws heavily on isolationist values inspired by various voices in the proto-referendum debate, coming from opposition and government supporters alike. The understanding of this broad context is crucial for the study of the UKIP Brexit discourse, which often addresses and benefits from the popular feeling of anxiety and uncertainty about Britain's political and economic sovereignty.

At the pragmalinguistic and lexical levels, Farage's rhetoric makes ample use of threat-constructing, coercive devices, which antagonise the Us/Them groups, legitimising the measures proposed to offset or prevent the projected immigration impact. The two most effective strategies are proximisation and conceptual metaphor, which both contribute to the deictic othering of immigrants, while at the same time mobilising the home group (i.e. British people) to accept political leadership and guidance of the speaker (Farage). In these goals, metaphor and proximisation complement each other remarkably well. Metaphor scenarios, particularly those involving the container schema, consolidate the Us camp, increase in-group allegiance and depict possible consequences of Them encroachment on the in-group. For their part, proximisation shifts construe direct and growing threats against the Us group, thus centralising the current moment and adding to the urgency of response. Not least, proximisation operations in the temporal domain lend useful credibility, in that they set up analogies referring to past events to endorse present and anticipated future scenarios.

Notes

1 This is evidenced by a number of opinion polls conducted in the months after the referendum. A major survey designed by the National Centre for Social Research (NCSR) and performed on 3,000 UK citizens in June 2017 reveals that nearly three-quarters (73 per cent) of those worried about immigration and its social effects (on security, employment, welfare, etc.) voted Leave, compared with 36 per cent of those who did not identify this as a concern. It also shows, more specifically, that the longer any given voter felt EU migrants should have lived in the UK before qualifying for welfare benefits, the more likely they were to vote to leave the EU. These findings demonstrate, according to the NCSR, that Britain's vote to leave the EU was the result of widespread anti-immigration sentiment, rather than a wider dissatisfaction with EU policies or politics in general (*Independent*, 2017).

2 For an extensive analysis of the speech, see Wodak (2016).

3 See e.g. Churchill's address to the House of Commons on 4 June 1940: "We shall defend our Island, whatever the cost may be; we shall fight on the beaches, we shall fight on the landing grounds, we shall fight in the fields and in the streets, we shall fight in the hills; we shall never surrender." (www.telegraph.co.uk/news/winston-churchill/11366880/Winston-Churchills-10-most-important-speeches.html)

4 This entails that, at the lexico-grammatical level, proximisation shifts are construed by verb phrases, which indicate the narrowing of the distance between the Us and Them entities,

which are construed by noun phrases. Thus, a linguistic representation of proximisation may be a single sentence such as "Saddam Hussein and his regime$_{NP}$ have set their course toward confrontation$_{VP}$ with America and all free world$_{NP}$" (G.W. Bush, 26 February 2003), though more often a longer discursive structure, in which the entities (Them, Us, or both) are not marked directly and – as will be seen in the data analysis below – need to be worked out anaphorically or inferred from the context. For a more detailed discussion of what Us and Them each comprise in different kinds of proximisation, see Cap (2013, chaps 4–5).

5 Recall, for instance, the phrase 'a September morning' used by G. W. Bush on various occasions after the 9/11 attacks (e.g. in Bush, 2003), to underscore the indefiniteness and thus presupposed continuity of the terrorist threat (cf. Cap, 2013, pp. 87–89).

6 Farage's comment in example (9) was made a week after an Islamic terrorist attack in which a truck was deliberately driven into crowds celebrating Bastille Day 2016 on the Promenade des Anglais in Nice, France, killing 84 people and injuring 434.

7 I have considered only the sequences meeting the following criteria: (a) the presence of a negatively charged nominal phrase designating Them in the first, 'ideological' segment of the sequence; (b) the presence of a nominal phrase designating Us in the second, 'material' segment; (c) the presence of a verbal phrase enacting the Them-toward-Us proximisation shift in the 'material' segment; (d) the overall length of the sequence not exceeding three sentences.

8 Farage refers to a series of coordinated terrorist attacks that occurred on Friday 13 November 2015 in Paris, leaving 130 people dead and another 413 injured.

References

Andersen, J. G., & Bjørklund, T. (1990). Structural changes and new cleavages: The progress parties in Denmark and Norway. *Acta Sociologica, 33*(3), 195–217. https://doi.org/10.1177/000169939003300303

Bush, G. W. (2003, 26 February). The President's address to the American Enterprise Institute. Available at www.whitehouse.gov, accessed 31 January 2018.

Cameron, D. (2013, 23 January). EU speech at Bloomberg. Available at www.gov.uk/government/speeches/eu-speech-at-bloomberg, accessed 31 May 2018. Contains public sector information licensed under the Open Government Licence v3.0.

Cap, P. (2006). *Legitimization in political discourse: A cross-disciplinary perspective on the modern US war rhetoric.* Newcastle-upon-Tyne: Cambridge Scholars Publishing.

Cap, P. (2008). Towards the proximization model of the analysis of legitimization in political discourse. *Journal of Pragmatics, 40*, 17–41. https://doi.org/10.1016/j.pragma.2007.10.002

Cap, P. (2010). Axiological aspects of proximization. *Journal of Pragmatics, 42*(2), 392–407. https://doi.org/10.1016/j.pragma.2009.06.008

Cap, P. (2013). *Proximization: The pragmatics of symbolic distance crossing.* Amsterdam: Benjamins.

Cap, P. (2017). *The language of fear: Communicating threat in public discourse.* Basingstoke: Palgrave Macmillan.

Charteris-Black, J. (2005). *Politicians and rhetoric: The persuasive power of metaphor.* Basingstoke: Palgrave Macmillan.

Chilton, P. (2004). *Analysing political discourse: Theory and practice.* London: Routledge.

Chilton, P. (2005). Discourse space theory: Geometry, brain and shifting viewpoints. *Annual Review of Cognitive Linguistics, 3*(1), 78–116. https://doi.org/10.1075/arcl.3.06chi

Chilton, P. (2010). From mind to grammar: Coordinate systems, prepositions, constructions. In V. Evans & P. Chilton (Eds), *Language, cognition and space: The state of the art and new directions* (pp. 640–671). London: Equinox.

Chilton, P. (2014). *Language, space and mind.* Cambridge: Cambridge University Press.

Chovanec, J. (2010). Legitimation through differentiation: Discursive construction of Jacques *Le Worm* Chirac as an opponent to military action. In U. Okulska & P. Cap (Eds), *Perspectives in politics and discourse* (pp. 61–82). Amsterdam: Benjamins.

Churchill, W. (1940, 4 June). Address to the House of Commons. Available at www.telegraph.co.uk/news/winston-churchill/11366880/Winston-Churchills-10-most-important-speeches.html, accessed 31 May 2018.

Cienki, A., Kaal, B., & Maks, I. (2010). Mapping world view in political texts using discourse space theory: Metaphor as an analytical tool. Paper presented at the RaAM 8 conference, Vrije Universiteit Amsterdam.

Daddow, O. J. (2006). Euroscepticism and the culture of the discipline of history. *Review of International Studies, 32*(2), 309–328. https://doi.org/10.1017/S0260210506007042

Dunmire, P. (2011). *Projecting the future through political discourse: The case of the Bush doctrine.* Amsterdam: Benjamins.

Farage, N. (2013, 19 September). Address at the UKIP autumn conference. Available at www.ukpol.co.uk/nigel-farage-2013-speech-to-ukip-conference, accessed 31 May 2018.

Farage, N. (2014a, 28 February). Address at the UKIP spring conference. Available at www.youtube.com/watch?v=A6JgyJp_QJw, accessed 31 May 2018.

Farage, N. (2014b, 25 May). Speech to the European Parliament. Available at www.youtube.com/watch?v=hkYO6hApXd8, accessed 31 May 2018.

Farage, N. (2015, 9 September). Speech to the European Parliament. Available at www.ukpol.co.uk/nigel-farage-2015-speech-at-the-state-of-the-union, accessed 31 May 2018.

Farage, N. (2016a, 29 February). Speech to the European Parliament. Available at www.ukpol.co.uk/nigel-farage-2016-speech-to-european-parliament, accessed 31 May 2018.

Farage, N. (2016b, 17 May). Interview at BBC station. Available at www.bbc.com/news/uk-politics-eu-referendum-36306681, accessed 31 May 2018.

Filardo Llamas, L. (2010). Discourse worlds in Northern Ireland: The legitimisation of the 1998 agreement. In K. Hayward & C. O'Donnell (Eds), *Political discourse and conflict resolution: Debating peace in Northern Ireland* (pp. 62–76). London: Routledge.

Filardo Llamas, L. (2013). Committed to the ideals of 1916: The language of paramilitary groups: The case of the Irish Republican Army. *Critical Discourse Studies, 10*(1), 1–17. https://doi.org/10.1080/17405904.2012.736396

Gavins, J. (2007). *Text world theory: An introduction.* Edinburgh: Edinburgh University Press.

Goodwin, M., & Heath, O. (2016). The 2016 referendum, Brexit and the left behind: An aggregate-level analysis of the result. *Political Quarterly, 87*(3), 323–332. https://doi.org/10.1111/1467-923X.12285

Hansard. (2013–2014). *House of Commons debates*, vols 565–571.

Hart, C. (2010). *Critical discourse analysis and cognitive science: New perspectives on immigration discourse.* Basingstoke: Palgrave Macmillan.

Hart, C. (2014). *Discourse, grammar and ideology: Functional and cognitive perspectives.* London: Bloomsbury.

Independent. (2017, 28 June). Brexit: People voted to leave EU because they feared immigration, major survey finds. Available at www.independent.co.uk/news/uk/home-news/brexit-latest-news-leave-eu-immigration-main-reason-european-union-survey-a7811651.html, accessed 31 May 2018.

Jowett, G. S., & O'Donnell, V. (1992). *Propaganda and persuasion.* Newbury Park, CA: Sage.

Kaal, B. (2012). Worldviews: The spatial ground of political reasoning in Dutch election manifestos. *CADAAD, 6*(1), 1–22.

Levelt, W. J. (1989). *Speaking: From intention to articulation.* Cambridge, MA: The MIT Press.

Levinson, S. C. (2003). *Space in language and cognition: Explorations in cognitive diversity.* Cambridge: Cambridge University Press.

Mann, W., & Thompson, S. (1988). Rhetorical structure theory: A theory of text organization. *Text, 8*, 243–281.
Marcussen, M., Risse, T., Engelmann-Martin, D., Knopf, H., & Roscher, K. (1999). Constructing Europe? The evolution of French, British and German nation state identities. *Journal of European Public Policy, 6*, 614–633. https://doi.org/10.1080/135017699343504
Musolff, A. (2004). *Metaphor and political discourse: Analogical reasoning in debates about Europe.* Basingstoke: Palgrave Macmillan.
Musolff, A. (2016). *Political metaphor analysis: Discourse and scenarios.* London: Bloomsbury.
Todd, J. (2015). *The British self and continental other: A discourse analysis of the United Kingdom's relationship with Europe.* Oslo: ARENA.
Tournier-Sol, K. (2017). UKIP, the architect of Brexit? *French Journal of British Studies.* Available at https://journals.openedition.org/rfcb/1378, accessed 31 May 2018.
van Dijk, T. (1998). *Ideology: A multidisciplinary approach.* London: Sage.
van Dijk, T. (2017). Socio-cognitive discourse studies. In J. Flowerdew & J. E. Richardson (Eds), *The Routledge handbook of critical discourse studies* (pp. 26–43). London: Routledge.
Werth, P. (1999). *Text worlds: Representing conceptual space in discourse.* Harlow: Longman.
Wodak, R. (2016). 'We have the character of an island nation': A discourse-historical analysis of David Cameron's 'Bloomberg speech' on the European Union. European University Institute working paper series RSCAS 2016/36. http://cadmus.eui.eu/bitstream/handle/1814/42804/RSCAS_2016_36.pdf?sequence=1&isAllowed=y.

6

'THE BRITISH PEOPLE HAVE SPOKEN'

Voter motivations and identities in vox pops on the British EU referendum

Marlene Miglbauer and Veronika Koller

Introduction

'The British people have spoken' has become a rallying cry ever since a slight majority of the British citizens who participated in the referendum voted to leave the EU on 23 June 2016. Proponents of the Leave vote – i.e. the campaign for the UK to leave the EU – have used the result consistently to make an argument *ad populum*, maintaining that the referendum result is binding (when the referendum was in fact advisory), that the UK should leave both the EU customs union and the single market and that parliament should not be involved in the Brexit process. In this chapter, we take the slogan literally and analyse a number of interviews with British voters conducted in public – known as vox pops ('voice of the people') – in the months before the referendum. In doing so, we aim to identify the topics that interviewees mention as influencing their voting intentions, some linguistic and nonverbal features they use to present those motivations as meaningful and the identities they construct for themselves when interacting with journalists. In addition, we are also interested in whether the vox pops reflect any motivations for supporting right-wing populist causes that British voters share with their counterparts elsewhere. We thus address three research questions in this chapter, which relate to the text, discourse practice and sociopolitical context level, respectively:

> RQ1: What topics and motivations are made relevant by people intending to vote to leave the EU?
>
> RQ2: What identities do interviewees construct for themselves?
>
> RQ3: Do the findings suggest reasons for supporting right-wing populist politics that are shared across European contexts?

To put these questions and our study in context, it is necessary to briefly sketch the background to the 2016 British EU referendum.

The UK's road to join what was then known as the European Economic Community (EEC) was less than straightforward, as membership applications were rejected twice in the 1960s. The 1963 and 1967 French vetoes on British membership were explained by the then French president Charles de Gaulle with his view that "England in effect is insular, she is maritime [and] has, in all her doings, very marked and very original habits and traditions" (quoted in Moore, 2016).[1] The UK did join the EEC in 1973, driven by the prospect of gaining access to the common market (Niedermeier & Ridder, 2017). Two years later, the electorate was asked to decide whether to stay or leave again and about two-thirds voted in favour of staying. Despite that result, Britain's relationship with the EU was always strained, involving numerous opt-outs, rebates and renegotiations, until in 2013, David Cameron fulfilled an election promise and announced another EU referendum, to be held on 23 June 2016. In that advisory plebiscite, slightly more than half of the votes (51.86 per cent) were in favour of leaving the European Union. On 29 March 2017, Prime Minister Theresa May sent the official notification to leave to the EU, starting two years of negotiations ending with Brexit, which is – at the time of writing (January 2019) – set to occur on 29 March 2019.

Support for leaving the EU did not just arise in the run-up to the referendum but needs to be seen against a long history of Euroscepticism in the UK, which some even define as an inherently Eurosceptic country (George, 2000): some researchers claim that Euroscepticism has been "fundamental to constituting Britain and Britishness in the post-imperial context, despite membership of the European Union" (Gifford, 2008, p. vii). More specifically, in order to redefine Britain in the wake of the imperial decline, an Other had to be defined, and this Other was the EU and the European integration project (ibid., p. 10), especially after the collapse of the Eastern bloc in 1989.

The foundation of the British brand of Euroscepticism is a type of nationalism that focuses on a dominant Anglosphere, which was regarded as being threatened by the European integration project (Niedermeier & Ridder, 2017, p. 4). Even Churchill, in his famous speech in 1946 on the possible establishment of a United States of Europe, referred to 'continental Europe' rather than to a Europe including the UK, which in his view would best remain one of the superpowers, next to the United States and the Soviet Union. This attitude towards Europe still exists and is part of British public discourse on Europe and the EU (Freeden, 2017, p. 1).

Discourse analysts started to address British Euroscepticism as early as the mid-1990s (Hardt-Mautner, 1995; Mautner, 2001). From a cognitivist point of view, Musolff (2000; see also Chilton & Ilyin, 1993) showed how the metaphor of the 'common European house', introduced into Western European public discourse in 1985 by the last president of the Soviet Union, Mikhail Gorbachev, experienced a semantic derogation throughout the 1990s, with British politicians and the press refocusing the metaphor on structural deficiencies. Other researchers demonstrated how tabloid media in particular fed the 'othering' of Europe, stoked fears about national identity and promoted stereotypes of other European nations. In her investigation of the debate about the 1992 Maastricht Treaty, Hardt-Mautner (1995, p. 199) already identified "a growing chasm between the discourse of the elites [. . .] and the lay discourse of the electorate". Anti-elite sentiment is a staple of populist politics (see next section) and the British tabloid press tapped into it both in the run-up to, and immediately after, the EU referendum (Koller & Ryan, 2019).

Recent studies (Nasti, 2012; Bijsmans, 2017) state that Euroscepticism has become mainstream in UK newspapers, both quality and tabloid. Taking a political sciences approach, Gifford (2006, 2008) regards the crisis in established British parties to be one of the main factors that have made Euroscepticism the mainstream in politics. As a result, Euroscepticism has been crucial in the campaigns – both Leave and Remain (see Wenzl, Chapter 3 this volume) – preceding the 2016 EU referendum. In this chapter, we are therefore interested if and how voters support populist topics and discourses when they voice their motivation for voting for Brexit (RQ1), how they position themselves as intended Leave voters (RQ2) and whether their motivations can also be observed in other national contexts (RQ3).

Right-wing populism and voter motivation

Populism has been defined in various ways (Weyland, 2001; Gidron & Bonikowski, 2013), and we regard two approaches to populism as relevant in this chapter: populism as ideology and populism as a discursive strategy. The former defines populism as "an ideology which pits a virtuous and homogeneous people against a set of elites and dangerous 'others' who are together depicted as depriving (or attempting to deprive) the sovereign people of their rights, values, prosperity, identity and voice" (Albertazzi & McDonnell, 2008, p. 3). Populism as a discursive strategy can be defined as a "latent set of ideas or a worldview [. . .] manifested in distinct linguistic forms and content that have real political consequences" (Hawkins, 2009, p. 1045). As such, it is a mode of political expression employed selectively and strategically by politicians (Kazin, 1995).

As a term, 'populism' has mostly been used for referring to right-wing populism, which comprises ideas expressed by parties and movements that have emerged on the right of the political spectrum in Europe since the 1980s (Decker, 2008, p. 122). Despite left-wing populism not having received as much attention in research (but see Demata, Chapter 8 this volume), we focus on right-wing populism as our data is primarily influenced by right-wing populist standpoints. If we therefore take the above definition of populism as ideology and apply it to right-wing populism, several inherent principles become apparent (Heinisch, 2008, p. 43; Wodak, 2015a, 2015b; Inglehart & Norris, 2016, pp. 6–7; Freeden, 2017, p. 4).

First, right-wing populists view society as ideally homogeneous, with an emphasis on nativist and revisionist tendencies. Any threat to the homogeneity of the 'good' people (Albertazzi & McDonnell, 2008, p. 6) is feared, because there are "enemies in their midst" (Freeden, 2017, p. 4), notably political elites and intellectuals, who are also often claimed to be corrupt (Nonhoff, 2017).[2] Perceptions of outside threats are fuelled by an increase in immigration, which results in the fear of economic inequality and loss of national culture (Inglehart & Norris, 2016). Another aspect of (right-wing) populism is the focus on governing in the interest of the people, who are regarded as sovereign and must (again) become "masters in their own homes" (Albertazzi & McDonnell, 2008, p. 6). The rise of right-wing populism in Western democracies has sparked interest in political and media discourse (e.g. Wodak et al., 2013; Wodak, 2015a, 2015b). The present chapter complements these previous studies in that we, instead of analysing politicians' language use, focus on the voices of voters. By doing so, we additionally build a bridge between populism being perceived as an ideology (Albertazzi & McDonnell, 2008) and as a discursive strategy (Kazin, 1995; Hawkins, 2009; Jowett & O'Donnell, 2015) by analysing linguistic markers and thus bringing linguistic concepts and sociopolitical concepts together.

This rise in right-wing populism is further related to a shift in voter motivation in elections: traditional aspects, i.e. social structural variables and party allegiance, have increasingly been trumped by short-term factors, i.e. topics that are regarded as crucial at the time of election (Denver et al., 2012; Kritzinger et al., 2013). Three decisive factors to cast votes for right-wing populist parties have been identified in the literature: fear of wage pressure and competition for welfare benefits, perception of immigration as a threat to national identity, and discontent with a country's democratic structures and processes (Mayer & Perrineau, 1992; Heinisch, 2008; Oesch, 2008). Among these, anti-immigrant attitudes and dissatisfaction with the country's politics tend to be the main driving factors for supporting right-wing populist parties (Billiet & Witte, 1995; Lubbers & Scheepers, 2000).

In the present chapter, we are analysing whether people intending to vote for leaving the EU refer to these driving factors and to populist ideas in general when explaining their voting behaviour. In the next section, we describe our vox pop data and methods in more detail.

Data and methods

Our data comprise vox pops, which can be defined as "interview fragments with ordinary people expressing their opinions on a particular issue in their own words" (Lewis et al., 2005, p. 70). Vox pops are often conducted to represent so-called ordinary people's reaction to, and views on, public events, but also as a complement to opinion polls in the run-up to elections or, as in our case, referenda. These spontaneous micro-interactions involve journalists accosting "random citizens who do not have a specific representative function or expertise" (Kleemans et al., 2017, p. 471) and as such add the news value of personalisation to media discourse (Bednarek, 2016, p. 34). In the second analysis subsection, we will address in how far vox pops are skewed towards interviewing people from particular demographics, e.g. by approaching them in certain locations, and explore in what way the interaction between journalists and wo/men on the street influences the interviewees' construction of their identities. For now, it should be noted that the focus of vox pops is less on what someone says but on the fact that the interviewee is shown as representing an 'ordinary person'. Seen as such, vox pops are mostly used to show "not what you say" but "what does someone like you say" (Myers, 2004, p. 209). In other words, it is less important to represent people's opinions than it is to represent people as such, with obvious repercussions for how and where interviewees are approached.

Our data show considerable variety, combining as they do 14 videos with voters in all parts of the United Kingdom (England, Northern Ireland, Scotland, Wales), although vox pops from different regions in England (North, East and West Midlands, South East, London, South West) account for almost two-thirds (64.28 per cent). The videos are further varied in that they comprise news features from the BBC, international (CNN, Russia Today) and regional news channels as well as private TV channels, individuals' YouTube channels and even student projects posted on the same platform. And finally, the formats in which the vox pops appear differ notably, with some taking the form of short question–answer sequences[3] while others are embedded in longer features along with a narrative by the interviewer. However different though, all vox pops were produced between 18 February and 22 June 2016, i.e. before and right up to the EU referendum. Table 6.1 presents an overview of our data and their sources.

In contrast to the findings by Brookes et al. (2004) in the run-up to the British general election 2001, i.e. that people on the street were mostly asked about who they thought would win, interviewees in our data were explicitly asked about their views on the EU referendum, how they intended to vote in it and also to provide reasons for their choice. While the videos represent the views of both Leave and Remain voters, the former are significantly underrepresented, at 40.26 per cent, while the latter are significantly overrepresented when compared to the actual referendum results ($p = 0.01993$).[4] While our data are therefore more balanced than the vox pops in political news investigated by Beckers et al. (2016), the overrepresentation of Remain voters in the videos we analysed could suggest that people planning to vote Leave were less willing to declare their intentions, perhaps wary of being perceived as racist if doing so. It should be noted though that opinions are not as clear-cut as the Leave/Remain dichotomy suggests: 12 interviewees were undecided while others gave opinions on issues raised in the referendum campaigns without declaring a voting intention. Yet others said that they would not vote, did not have enough information to have an opinion, questioned the point of having a referendum in the first place or refused to speak to the interviewer.[5] In the following section, we analyse the contribution by the 31 declared Leave voters only. The reason for this is as much personal as it is political: although neither of us was eligible to vote in the referendum, we both supported the Remain cause, so analysing why voters opted for Leave would help us to understand viewpoints

TABLE 6.1 Vox pop data and sources

Location	*Date*	*Producer*	*Source*	*Mnemonic*
Belfast	27 May 2016	Clipstorm/*Belfast Telegraph*	www.youtube.com/watch?v=k6Le6snNeSQ	BR1, BR2
Boston	19 May 2016	CNN	http://edition.cnn.com/videos/business/2016/06/15/boston-england-brexit-vote-dnt-quest.cnn	BR3, BR4, BR5
Bridgend	10 May 2016	BBC	www.bbc.co.uk/news/av/uk-wales-36257774/eu-referendum-views-from-over-the-farm-fence-in-wales	BR6
Brighton	9 April 2016	The Latest TV	www.youtube.com/watch?v=GizxuOrAjHQ	BR7, BR8
Cardiff	20 June 2016	WalesOnline	www.walesonline.co.uk/news/politics/asked-people-cardiff-theyre-voting-11500745	BR9
Coventry	1 March 2016	bhodds	www.youtube.com/watch?v=TpJyCSDWdio	BR10
Dover	19 February 2016	Russia Today UK	www.youtube.com/watch?v=lCI3jnjpcQA	BR11
Dundee	22 June 2016	Graham Phillips	www.youtube.com/watch?v=8z7CtX3R3zY [no longer available]	BR12, BR13, BR14, BR15
Eastbourne	21 June 2016	Dale McCartney	www.youtube.com/watch?v=ROUi4d6ZkTs	BR16, BR17, BR18
Glasgow	18 February 2016	Strath Media	www.youtube.com/watch?v=Ac6dYPcoLhs	BR19
London	31 May 2016	Crunch TV	www.youtube.com/watch?v=cvWWMJhNT_Y	BR20, BR21, BR22
Nottingham	19 May 2016	LeftLion	www.youtube.com/watch?v=_h1X9HZfOBs	BR23, BR24, BR25
Penzance	15 April 2016	BBC	www.youtube.com/watch?v=DLTBQyV4KJw	BR26, BR27, BR28
Sheffield	25 April 2016	Bradley Guest	www.youtube.com/watch?v=FKH93eJc4n0	BR29, BR30, BR31

different from our own. More generally, our analysis seeks to shed light on causes for the surge of populism in Western democracies, using interviews with voters as an entry point.

In order to conduct the analysis, we investigated a number of content and language features. Relating to the text level, our first research question queries what topics and motivations are made relevant by people intending to vote for leaving the EU. In order to answer this question, we first manually identified the topics that interviewees mentioned as motivating their voting intentions. We then linked this content analysis to which social actors were mentioned in relation to the upcoming referendum and how they were referred to (van Leeuwen, 1996; 2008, pp. 23–54). This part of the analysis is again data driven, coming up with *ad hoc* labels for social actors. Finally, we also analysed how the various actors as well as the Remain and Leave options were appraised (Martin & White, 2005). While social-actor representation and appraisal are not unlike nomination and predication (Reisigl & Wodak, 2005), they allow for a more detailed analysis. Example (1) foregrounds a topic influencing the interviewee's voting intention and also represents and appraises social actors:

(1) At the moment we are paying £6 billion as a UK government into the cap in Brussels. We are only getting £3.8 billion back. What the hell is happening with these other £2.2 billion? It's not fair on us at all is it? (BR6)

The topic of the UK's contribution to the EU budget is linguistically realised through a material process carried out by the social actor 'UK government' ('we are paying £6 billion pounds as a UK government') and a negative value of propriety ('It's not fair on us'). In the section on appraisal analysis, we have annotated the transcripts according to what aspect is evaluated and whether the evaluation is negative or positive, e.g. as [–Propriety] or [+Benefit].

In addition to identifying topics and analysing linguistic features, we also annotated the transcribed data for gesture, body movement and facial expression to account for the visual medium of vox pop videos. Systematic analysis of the data showed that those nonverbal features have a number of reinforcing and indicative functions:[6]

- reinforce prosodic and lexical emphasis;
- reinforce voting intention;
- reinforce appraisal;
- indicate geographical distance and movement;
- indicate metaphorical distance to Other;
- indicate metaphorical movement;
- indicate obvious nature of voting intentions and reasons;
- indicate personal nature of voting intention and reasons;
- indicate embarrassment or awkwardness.

In example (1) above, for instance, the interviewee tilts his head to the right when saying 'in Brussels', thereby indicating a metaphorical distance in that the EU – metonymically referred to as 'Brussels' – is outside of his personal space, i.e. an Other.

Our second research question pertains to the identities that interviewees construct for themselves, thus taking the study to the discourse practice level. We drew on positioning theory (Harré & van Langenhove, 1999), together with an analysis of pronoun use, to address this second question. For instance, example (2) alternates between the first-person singular pronoun to reference the voter herself and the first-person plural pronoun to index, presumably, all British people, a group with which the interviewee thereby identifies. In addition, she positions the British people as disempowered, rendering a Leave vote an act of national self-empowerment.

(2) I will be voting to leave the EU purely because we've lost control on immigration and I don't want to lose sovereignty. (BR31)

Taken together, the results from the analysis enabled us to answer our third research question – relating to the sociopolitical context of the EU referendum – about whether the findings suggest reasons for supporting right-wing populist politics that the British context shares with other countries (see e.g. Mayer & Perrineau, 1992; Heinisch, 2008; Oesch, 2008; Schumacher & Rooduijn, 2013).

First, however, we will present the findings from our analysis of the texts and of the discourse practices in which they are embedded.

Findings

Text level: topics, social actors and appraisal

We will begin our presentation of the findings with a look at the content of the videos, showing what topics are made relevant by the interviewees as informing their voting intentions. This will be followed by a linguistic analysis of how they represent social actors, and how they appraise them and the current and future situation of Britain as part or outside of the EU. Nonverbal features and their functions will be considered throughout.

Topics

The topic that intending Leave voters foreground most frequently in connection with the EU referendum is British sovereignty (10 mentions), as in example (3):

(3) What is the point of we electing our own MPs and our own leaders to make rules and laws for us while everything is being done in Brussels what's the point? (BR21)

This is followed by immigration and border control (8 mentions), and a topic cluster we could call business/economy/money (7 mentions). The latter comprises concerns for particular industries, such as farming, alongside a belief that the UK would benefit from agreeing trade deals with non-EU countries and resentment about paying contributions to the EU budget. As for other topics, four interviewees express their dislike for the policies, processes and structures of the EU, while five interviewees gave no reason for their voting intention and four gave only unspecified reasons (e.g. 'if we vote yes the country's going to get worse', BR25). The most frequent topics echo previous findings (e.g. Mayer & Perrineau, 1992; Oesch, 2008; Schumacher & Rooduijn, 2013; Rooduijn, 2018) that show 'taking control' and a perceived threat from outside as central motivations for voters of right-wing populist parties and causes. Left-wing populist reasons for voting Leave (see Demata, Chapter 8 this volume), such as disagreement with EU policies on market competition and the environment, are mentioned less often (BR8, BR9). This suggests that the Leave campaign resonated most with supporters of right-wing populism. Further evidence for this can be found in some interviewees' objection to the UK's net contribution to the EU budget:

(4) We need to pay more attention to our own country and not donating so much money to other countries. (BR18)
(5) I don't see why we should pay money to somebody else and not get our own back. (BR28)

Voter motivations such as the ones quoted above argue for a primacy of the national in-group's interests at the expense of supranational collaboration. This focus can be further reduced to 'smaller life worlds', such as "personal space, family, and friends, result[ing] in growing concerns about personal safety and security" (Heinisch, 2008, p. 49). Example (6) illustrates this focus on the personal and how it can be reinforced by the consequences of fiscal austerity:

(6) I was homeless from November to February I was told that we couldn't get any help because the migrants come in and Brighton and Eastbourne is housing a thousand of them. (BR18)

Gestures and body movement can reinforce the interviewees' verbal expressions of voting intention and also present those as obvious. Examples (7) and (8) illustrate these functions:

(7) I don't like the turn of events in Europe {raises eyebrows}. I don't like the tendency of confrontation with Russia and again {raises eyebrows} the lack of democracy within Europe itself. (BR17)
(8) The other [driving force] is just {raises left shoulder} to take back our own country you know. (BR4)

After identifying the main topics influencing the interviewees' voting intentions, we will now turn to how they represent different social actors.

Social actors

The most frequently mentioned social actor is the collective self, referred to by toponyms (Britain, our/this/the country)[7] or in a collectivised way (the British, our community). Relational identifications of previous generations (our forefathers, grandparents) evoke national myths of British freedom being defended in the Second World War. The prominent in-group is referred to 13 times, followed by the Other against which it is identified, i.e. a collectivised EU, which is sometimes conflated with Europe (10 mentions). The Other is also collectivised with another toponym, namely 'countries/other countries', and as 'somebody else' (a combined 8 mentions). Expressed as such, the collective self and its Other are the linguistic representation of the topic that is most frequently mentioned as relevant for voting intentions, namely British sovereignty.

Another social actor group is politicians, who can be nominated – e.g. then Prime Minister David Cameron – or identified in collectivisations such as MPs, ministers, parliamentarians, different parties. Alternatively, politicians are also functionalised collectively, and referred to as leaders and the UK government. Interestingly, politicians are related to the in-group when contrasted with perceived interference by the EU (e.g. 'our own MPs and our own leaders', BR21) but otherwise they are constructed as an out-group that cannot be trusted (e.g. 'all these parliamentarians all these ministers they're saying one thing really but you know how politics goes', BR22). The final social actor group though is definitely an out-group, being referred to in collectivised or abstracted ways as refugees, migrants and immigration.

Nonverbal features, and in particular gestures, support social actor representation in that they can indicate geographical or metaphorical distance and movement. Examples (9–11) illustrate this function:

(9) These people if they were at home they would be earning ten times less {extends left arm sideways} coming here {left hand towards chest} to get money to send home {extends left arm sideways}. (BR20)

(10) We need to pay more attention to our own country and not donating so much money to other countries {extends right hand forward and upward in an arch}. (BR18)

(11) No doubt get out {points with left thumb over left shoulder}. (BR20)

Appraisal

Before we draw on appraisal theory (Martin & White, 2005) to show what different types of appraisal are evidenced in the vox pops, we can state in general terms that interviewees reserve negative evaluation for the EU (14 instances) and the UK as part of it (11 instances). Conversely, leaving the EU is positively evaluated in 17 instances. (The UK political establishment plays only a minor role, being mentioned 5 times, 4 of which show negative evaluation.) Given that we analysed only the vox pops featuring voters intending to opt for Leave, this is of course unsurprising. Likewise, the genre of the vox pop means that appraisal is overwhelmingly authorial and monoglossic, i.e. representing the opinions of the interviewees without integrating any other voices.

However, if we look more closely at what types of appraisal are used to positively evaluate leaving the EU and negatively talk about staying in it, we can see that speakers mostly talk about benefit and capacity:

(12) I'm out . . . we need a better [+Benefit] deal I think. (BR11)
(13) No doubt get out . . . I don't think it's good [–Benefit] for anybody. (BR20)
(14) If we're out from European Union then people can check [+Capacity] if the right person is coming back or not. (BR15)
(15) I'm out because . . . we're no longer in control [–Capacity]. (BR3)

Apart from such appreciation, we also find negative judgement of the EU, chiefly in terms of propriety. This is sometimes combined with the speaker's emotional response to EU policies, processes and structures (a topic mentioned as relevant for voting intentions):

(16) I don't like [–Happiness] the tendency of confrontation with Russia and again the lack of democracy [–Propriety] within Europe itself. (BR17)
(17) I don't like [–Happiness] Europe I think they're fascists [–Propriety] I think they're anti-democratic [–Propriety]. (BR29)

Since the EU is judged as lacking propriety, being or staying part of it is judged as harmful:

(18) There's so many strangleholds [–Harm] the EU has over [Britain]. (BR8)
(19) I think it's costing us too much [–Harm]. (BR10)

Once again, appraisal is reinforced through nonverbal features:

(20) The original idea was great {nods} but now it isn't anymore {shakes head}. (BR12)

Together, the analyses of topics, social actors and appraisal show a focus on British sovereignty, which is expressed in references to a collective self that is harmed by being in the EU and would benefit from leaving it. Negative aspects of remaining are costs and the issue of immigration, with leaving the EU being constructed as increasing the capacity of British people to spend less money on the EU budget and controlling immigration. This focus on sovereignty is coupled with a dislike of the EU, which is represented as an immoral collective Other that evokes negative feelings in the interviewees.

Discourse practice: citizens' identities

We draw upon positioning theory (Harré & van Langenhove, 1999) for investigating how people position themselves in the vox pops. The aim of the vox pops we investigate is to ask the interviewees to voice their opinions and attitudes, in particular, "more deeply felt social and political attitude[s]" (Ekström & Tolson, 2017, p. 225) on Britain's membership in the EU. In this section we investigate how these articulations contribute to the construction of the interviewees' identities.

First of all, it is important to take into consideration the nature and the context of the interaction, both of which influence the construction of the interviewees' identities. There is the context of people on the street or "ordinary individuals with no affiliation, expert knowledge or exclusive information" (Beckers et al., 2016, p. 284). The people in the vox pops were interviewed during the daytime in public places such as shopping streets, markets and promenades. Despite purporting to ask a cross-section of people, our data suggest that some interviewers chose specific places where they expected to interview certain voters (e.g. a street market in Boston, a Leave stronghold – even though the presenter acknowledged that it was not typical of the UK as a whole). This contrasts with how Beckers et al. (2016, p. 284) regard vox pop interviewees, i.e. as "randomly chosen". Rather, the choice is determined or "dictated by the media" (Hermes, 2006, p. 297). Additionally, the perceived political opinion of the interviewer and the interviewer's question may well influence the self-positioning of the interviewees.

The interviewees are asked about their voting decision (see note 3) and are thus positioned by the interviewers as eligible voters in the EU referendum. As expected, the first-person singular 'I' is used in connection with directly voicing one's voting decision:

(21) I'm out {nods} (BR11)
(22) I'm I'm gonna to vote to {chin back} leave. (BR23)

Nonverbal features such as nodding are applied to support one's decision and thus also one's identity construction. Some of the interviewees position themselves as self-confident voters who have made their decision, others, as in example (22), construct an identity as defensive voters: the nonverbal feature of tucking in the chin hints at the voter as being "aware of possible challenges to what they say and how they say it" (Myers, 2000, p. 183).

The interviewees in our data have all agreed to be interviewed. Yet, despite being willing to voice their voting decision, some interviewees still seem embarrassed. The following example includes nonverbal features that support this:

(23) and no disrespect I'm not being racist {hands moved downwards with palms touching} when I say this (BR18)

The phrase 'I'm not a racist, but . . .', or any variation thereof, is usually analysed as an argumentative disclaimer followed by a racist statement (e.g. Bonilla-Silva & Forman, 2000). In the above example, however, the pleading body language suggests that the speaker is aware of, and distances himself from, discourse participants who preposition him as racist.

In our data, most interviewees display a strong alignment to a group of people when voicing and reasoning for their own voter intention, i.e. they position and identify themselves as members of an in-group of British people. By switching the pronoun from first-pronoun singular to first-pronoun plural, they move from their identity as interviewees, which is also foregrounded by the context of the interviews, to their identity as British citizens.

(24) I'll be voting to leave the EU purely because we've lost control on immigration and I don't want to lose sovereignty. (BR30)

(25) I'm out because I remember when Britain used to be a community and we're no longer in control. (BR3)

Interviewees show a strong alignment with the British and Britain, thus foregrounding their collective identities as British citizens. In addition, the British and Britain are constructed as helpless and disadvantaged. Constructing the EU as Other and the 'threat from outside' reflects the Euroscepticism promoted in the media and by populists: sovereignty is important for the nation and needs to be protected, so people need to 'take back control'. Consequently, interviewees construct their identity as one of self-confident voters who are regaining power as British people by overcoming their helplessness and being disadvantaged by the Other, i.e. the EU. These voters thereby re-define British identity during the transition of the UK from an EU member state to an ex-EU member state.

Discussion and conclusion

In this chapter, we have investigated what topics and motivations are made relevant by people intending to vote to leave the EU, what identities those interviewees construct for themselves and whether there are reasons for supporting right-wing populist politics that are shared across European contexts. To answer the first research question, the most decisive factor to vote Leave in our dataset is British sovereignty and regaining control of the country, including immigration and the economy. The status quo of having to deal with the EU and its policies is regarded as harmful and hence undesirable. This pertains to policies that are perceived to negatively affect life in Britain, leading to the impression of being ruled by an outside force, i.e. the EU, which is rejected as a morally deficient Other. It follows that voting Leave is seen as resulting in increased capability; most interviewees trust that a Leave vote means they will finally be able to change the harmful status quo and boost the power of the in-group.

Concerning the second research question, our analysis also revealed that the intended voting behaviour is not only heavily influenced by short-term factors, but also impacts on the identity construction of interviewees in the vox pops. Our findings disclose in-group bias and an emphasis on "smaller life worlds" (Heinisch, 2008, p. 49) since the interviewees show a considerable alignment with British citizens and the UK. By doing so, they construct idealised and homogenised versions of British identity and also position themselves as members of a group who is disadvantaged and victimised vis-à-vis the EU. They strongly identify with collective identities when voicing their personal and individual reasons for their decision to vote for Brexit. Further, they use the EU as Other to construct a dual identity both as helpless British citizens and self-confident voters, who can finally take control over their lives and country again. While this identity seems contradictory, the two aspects are reconciled by presenting the EU referendum as enabling interviewees to move from being a victim to being an agent.

In answer to the third research question, our findings on voting intentions and motivations resemble previous research findings on voter motivation for right-wing populist parties elsewhere (e.g. Mayer & Perrineau, 1992; Billiet & Witte, 1995; Heinisch, 2008; Oesch, 2008). First, in our data, some interviewees represented previous generations to refer to founding myths of the nation by highlighting British efforts in fighting for the country's freedom during the Second World War. There is a strong in-group bias with a fear from 'the enemy from outside'. In our data, this 'enemy from the outside' is the EU or Europe – the two terms are used synonymously by the interviewees – and to some extent immigrants/migrants. Interestingly, another characteristic of (right-wing) populism, the threat from 'enemies in their midst' (Freeden, 2017, p. 4), i.e. political elites and intellectuals, is not as dominant in our data. However, it could be claimed that the EU and British (pro-)EU politicians may be regarded as such and there is a slight conflation of what counts as 'inside and outside'. The view of taking control and becoming "masters in their own homes" (Albertazzi & McDonnell, 2008, p. 6) is also quite prevalent in our data.

Our findings thus provide further evidence for the shared recontextualisation of right-wing populist ideas and rhetoric across different contexts in Europe. Despite the different natures of elections and contexts, right-wing populist ideas have entered the political landscape in Europe (Rooduijn, 2018). In particular, it seems as if shared topics across the EU such as a perceived threat from outside – in our case, mostly the EU – and a sense of victimhood constitute (or are presented by journalists as constituting) one of the most relevant topics in elections and referenda and thereby contribute to the success of various right-wing populist parties and causes.

Notes

1 This belief is echoed in a speech made 50 years later by former British Prime Minister David Cameron, in which he argued that "we have the character of an island nation" (Wodak, 2016, p. 18; Cap, Chapter 5 this volume).
2 In this context, Nonhoff (2017) draws an important distinction between promises of equality and self-rule, which he recognises as democratic, and promises of toppling corrupt elites, which can be seen as populist.
3 Not all videos feature the questions of the interviewer. Those that do include one question for clarification ('So you'll vote that way [out]?' BR28), a number of follow-up questions (e.g. 'And do you have any reason why?' BR20) and only rarely a direct question as to the interviewee's voting behaviour (e.g. 'How will you be voting in the EU referendum?' BR10). As far as we can tell, interviewers did not foreground particular topics or reasons for interviewees' voting intentions.
4 It is noteworthy that the data are also skewed for gender: less than a third of people interviewed (31.17 per cent) are women, which makes them significantly underrepresented ($p = 0.00017$). This could be due to women being less willing to speak to strangers or in public, and/or be an effect of the mostly male interviewers – nine of the interviewers who feature in their vox pops are male and only one is female – exhibiting an in-group bias. Interestingly, two-thirds of women in the vox pops declared that they would vote Remain, compared to 51 per cent in the actual referendum (Ipsos MORI, 2016), a significant overrepresentation ($p = 0.00172$). This could suggest that, if women were less willing to be interviewed, it was female Leave voters in particular who did not state their voting intentions. Women's reluctance to speak in public may here be compounded by a stigma attaching to the Leave vote before the referendum.
5 A few others did not speak sufficient English to answer the interviewer's questions and/or were not eligible to vote in the referendum.
6 Although Montgomery (2007, p. 177) has observed that "short on-the-spot interviews amongst bystanders – vox pops – play an important role in offering a range of emotional reactions to [an] event", we could find no emotion-related function of nonverbal features in our vox pops on voting intentions and motivations. For future research, it will be interesting to see whether nonverbal features differ across cultures and whether they become more pronounced along with intensification in the spoken language.
7 Outside England, interviewees distinguish between Northern Ireland and the UK mainland (BR2) or deictically locate the self as 'here in Wales' (BR6).

References

Albertazzi, D., & McDonnell, D. (2008). Introduction: The sceptre and the spectre. In D. Albertazzi & D. McDonnell (Eds), *Twenty-first century populism: The spectre of Western European democracy* (pp. 1–14). Basingstoke: Palgrave Macmillan.

Beckers, K., Walgrave, S., & Van den Bulck, H. (2016). Opinion balance in vox pop television news. *Journalism Studies, 19*(2), 284–296. http://dx.doi.org/10.1080/1461670x.2016.1187576

Bednarek, M. (2016). Voices and values in the news: News media talk, news values and attribution. *Discourse, Context & Media, 11*, 27–37. http://dx.doi.org/10.1016/j.dcm.2015.11.004

Bijsmans, P. (2017). EU media coverage in times of crisis: Euroscepticism becoming mainstream? In M. Caiani & S. Guerra (Eds), *Euroscepticism, democracy and the media: Communicating Europe, contesting Europe* (pp. 73–94). Basingstoke: Palgrave Macmillan.

Billiet, J., & Witte, H. (1995). Attitudinal dispositions to vote for a 'new' extreme right-wing party: The case of 'Vlaams Blok'. *European Journal of Political Research, 27*(2), 181–202. http://dx.doi.org/10.1111/j.1475-6765.1995.tb00635.x

Bonilla-Silva, E., & Forman, T. (2000). 'I am not a racist but . . .': Mapping white college students' racial ideology in the USA. *Discourse & Society*, *11*(1), 50–85.

Brookes, R., Lewis, J., & Wahl-Jorgensen, K. (2004). The media representation of public opinion: British television news coverage of the 2001 General Election. *Media, Culture & Society*, *26*(1), 63–80. http://dx.doi.org/10.1177/0163443704039493

Chilton, P., & Ilyin, M. (1993). Metaphor in political discourse: The case of the common European house. *Discourse & Society*, *4*(1), 7–31. https://doi.org/10.1177/0957926593004001002

Decker, F. (2008). Germany: Right-wing populist failures and left-wing successes. In D. Albertazzi & D. McDonnell (Eds), *Twenty-first century populism: The spectre of Western European democracy* (pp. 119–134). Basingstoke: Palgrave Macmillan.

Denver, D., Carman, C., & Johns, R. (2012). *Elections and voters in Britain*. Basingstoke: Palgrave Macmillan.

Ekström., M., & Tolson, A. (2017). Citizens talking politics in the news: Opinions, attitudes and (dis)engagement. In M. Ekström & J. Firmstone (Eds), *The mediated politics of Europe: A comparative study of discourse* (pp. 201–227). Cham: Palgrave Macmillan.

Freeden, M. (2017). After the Brexit referendum: Revisiting populism as an ideology. *Journal of Political Ideologies*, *22*(1), 1–11. http://dx.doi.org/10.1080/13569317.2016.1260813

George, S. (2000). Britain: Anatomy of a Eurosceptic state. *Journal of European Integration*, *22*(1), 15–32.

Gidron, N., & Bonikowski, B. (2013). Varieties of populism: Literature review and research agenda. *Working Paper. Weatherhead Center for International Affairs 13(0004)*. Cambridge, MA: Harvard University.

Gifford, C. (2006). The rise of postimperial populism: The case of right-wing Euroscepticism in Britain. *European Journal of Political Research*, *45*(5), 851–869. http://dx.doi.org/10.1111/j.1475-6765.2006.00638.x

Gifford, C. (2008). *The making of Eurosceptic Britain: Identity and economy in a post-imperial state*. Aldershot: Ashgate.

Hardt-Mautner, G. (1995). How does one become a good European? The British press and European integration. *Discourse & Society*, *6*(2), 177–205. https://doi.org/10.1177/0957926595006002003

Harré, R., & van Langenhove, L. (1999). *Positioning theory*. Oxford: Blackwell.

Hawkins, K. A. (2009). Is Chávez populist? Measuring populist discourse in comparative perspective. *Comparative Political Studies*, *42*(8), 1040–1067.

Heinisch, R. (2008). Austria: The structure and agency of Austrian populism. In D. Albertazzi & D. McDonnell (Eds), *Twenty-first century populism: The spectre of Western European democracy* (pp. 67–83). Basingstoke: Palgrave Macmillan.

Hermes, J. (2006). Citizenship in the age of the Internet. *European Journal of Communication*, *21*(3), 295–309. http://dx.doi.org/10.1177/0267323106066634

Inglehart, R. F., & Norris, P. (2016). Trump, Brexit, and the rise of populism: Economic have-nots and cultural backlash. *Harvard Kennedy Working Paper Series*. Available at https://faculty.uml.edu/sgallagher/Trump_Populism_Norris.pdf, accessed 18 March 2018.

Ipsos MORI (2016). How Britain voted in the 2016 EU referendum. Available at www.ipsos.com/ipsos-mori/en-uk/how-britain-voted-2016-eu-referendum, accessed 14 March 2018.

Jowett, G. S., & O'Donnell, V. (2015). *Propaganda and persuasion* (6th ed.). Thousand Oaks, CA: Sage.

Kazin, M. (1995). *The populist persuasion: An American history*. Ithaca, NY: Cornell University Press.

Kleemans, M., Schaap, G., & Hermans, L. (2017). Citizen sources in the news: Above and beyond the vox pop? *Journalism: Theory, Practice & Criticism, 18*(4), 464–481. http://dx.doi.org/10.1177/1464884915620206

Koller, V., & Ryan, S. J. (2019). 'A nation divided': Metaphors and scenarios in the media coverage of the 2016 British EU referendum. In C. Hart (Ed.), *Cognitive linguistic approaches to text and discourse: From poetics to politics*. Edinburgh: Edinburgh University Press.

Kritzinger, S., Lewis-Beck, M., Nadeau, R., & Zeglovits, E. (2013). *The Austrian voter*. Göttingen: V&R unipress.

Lewis, J., Inthorn, S., & Wahl-Jorgensen, K. (2005). *Citizens or consumers? What the media tell us about political participation*. Maidenhead: Open University Press.

Lubbers, M., & Scheepers, P. (2000). Individual and contextual characteristics of the German Republikaner vote: A test of complementary theories. *European Journal of Political Research, 38*(1), 63–94. https://doi.org/10.1111/1475-6765.00528

Martin, J. R., & White, P. R. R. (2005). *Appraisal in English*. Basingstoke: Palgrave Macmillan.

Mautner, G. (2001). British national identity in the European context. In A. Musolff, C. Good, P. Points, & R. Wittlinger (Eds), *Attitudes towards Europe: Language in the unification process* (pp. 3–22). Aldershot: Ashgate.

Mayer, N., & Perrineau, P. (1992). Why do they vote for Le Pen? *European Journal of Political Research, 22*(1), 123–141. http://dx.doi.org/10.1111/j.1475-6765.1992.tb00308.x

Montgomery, M. (2007). *The discourse of broadcast news: A linguistic approach*. London: Routledge.

Moore, C. (2016, 20 April). De Gaulle knew it: Britain does not belong in the EU. *The Spectator*. Available at www.spectator.co.uk/2016/04/de-gaulle-knew-it-britain-does-not-belong-in-the-eu, accessed 18 March 2018.

Musolff, A. (2000). Political imagery of Europe: A house without exit doors? *Journal of Multilingual and Multicultural Development, 21*(3), 216–229. https://doi.org/10.1080/01434630008666402

Myers, G. (2000). Entitlement and sincerity in broadcast interviews about Princess Diana. *Media, Culture & Society, 22*(2), 167–185. http://dx.doi.org/10.1177/016344300022002003

Myers, G. (2004). *Matters of opinion: Talking about public issues*. Cambridge: Cambridge University Press.

Nasti, C. (2012). *Images of the Lisbon Treaty debate in the British press: A corpus-based approach to metaphor analysis*. Newcastle-upon-Tyne: Cambridge Scholars Publishing.

Niedermeier, A., & Ridder, W. (2017). *Das Brexit Referendum: Hintergründe, Streitthemen, Perspektiven* [*The Brexit referendum: Background, controversies, perspectives*]. Wiesbaden: Springer.

Nonhoff, M. (2017). Populism and the promise of radical democracy. Paper presented at DiscourseNet Congress 2, 13–15 September, Warwick, UK.

Oesch, D. (2008). Explaining workers' support for right-wing populist parties in Western Europe: Evidence from Austria, Belgium, France, Norway, and Switzerland. *International Political Science Review, 29*(3), 349–373. http://dx.doi.org/10.1177/0192512107088390

Reisigl, M., & Wodak, R. (2005). *Discourse and discrimination: Rhetorics of racism and antisemitism*. London: Routledge.

Rooduijn, M. (2018). What unites the voter bases of populist parties? Comparing the electorates of 15 populist parties. *European Political Science Review, 10*(3), 351–368. http://dx.doi.org/10.1017/S1755773917000145

Schumacher, G., & Rooduijn, M. (2013). Sympathy for the 'devil'? Voting for populists in the 2006 and 2010 Dutch general elections. *Electoral Studies, 32*(1), 124–133. http://dx.doi.org/10.1016/j.electstud.2012.11.003

van Leeuwen, T. (1996). The representation of social actors. In C. R. Caldas Coulthard & M. Coulthard (Eds), *Text and practices: Readings in critical discourse analysis* (pp. 32–70). London: Routledge.

van Leeuwen, T. (2008). *Discourse and practice: New tools for critical discourse analysis*. Oxford: Oxford University Press.

Weyland, K. (2001). Clarifying a contested concept: Populism in the study of Latin American politics. *Comparative Politics*, *34*(1), 1–22.

Wodak, R. (2015a). 'Normalisierung nach rechts': Politischer Diskurs im Spannungsfeld von Neoliberalismus, Populismus und kritischer Öffentlichkeit ['Normalising towards the right': Political discourse between neoliberalism, populism and a critical public]. *Linguistik online*, *73*(4), 27. http://dx.doi.org/10.13092/lo.73.2191.

Wodak, R. (2015b). *The politics of fear: What right-wing populist discourses mean*. Los Angeles, CA: Sage.

Wodak, R. (2016). 'We have the character of an island nation': A discourse-historical analysis of David Cameron's 'Bloomberg speech' on the European Union. *European University Institute Working Paper Series RSCAS 2016/36*. Available at https://papers.ssrn.com/sol3/papers.cfm?abstract_id=2870570, accessed 6 December 2018.

Wodak, R., KhosraviNik, M., & Mral, B. (Eds) (2013). *Right-wing populism in Europe*. London: Bloomsbury.

7

'FRIENDS DON'T LET FRIENDS GO BREXITING WITHOUT A MANDATE'

Changing discourses of Brexit in *The Guardian*

Ursula Lutzky and Andrew Kehoe

Introduction

While discussions surrounding Brexit increased in the months leading up to the referendum in June 2016 and have continued to dominate the news ever since, the term 'Brexit' and the corresponding discourse of the United Kingdom leaving the European Union have existed for several years. The first attestation of 'Brexit' in the UK newspaper *The Guardian* was on 9 August 2012. It was used in an article in the Business section that discussed the eurozone crisis and indicated that the then Prime Minister David Cameron might call for a referendum on Britain's membership of the European Union:

> In short, David Cameron's falling popularity could persuade him to call an in–out referendum, at a time when the eurozone crisis is fuelling euroscepticism. Europe's efforts to fix the crisis also risk triggering a *Brexit*,[1] with issues such as banking union and financial regulation looming.[2]

In this chapter, we take a closer look at the development in the discourses of Brexit in *The Guardian*, with a view to gaining further insights into discursive changes that have occurred since 2012. The analysis traces the diachronic development of the word 'Brexit' in the 1.3 billion-word *Guardian* corpus (see section on data below) and links its distribution in this corpus to the main political changes that influenced the frequency of its attestation. Additionally, we discuss Brexit-related terms, such as 'Brexiteers' and 'Brexiters', to show which types of neologism the discussion of this topic has triggered (see also Lalić-Krstin & Silaški, Chapter 14 this volume).

By taking a corpus-linguistic approach, we aim to show the extent to which the topic was discussed in *Guardian* articles, pre- and post-referendum, and how Brexit was discursively constructed in different sections of the newspaper, especially after the Leave result of the referendum. To this end, we study the use of Brexit-related terms in two sections of *The Guardian*, the Business section and Comment Is Free, which are, apart from Politics, the two sections in our data in which the terms appear with the highest frequencies. By doing so, we aim to uncover differences in the discourse surrounding the terms to see how the concept of Brexit was discussed in a traditional section of the newspaper focusing on the topic of business, as opposed to a newer section of a blog-like nature that encourages both journalists and external contributors to express their opinion on a variety of topics.

News discourse

While the UK's leaving of the European Union (EU) is primarily the result of a political decision, its impact transcends the sphere of politics and is reflected in a variety of related discourses. Thus, Brexit has been discussed repeatedly in national and international news (e.g. Ridge-Newman et al., 2018), it has been studied with regard to its effects on the British and international economy (e.g. Blackaby, 2018), and people have reacted to it on social media and expressed their supportive or opposing opinion (see Bouko & Garcia, Chapter 11 this volume). These discussions of and reflections on the phenomenon of Brexit have happened both in offline and online contexts and pertained to different expressive dimensions, including various multimodal elements.

In this study, we focus on the discussion of Brexit in online news discourse. While online news is nowadays generally multimodal in nature, including photographs, videos or hyperlinks to related news stories (see e.g. Bednarek & Caple, 2012, pp. 2–5; Landert, 2015, pp. 29–30), our study is based only on the words used in the context of reporting on Brexit. We therefore follow a narrow definition of discourse by taking only textual elements into account and excluding multimodal or multisemiotic features. However, language use in newspapers cannot be regarded as "a single, homogeneous object of study" either (Semino, 2009, p. 439). This is due to the fact that newspapers comprise a variety of different genres, such as news reports, editorials or reviews, and that they are organised into different sections, each of which addresses a particular topic, including for example, Politics, Business or Sports. At the same time, newspaper articles do not only inform readers about events and issues but also provide "a particular perspective and evaluation" (ibid., p. 453).

This is also reflected in the quote below from the Comment Is Free section of *The Guardian*, published on 20 December 2012. In addition to explicitly referring to the power of the media in shaping people's opinions, it includes an example of the competing term 'Brixit' that appeared in the early months of the use of 'Brexit':

> I do not believe the brains of the British people have been so addled by the *Sun* and *Daily Mail* that they will, confronted with the facts about what it is really like to be Norway (without the oil) or Switzerland, decide that exit – *Brexit or Brixit* – is the best option for this country.[3]

Previous research on news discourse has investigated the diachronic development of collocational patterns to gain further insight into their distribution over time and demonstrate how their use reflects extralinguistic changes. For instance, Kehoe and Gee (2009) traced the history of the phrase 'credit crunch' from the 1920s to the present day using a combination of conventional corpora such as Brown (Kucera & Francis, 1967), online news archives and an earlier version of the *Guardian* corpus used in this study. They showed occurrences of the phrase to be cyclical, reflecting real-world events, and found that, during each cycle, the phrase tends to be introduced in quotation marks with a full gloss before gradually falling into common use and even being shortened to 'the crunch'. Additionally, several studies have examined the discourse and representation of Europe in British newspapers. Thus, Mautner (2000) focused on the first 20 years of the UK's membership of the European Community and later the European Union, Bednarek (2006) studied the evaluation of Europe 10 years later (i.e. in 2003–2004) and Buckledee (2018) investigated language use leading up to the referendum and its result in 2016. Our study of the discourse of Brexit in *The Guardian* aims to contribute to this line of research by focusing on its diachronic development and in particular the period following the referendum, when the topic was discussed increasingly in the news, as our analysis will show.

Data and methodology

The corpus used in this study was compiled by the Research and Development Unit for English Studies at Birmingham City University (UK). It is part of a larger monitor corpus of UK newspapers, updated annually and searchable through the WebCorp Linguist's Search Engine (WebCorpLSE).[4] Our focus here is on the *Guardian* corpus which, at the time of writing, includes every article published on the *Guardian* website between January 2000 and December 2017, comprising 1.9 million articles and a total of 1.3 billion words. The articles were downloaded using the specialist web crawling tools built into WebCorpLSE. The resulting corpus is segmented by month and by section of the newspaper, allowing us to pinpoint exactly when a term was first used and to examine the context in which it appeared. It is worth noting that although *The Guardian* still exists as a print newspaper (and we refer to it as a newspaper for this reason), the vast majority of readers now access its content online. In fact, many more people now access *The Guardian* online than ever read the print version in the past, and these readers are spread across the world, with the *Guardian* website consistently among the top 150 most accessed worldwide.[5]

In order to gain further insights into the discursive construction of Brexit in *The Guardian*, we will study patterns of language use through corpus-linguistic means. In previous research, Baker (2006) showed, for example, that the study of concordances allowed further insights into the discourses of refugees in a corpus of newspaper articles (see also Baker & McEnery, 2005). He concluded that "the context of a word is important in how it contributes towards particular discourses" (Baker, 2006, p. 89). It is this context of occurrence that we will refer to in our study of collocational patterns and clusters. Additionally, through a keyword analysis, we aim to uncover statistically significant differences between sections of *The Guardian* with regard to their discussion of Brexit.

A *Guardian* section of particular interest to us is the Comment Is Free blog. This was launched in March 2006 as "the first collective comment blog by a British newspaper website".[6] It was designed to allow existing *Guardian* writers as well as "outside contributors – politicians, academics, writers, scientists, activists and of course existing bloggers" to discuss issues in the news. We find that 102,383 (5 per cent) of the 1.9 million articles in our *Guardian* corpus (2000–2017) come from the Comment Is Free section, which is a considerable portion given that the section did not exist for the first six years of the period. One of the aims of our study is to examine whether descriptions of and attitudes to Brexit found in Comment Is Free differ significantly from those found in other sections of the newspaper.

Analysis

We will begin our analysis by studying the diachronic distribution of the word 'Brexit' in our data. Figure 7.1 traces the use of 'Brexit' in the *Guardian* corpus, from its first attestation in 2012 to the end of 2017. The dotted line is the scaled frequency (per million words) plotted on a monthly basis, while the solid line is a 12-month moving average. As can be seen in Figure 7.1, the frequency of 'Brexit' was rather low until the beginning of 2016, with a small increase in May 2015 around the time of the UK general election when David Cameron first promised a referendum on EU membership. After the Conservative party had won this election with a majority, Cameron announced in February 2016 that the referendum was to be held on 23 June that year. This is also reflected in our data, as Figure 7.1 shows an increase in the use of the word 'Brexit' at the beginning of 2016 and a peak in attestations at the time of the referendum. However, 'Brexit' reaches an even higher frequency in the second half of that year, when the new Prime Minister Theresa May announced that she would trigger Article 50 by the end of March 2017 to start the formal negotiations of leaving the EU. Consequently, there is a further peak in usage around that time in 2017 and the word 'Brexit' then reaches its highest overall frequency in the corpus in the second quarter of 2017, which was the time when the first round of Brexit talks took place between the UK and EU negotiators.

'Brexit' word-formations*

While 'Brexit' is the main form used when referring to the process of the UK leaving the EU, it has also sparked the creation of new words since its first occurrence. Table 7.1 lists the top 20 'Brexit*' word-formations in our data. The wildcard here matches any combination of letters following the base form 'Brexit' (in upper or lower case). Some of the rows in Table 7.1 include spelling and hyphenation variants, with the frequencies of these variants indicated in parentheses.

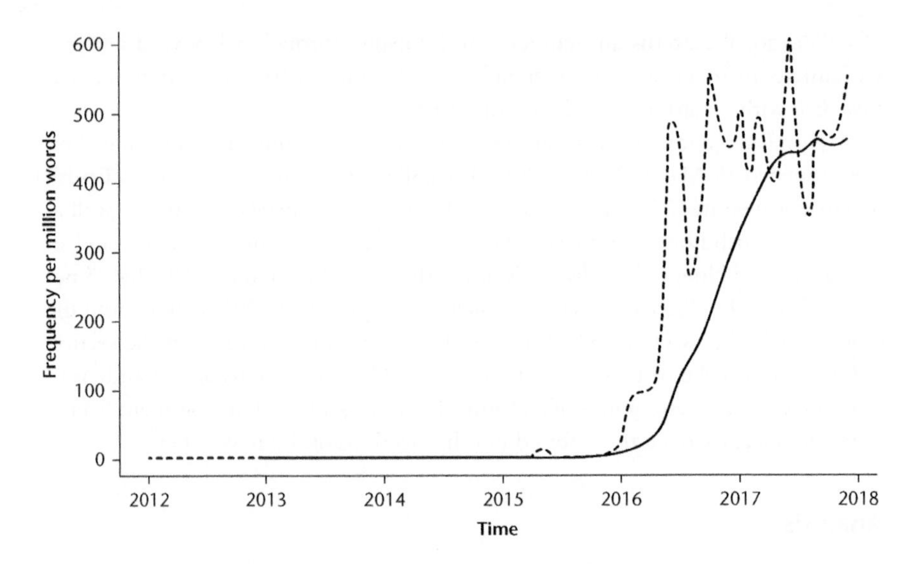

FIGURE 7.1 Distribution of 'Brexit' in the *Guardian* corpus

Not surprisingly, Table 7.1 shows that 'Brexit' is the most frequent form in the *Guardian* corpus overall, appearing 56,082 times. In addition to the singular form, it is also attested in the plural (see rank 10 in Table 7.1) and is then used to refer to different Brexit scenarios, which have been described as soft, medium or hard, as examples (1) and (2) illustrate. In other words, the plural form denotes possible outcomes of the Brexit negotiations and the ensuing consequences for Britain, for instance in terms of control of its borders or access to the single market and the customs union.

(1) All this stuff about soft *Brexits* and medium *Brexits* is pie in the sky (11 December 2016).
(2) Instead, Theresa May is opting for the hardest of hard *Brexits* with no regard for the consequences (4 April 2017).

The remaining word formations in Table 7.1 appear with notably lower frequencies when compared to their base form 'Brexit'. The two forms immediately following 'Brexit' are 'Brexiters' and 'Brexiteers', at ranks 2 and 3 in Table 7.1, together with their singular forms at ranks 4 and 5. 'Brexiters' and 'Brexiteers' would appear to be two competing terms, both used to describe the same group of people: those who are in support of Brexit. The former is considerably more frequent than the latter in our data, which would seem to suggest it is the preferred form amongst *Guardian* writers. Indeed, *The Guardian*'s online style guide comments specifically on usage of this word[7]:

Brexiter

Only use Brexiteer if quoting someone

Despite the fact that *Guardian* writers are instructed not to use 'Brexiteer' (and presumably not 'Brexiteers' either) we still found 1,084 examples of the singular and plural forms combined in our *Guardian* corpus. It seemed unlikely that all of these examples appeared in quotes (the only situation where the style guide permits the use of 'Brexiteer/s') so we carried out further analysis of the concordance lines to determine what was going on. This revealed that just under half the instances of 'Brexiteer/s' (507) appeared in Comment Is Free, the section containing contributions from non-journalists. It is not surprising, therefore, that writers in this section seem to be ignoring *The Guardian*'s style guide. Indeed, the style guide does not appear to apply to this section at all, as indicated by a remark by Comment Is Free founding editor Georgina Henry in the week the section was launched:

> We've invited several hundred people to blog as and when they want on any subject they choose and at any length. Instead of tight copy-editing – back and forth to writers, asking them to elaborate arguments, change introductions, and cut copy to fit – we're checking mainly just for libel.[8]

TABLE 7.1 Top 20 'Brexit*' word-formations

	Brexit (case insensitive)*	*Frequency*
1	Brexit/bREXit (1)	56,082
2	Brexiters/Brexit-ers (2)/brexiters (1)	1,425
3	Brexiteers/brexiteers (1)	849
4	Brexiter/Brexit-er (3)/BREXITER (1)	286
5	Brexiteer/brexiteer (3)/BREXITEER (1)	235
6	Brexit-related	208
7	Brexit's	183
8	Brexit-supporting	112
9	Brexit-induced	56
10	Brexits/brexits (1)	53
11	Brexit-backing	39
12	Brexiting	29
13	Brexited/Brexit-ed (1)/brexited (1)	26
14	Brexit-inspired	23
15	Brexit-voting	22
16	Brexity/Brexit-y (4)/Brexitty (3)	28
17	Brexitland	17
18	Brexit-themed	14
19	Brexiteering	14
20	Brexit-style	11

Examples (3) and (4) are typical of the occurrences found in the different sections of the *Guardian* corpus, with 'Brexiters' used in sections written predominantly by *Guardian* journalists (Politics in example 3) and 'Brexiteers' used in Comment Is Free (example 4). However, there are exceptions, such as example (5), which sees 'Brexiter' appear in Comment Is Free, and example (6), which sees 'Brexiteer' appear in the Football section (where it does not appear in a quote). Example (3), furthermore, illustrates that while the noun 'Brexite(e)r' is almost exclusively capitalised in the corpus, this is not to the same extent the case for the form 'remainer', which here immediately follows the form 'Brexiter' but is attested in lower-case.

(3) May will aim to strike a note of reconciliation when she addresses the Commons, claiming this is the time for *Brexiters* and remainers to come together after holding an early-morning meeting of her cabinet (29 March 2017, Politics).
(4) The slogan of the year, and perhaps the century, is the one about the need to take back control. Those intoxicating words took centre stage in the EU referendum and won the vote for the *Brexiteers* (19 December 2016, Comment Is Free).
(5) For example, someone who identifies as a *Brexiter* might feel schadenfreude from the gradual economic collapse of Brexit Britain, if they felt it was making some stuck-up Londoners very miserable (2 May 2017, Comment Is Free).
(6) Lobotomised Leicester are treating their opponents in Europe with all the disdain of a *Brexiteer* telling his Italian counterpart that he once took a prosecco-making course, so everything's absolutely fine, bugger off (22 November 2016, Football).

In addition to 'Brexite(e)r(s)', Table 7.1 includes one further example of derivation, the form 'Brexity', which is also occasionally spelled 'Brexit-y' or 'Brexitty' in our data. As examples (7) and (8) illustrate, the adjective 'Brexity' is used to express that something is related to Brexit, such as the level of hardness or softness of the Brexit deal or that someone is more or less in support of Brexit, such as the population of London compared to that of Scotland.

(7) The ongoing debate over the optimum level of *Brexity* hardness or softness, from ragingly tumescent to apologetically flaccid, has divided the nation all year (29 December 2017).
(8) In last year's EU referendum, just under 60% of Londoners voted remain: only Scotland was less *Brexity*, and there only slightly (30 October 2017).

Furthermore, Table 7.1 includes examples of conversion that show that by mid-2016 the noun 'Brexit' was also used as a verb, as in 'Brexits', 'Brexited' and 'Brexiting' in examples (9) to (12), with the form being capitalised throughout. It should be noted, however, that the form 'Brexits' is primarily used as a plural noun rather than as a verb in the present tense in the *Guardian* corpus.

(9) I am 100% certain that if the UK *Brexits* out of the single market, it can wave ¾ of its car industry goodbye within 5 years (6 October 2016).

(10) Has the UK *Brexited* yet? No. And according to the Austrian finance minister Hans Jörg Schelling, perhaps it never will (5 July 2016).

(11) Friends don't let friends go *Brexiting* without a mandate. But where are Theresa May's friends? (14 June 2017).

(12) Shorten is making the point Turnbull used the Brexit vote to urge Australia to maintain stable government and not change to Labor. 'He *Brexited* himself . . . He leads a divided party, he has had an election and he has delivered an inferior and unstable outcome' (4 July 2016).

Example (12) is particularly interesting as 'Brexit' is here used as a reflexive verb. The leader of the Australian Labor party, Bill Shorten, commented on the leader of the Liberal party and then Prime Minister of Australia, Malcolm Turnbull, by saying that the latter had 'Brexited himself'. He also called him the 'David Cameron of the southern hemisphere',[9] comparing Turnbull to the former British Prime Minister, who had won the 2015 general election with a majority but then decided to resign due to the outcome of the referendum. Shorten urged Turnbull to resign too, following the very narrow results of the Australian federal election in July 2016.[10]

At the same time, the participle forms 'Brexited', 'Brexiting' and 'Brexiteering' appear as modifiers, as in examples (13) to (15), where they are used to describe Britain and the Conservative government.

(13) [W]hat would Boris's *Brexited*, Broken Britain actually feel like to live in? (29 March 2016)

(14) Even the most ardent of the Outers have to acknowledge that a *Brexiting* Britain couldn't just cast off from its continent and drift into the mid-Atlantic (29 May 2016).

(15) Between a *Brexiteering* Conservative government and Corbynista Labour, there are acres of unoccupied political real estate (18 September 2016).

The remaining forms in Table 7.1 include several compounds. For example, the adjectives 'Brexit-related' and 'Brexit-induced' indicate that a feeling such as uncertainty or a situation such as economic recession may be caused by Brexit, as illustrated by examples (16) and (17). Additionally, there are the adjectives 'Brexit-supporting', 'Brexit-voting' and 'Brexit-backing', which express a view in support of leaving the EU and may be used to describe a group of people or an area in the UK, as shown by examples (18) to (20).

(16) [C]onsumer spending is likely to be weighed down by weak wage growth and investment spending held back by *Brexit-related* uncertainty (10 August 2017).

(17) However, the unprecedented uncertainty means we could still see radical steps taken in the coming weeks to ward of [*sic*] a *Brexit-induced* recession (14 July 2016).

(18) Impatience is growing, too, among *Brexit-supporting* business leaders, who will also use the Birmingham meeting to demand more clarity (1 October 2016).

(19) What a dismal spectacle to see life-long pro-Europeans in *Brexit-voting* constituencies crumpling to respect the will of the people for fear of losing their seats (31 January 2017).

(20) The move secured 7,000 jobs in the *Brexit-backing* city, but prompted questions over whether a so-called sweetheart deal had been struck between the carmaker and the government (1 December 2016).

'Brexit-inspired', 'Brexit-themed' and 'Brexit-style', on the other hand, describe the influence that Brexit has had on specific events. Example (21), for instance, refers to the mural that the artist Banksy created in Dover; example (22) mentions an event about the implications of Brexit on different professional groups; and example (23) reports on President Erdoğan's suggestion that Turkey could hold a similar referendum to decide if they still wanted to become a member state of the EU. Finally, in addition to these hyphenated constructions, Table 7.1 also includes the form 'Brexitland', which refers to the general subject area of Brexit and the issues surrounding it and was first attested in the *Guardian* corpus on 23 August 2016, as illustrated in example (24).

(21) A *Brexit-inspired* mural by Banksy showing a metalworker chipping away at a star on the EU flag has appeared in Dover (8 May 2017).

(22) In this *Brexit-themed* event, we'll explore the most pressing issues for small business – from staffing to tariffs – and hear from entrepreneurs and academics on their view (4 December 2017).

(23) In an interview published on Sunday, Erdoğan suggested he may stage a *Brexit-style* referendum to decide if his country should continue to seek membership of EU, saying his country's patience is not infinite (13 November 2016).

(24) Whatever is (or is not) going on in *Brexitland*, however, everything is going to work out just fine because, as the *Sunday Times* reported, Britain's remarkable performance in the Rio Olympics will serve as an inspiration to all (23 August 2016).

'Brexit' in* The Guardian*'s sections*

As we mentioned in the introduction, the form 'Brexit' was first attested in the *Guardian* in an article appearing in the Business section on 9 August 2012. In the following, we will take a closer look at the distribution of Brexit-related word-formations in different sections of the newspaper. Table 7.2 shows the top 20 sections in which the word 'Brexit' and its derived forms appear in the *Guardian* corpus.

Not surprisingly, the word 'Brexit' and its derived forms appear most frequently in the Politics section. This is followed immediately by Comment Is Free, the section of the newspaper designed to encourage debate and motivate readers to voice their opinions. As Table 7.2 shows, the topic of Brexit has sparked contributors' interest and resulted in a frequency of Brexit-derived words in this section that amounts to almost half of that in Politics. What we also see in Table 7.2 is that the 'Brexit' words have spread to a wide range of other sections, including Education, Music and Stage. In fact, our analysis shows that by December 2017 the words had even appeared in the Crossword section on 12 occasions.

The two sections that stand out in Table 7.2 in terms of frequency next to Politics are Comment Is Free and Business, which is why we will focus on these two sections in the following analysis. In particular, we will examine the discourse surrounding the term 'Brexit' and its related word-formations in these sections and compare our findings to *The Guardian* as a whole. In order to do so, we first used WebCorpLSE to extract the collocates of each of the words included in our 'Brexit*' search within a span of four words to the left and four words to the right. In the following sections, this collocational window is used as the basis of a keyword analysis to reveal which collocates occur more frequently than expected in one section of the newspaper compared to all other sections. Our analysis follows the same underlying principles as a standard keywords analysis (popularised by WordSmith Tools; Scott, 1996) but the corpus and reference corpus we use contain only the immediate contexts (span 4) of the 'Brexit*' words. We refer to this below as a key collocate analysis.

TABLE 7.2 Top 20 sections for 'Brexit*' in the *Guardian* corpus

	Section	*Frequency*
1	Politics	26,351
2	Comment Is Free	12,093
3	Business	8,388
4	World	2,480
5	UK News	1,797
6	Media	992
7	US News	612
8	Environment	511
9	Society	497
10	Books	486
11	Life and Style	473
12	TV and Radio	442
13	Education	438
14	Money	436
15	News	344
16	Science	282
17	Global	251
18	Music	250
19	Stage	246
20	Small Business Network	229

'Brexit' in the* Guardian *Business section*

Table 7.3 presents the results of our first key collocate analysis, in which we compare the collocates of 'Brexit*' in the Business section to the collocates of 'Brexit*' in all other sections of *The Guardian* combined.

As we might expect, Table 7.3 includes several examples that are part of the semantic field of business. These include 'pound', 'bank', and 'sterling' among the top 10, but also 'economy', 'investors' and 'consumer' at ranks 16, 18 and 20 respectively. Additionally, Table 7.3 includes the proper noun 'Carney', which refers to the economist Mark Carney. Thus, business articles on the topic of Brexit refer to the Governor of the Bank of England, a position Carney has held since July 2013, or quote him to a significantly higher extent than articles appearing in other sections of *The Guardian*.

However, the most significant key collocate in the Business section is 'vote'. We find that it is most frequently attested in the two-word cluster 'Brexit vote' (1,947 occurrences) and the three-word cluster 'the Brexit vote' (1,647 occurrences). When expanding this cluster and studying 4-grams, we notice that they include temporal references, such as 'after the Brexit vote' (227 occurrences) or 'following the Brexit vote' (165 occurrences). This indicates that the business articles in *The Guardian* are concerned mainly with the developments resulting from the outcome of the referendum. This is also reflected in the key collocates 'since', 'following' and 'June', which appear in Table 7.3 at ranks 3, 8 and 12.

TABLE 7.3 Top 20 key collocates of 'Brexit*' in the *Guardian* Business section

	Key collocate	*Frequency*	*Keyness*
1	vote	2,144	2,025.04
2	uncertainty	452	856.11
3	since	457	609.93
4	pound	249	569.02
5	the	7,137	450.66
6	bank	115	297.61
7	fears	163	296.28
8	following	257	269.92
9	sterling	103	257.22
10	growth	95	196.77
11	impact	307	195.36
12	June	159	193.07
13	related	125	187.46
14	Carney	69	182.73
15	worries	75	172.16
16	economy	164	158.61
17	hit	99	153.98
18	investors	60	152.17
19	concerns	106	140.89
20	consumer	46	131.48

The word 'impact' also appears among the key collocates in the Business section, occupying rank 11 in Table 7.3. In fact, among the top five 5-grams of 'vote' in the data, we find 'impact of the Brexit vote' (77 occurrences) as well as 'aftermath of the Brexit vote' (71 occurrences) and 'wake of the Brexit vote' (70 occurrences), all of which pertain to the consequences the referendum has had or will have. At the same time, Table 7.3 includes several examples with slightly more negative connotations than 'impact', including 'uncertainty' at rank 2 but also 'fears', 'worries' and 'concerns', at ranks 7, 15 and 19 respectively. This indicates that, compared to the rest of the *Guardian* corpus, the articles appearing in the Business section explicitly address the unclear future outlook that the Brexit result entails (see also Kopf, Chapter 10 this volume). Thus, one-third of the instances of the word 'uncertainty' appear in the cluster 'Brexit uncertainty' (154 occurrences), and the most frequent trigram in which it occurs is 'uncertainty over Brexit' (40 occurrences). Likewise, the section contains the frequent clusters 'Brexit fears' (70 occurrences), 'Brexit worries' (43 occurrences) and 'Brexit concerns' (20 occurrences) as well as longer constructions, such as 'fears of a hard Brexit' (15 occurrences), 'worries about Brexit' (13 occurrences) and 'concerns about/over Brexit' (19/14 occurrences).

The form 'hit' also falls into this group of negatively connotated words. According to the *Oxford English Dictionary* (OED), the verb (s.v. *hit*, v. I.8a.) means, in its figurative sense, "[t]o affect the conscience, feelings, comfort, prosperity, etc. of (any one) in a way analogous to physical hitting; to affect sensibly, painfully, or injuriously; to smite, wound, hurt". The Business section includes examples such as 'Brexit would/could/will/has hit growth/investment/wages/British exports/ the economy/consumer and business confidence', which indicate that these areas would be negatively affected. This is further illustrated by examples (25) and (26).

(25) The trade union federation, which is campaigning to persuade voters to remain part of the EU, said *Brexit would hit* wages, jobs and workers' rights and warned of a devastating blow to Britain's manufacturing sector, where highly skilled jobs would be lost (1 June 2016).

(26) Meanwhile in the UK, we have seen more signs that *Brexit has hit* investment in the building sector (4 September 2017).

Example (25), which appeared in an article that was published prior to the referendum in June 2016, represents a statement by the Trade Union Federation, which warned of the economic effects a Leave vote would have for the country. Example (26), on the other hand, was published more than a year after the Brexit vote and reports on one specific effect that has been observed, namely a downturn in the building sector.

The study of the top 20 keywords among the span 4 collocates of 'Brexit*' in the Business section has thus shown that this section of *The Guardian*, on the one hand, discusses the topic of Brexit in the context of several business-related concepts, as was to be expected. On the other hand, we were able to identify several key collocates with negative connotations and temporal references to the time after the referendum. Thus, when referring to Brexit the Business section mainly shows an interest in the (economic) consequences of the Leave vote and generally expresses a rather negative view of what these could be or have been to date.

'Brexit' in the* Guardian *Comment Is Free section*

As mentioned above (see Table 7.2), the Comment Is Free section includes even more Brexit-related words than the Business section. Table 7.4 therefore lists the results of our second key collocate analysis, in which we compare the collocates of 'Brexit*' in the Comment Is Free section to all other sections of *The Guardian*.

What is immediately noticeable is that the key collocates from the Comment Is Free section differ considerably from those in the Business section. Apart from collocates pertaining to the topic of Brexit, such as 'hard', which mainly appears in the cluster 'hard Brexit' (513 occurrences), we cannot identify a specific semantic field from which most collocates stem. Instead, many of the examples in Table 7.4 are of a more general nature, including pronouns such as 'it' and 'they', modal verbs such as 'must' and 'can', and adverbs such as 'all' and 'many'. This may be related to the nature of this section, which is not as focused as some of the other sections (e.g. Politics or US news) but that allows journalists as well as external contributors to voice their opinions on a wide range of topics.

The key collocates of 'Brexit*' in the Comment Is Free section include several words that relate to the people involved in the Brexit discourse. The most significant is 'Brexiteers' (see Table 7.4, rank 1), followed by 'Brexiters' at rank 3 and the singular 'Brexiteer' at rank 20. Additionally, the personal pronoun 'they' appears among the top 20, as does the proper noun 'Tory', and the address form 'Mrs', which mainly collocates with Prime Minister May's last name. As keywords reveal "important concepts in a text (in relation to other texts)" (Baker, 2004, p. 347), we may thus note that the focus of the Comment Is Free section is on the participants in the Brexit process. This includes the supporters of Brexit as well as the main agents in provoking Brexit and determining its specific form. The word 'Tory' is here used in more than half of its attestations to modify the word 'Brexit' (58 occurrences), 'Brexiters' (38 occurrences) and 'Brexiteers' (16 occurrences), indicating that there is a strong association in the Comment Is Free section between Brexit and the Conservative party, despite the fact that supporters of Brexit are not limited to this party. Again, this may relate to the nature of the Comment Is Free section, where strong opinions are encouraged and the usual *Guardian* guidelines do not apply.

In addition to these terms of reference, Table 7.4 also includes the time adverbial 'now', which, like the forms 'since' and 'following' in Table 7.3, expresses a temporal reference. However, instead of focusing on the post-Brexit period, the emphasis here is on current affairs. Furthermore, we find the third-person singular form of the verb 'to be' as well as the modal verbs 'can', 'will' and 'must' among

TABLE 7.4 Top 20 key collocates of 'Brexit*' in the *Guardian* Comment Is Free section

	Key collocate	*Frequency*	*Keyness*
1	brexiteers	423	353.09
2	is	1,911	335.11
3	brexiters	561	261.54
4	this	483	82.58
5	that	1,829	82.16
6	can	210	78.17
7	hard	723	73.99
8	it	846	70.76
9	they	360	70.48
10	so	283	63.95
11	all	271	61.50
12	Mrs	45	59.54
13	Tory	196	54.71
14	will	818	53.52
15	Britain	334	52.17
16	brexit's	81	51.98
17	must	122	41.25
18	many	161	40.30
19	now	251	37.76
20	brexiteer	89	36.55

the top 20 key collocates in the Comment Is Free section. When studying the two-word clusters in which they predominantly occur, it turns out that they mainly collocate with the noun 'Brexit'. In fact, around one-third of the attestations of 'is' and 'will' are attested in the cluster 'Brexit is/will' and around one-fifth of the instances of 'can' and 'must' appear as 'Brexit can/must' (see also Buckledee, 2018 on the use of modal verbs in the Remain versus Leave campaigns).

In the Comment Is Free section, Brexit is described as 'a bold step', 'a disaster', 'a terrible idea', 'a golden opportunity', 'a doomed path', or 'a civil war'. At the same time, it is referred to as 'not mysterious', 'not over', 'not just daft', 'not going away', and as 'not yet irrevocable'. Thus, in this section, writers elucidate what they believe defines Brexit. They state what Brexit is, as examples (27) and (28) illustrate, which equate Brexit with a failure and a recipe for a nationalist Britain, respectively. At the same time, they say what Brexit is not, as in examples (29) and (30), although negative definitions of this kind are considerably less frequent than positive ones.

(27) *Brexit* is a failure before it has started (15 February 2017).

(28) Clearly, whatever the claims of the leave camp – reiterated at the launch of a new free trade thinktank on Wednesday – *Brexit is* a recipe not for an outward-looking global Britain but an inward-looking, nationalist, protectionist one (28 September 2017).

(29) The prime minister wanted to reassure her continental counterparts that *Brexit is not* a wrecking project akin to Trumpism (3 February 2017).

(30) Indeed this reinforces the view that *Brexit is not* the immigration silver bullet that some hope and expect it to be (25 May 2017).

Summary and conclusion

In this chapter, we studied the discourse of Brexit in the *Guardian* corpus following the first appearance of the term in 2012. We began by tracing the diachronic development of the term 'Brexit' through our data and mapped increases in its use to extralinguistic events in politics. Additionally, we discussed new words derived from the base form 'Brexit', which demonstrate the discursive spread of the concept and illustrate the need for further expressions to allow for the relevant narratives on the UK's leaving the EU to be construed. These creations included forms to denote the supporters of Brexit, with 'Brexiters' being considerably more frequent in the newspaper than 'Brexiteers', conversion turning the noun into a verb ('to Brexit') and derived forms to further describe a 'Brexiting' Britain, 'Brexit-related' uncertainty or 'Brexit-themed' events.

In the second part of our analysis we then contextualised these forms by studying their use in two sections of the newspaper in which they appear with particularly high frequencies. Thus, we carried out a key collocate analysis on the Brexit-related words in the Business and Comment Is Free sections and found that writers in these sections differ significantly in the way they construct their version of the discourse of Brexit. While the Business section is focused on a future perspective discussing the impact that Brexit will have and the economic developments following the referendum, the Comment Is Free section is concerned mainly with the participants in the Brexit process and with defining what Brexit is, can or must involve.

Our study has therefore shown that the discursive construction of Brexit in the *Guardian* newspaper does not only reflect extralinguistic developments but has also necessitated the creation of a range of new words that assist in discussing a process which, according to the Business section, entails a notable degree of uncertainty and negative implications. In the Comment Is Free section, on the other hand, in which writers are encouraged to voice their opinions, this uncertainty has led people to come up with their own definitions of what Brexit could be. Thus, the discourses of Brexit in *The Guardian* illustrate different ways of coming to terms with a political phenomenon that will have a lasting effect on the future of the UK.

While these findings are based on the study of one newspaper only and may not reflect the breadth of news media in the UK they do show that, even within a single newspaper, there are different approaches to representing Brexit. This, therefore, underlines the importance of contextualising newspaper data and of carrying out fine-grained analyses. At the same time, our study contributes to a more complete understanding of the discussion of Brexit in newspaper discourse by providing insights on a large-scale basis, including the analysis of 1.9 million articles and over a billion words. It offers a diachronic view of the discursive development of Brexit, examining not only the period preceding the referendum – going back as far as 2012 – but also the year and a half following the Leave vote. It therefore complements previous studies that focused on media coverage immediately before and shortly after the referendum (see Ridge-Newman et al., 2018). Based on a large data set, our analysis has demonstrated that the outcome of the referendum triggered a sharp increase in discussion of the topic which lasted several months and reached its peak only a year later. Future studies will need to continue quantitatively assessing trends in the discourses of Brexit in other media outlets and investigate in particular the period following the referendum.

Notes

1 The italics here and in all following examples are ours.
2 www.theguardian.com/business/2012/aug/09/eurozone-crisis-ecb-credit-crunch-china (accessed 7 July 2018).
3 www.theguardian.com/commentisfree/2012/dec/20/referendum-europe-bring-it-on (accessed 7 July 2018).
4 www.webcorp.org.uk/lse. For copyright reasons the newspaper corpus is available to registered partners only.
5 www.alexa.com/siteinfo/theguardian.com (accessed 7 July 2018).
6 www.theguardian.com/commentisfree/2006/mar/14/welcometocommentisfree (accessed 7 July 2018).
7 www.theguardian.com/guardian-observer-style-guide-b (accessed 7 July 2018).
8 www.theguardian.com/commentisfree/2006/mar/18/editorsweek (accessed 7 July 2018).
9 www.theguardian.com/australia-news/2016/jul/04/malcolm-turnbull-cannot-command-his-party-and-should-resign-bill-shorten-says (accessed 7 July 2018).
10 www.theguardian.com/australia-news/live/2016/jul/04/australian-election-2016-labor-coalition-independents-politics-live (accessed 7 July 2018).

References

Baker, P. (2004). Querying keywords: Questions of difference, frequency, and sense in keyword analysis. *Journal of English Linguistics*, *32*(4), 346–359. https://doi.org/10.1177/0075424204269894

Baker, P. (2006). *Using corpora in discourse analysis*. London: Bloomsbury.

Baker, P., & McEnery, T. (2005). A corpus-based approach to discourses of refugees and asylum seekers in UN and newspaper texts. *Journal of Language and Politics*, *4*(2), 197–226. https://doi.org/10.1075/jlp.4.2.04bak

Bednarek, M. (2006). Evaluating Europe: Parameters of evaluation in the British press. In C. Leung & J. Jenkins (Eds), *Reconfiguring Europe: The contribution of applied linguistics* (pp. 137–156). London: Equinox.

Bednarek, M., & Caple, H. (2012). *News discourse*. London: Bloomsbury.

Blackaby, D. (2018). The UK economy and Brexit. In Y. K. Dwivedi, N. P. Rana, E. L. Slade, M. A. Shareef, M. Clement, A. C. Simintiras, & B. Lal (Eds), *Emerging markets from a multidisciplinary perspective: Challenges, opportunities and research agenda* (pp. 37–45). Chaim: Springer.

Buckledee, S. (2018). *The language of Brexit: How Britain talked its way out of the European Union*. London: Bloomsbury.

Kehoe, A., & Gee, M. (2009). Weaving web data into a diachronic corpus patchwork. In A. Renouf & A. Kehoe (Eds), *Corpus linguistics: Refinements and reassessments* (pp. 255–279). Amsterdam: Rodopi.

Kucera, H., & Francis, W. N. (1967). *Computational analysis of present-day American English*. Providence, RI: Brown University Press.

Landert, D. (2015). Reportable facts and a personal touch: The functions of direct quotes in online news. In J. Arendholz, W. Bublitz, & M. Kirner-Ludwig (Eds), *The pragmatics of quoting now and then* (pp. 29–52). Berlin: de Gruyter.

Mautner, G. (2000). *Der britische Europa-Diskurs: Methodenreflexion und Fallstudien zur Berichterstattung in der Tagespresse*. Vienna: Passagen Verlag.

Oxford English Dictionary. www.oed.com (accessed 7 July 2018).

Ridge-Newman, A., León-Solís, F., & O'Donnell, H. (Eds) (2018). *Reporting the road to Brexit: International media and the EU referendum 2016*. Basingstoke: Palgrave Macmillan.

Scott, M. (1996). *WordSmith tools*. Oxford: Oxford University Press.

Semino, E. (2009). Language in newspapers. In J. Culpeper, F. Katamba, P. Kerswill, R. Wodak, & T. McEnery (Eds), *English language: Description, variation and context* (pp. 439–453). Basingstoke: Palgrave Macmillan.

PART II

Discursive consequences of the Brexit vote

8

'THE REFERENDUM RESULT DELIVERED A CLEAR MESSAGE'

Jeremy Corbyn's populist discourse

Massimiliano Demata

Introduction

This chapter analyses some of the discourse strategies at the core of Jeremy Corbyn's policies in 2016–2017, a period that witnessed the EU membership referendum (23 June 2016) and the General Election (8 June 2017) called by UK Prime Minister Theresa May in a bid to capitalise on the results of the referendum. The chapter discusses how the language of the Labour leader in this period bore the signs of certain discursive patterns that are usually associated with populism and that, to a large extent, derived from the discourse surrounding the referendum itself.

The first part of this chapter will look into the EU referendum in the context of the modern concept of populism. In a historical context in which referenda have become a favourite political tool for populists (Topaloff, 2017), this section will summarise the root causes of the success of the Leave campaign and Corbyn's own ambiguous position on Europe. The second part of the chapter will look at Corbyn's speeches, newspapers articles written by him and official Labour statements from 2016–2017. It will specifically analyse the evolution of Corbyn's discourse during the period between the referendum and the General Election, looking at how certain choices within his discourse may be related to populism. The key argument developed in the chapter is that in his discourse Corbyn responded to the wave of populist politics that caused the Leave victory in the EU referendum by using the key concept of populism and of Brexit rhetoric, i.e. the 'people', in a politically progressive manner.

Corbyn, Brexit and populism

The rather surprising and, to many, deeply unsettling outcome of the 2016 EU referendum has been interpreted as major evidence of the rise of populism and nationalism all over Europe (Ford & Goodwin, 2017). The agenda for the referendum, largely set by the Leave campaign, mainly consisted of three points: immigration, sovereignty (i.e. control of national borders and not following EU laws anymore) and financial concerns over Britain's membership in the EU (Evans & Menon, 2017, pp. 75–78; Ford & Goodwin, 2017, pp. 9–10; Miglbauer & Koller, Chapter 7 this volume). The Leave campaign managed to raise a widespread sense of social alarm and to assign blame to the EU for the threats posed to Britain in these areas (Evans & Menon, 2017). Indeed, these three arguments are also at the core of the contemporary populist agenda: the Leave campaign appealed to the typical fears promoted by right-wing populist movements both on the Continent and in the United States, namely fear of migrants, loss of jobs and economic uncertainty on the one hand, and threats to national boundaries and sovereignty on the other (Wodak, 2015, pp. 3–7).

Populism claims to be a programme that fulfils the interests and the will of the majority of the ordinary people, and to do so, it puts "into question the institutional order by constructing an underdog as an historical agent – i.e. an agent which is an Other in relation to the way things stand" (Laclau, 2005, p. 47). According to Mudde and Kaltwasser's famous definition,

> [p]opulism is a "thin-centred" ideology that considers society to be ultimately separated into two homogenous and antagonistic groups, "the pure people" and "the corrupt elite," and which argues that politics should be an expression of the *volonté générale* (general will) of the people.
>
> *(Mudde & Kaltwasser, 2012, p. 8)*

At its most basic and in all its different national applications, populism revolves around three core concepts: the people, the elite and the general will (Mudde & Kaltwasser, 2017, pp. 9–19). The 'people' is a discursive construction in which they are seen as 'pure' and as the combination of the people as sovereign, the common people and the nation. The 'elite', on the other hand, is considered 'corrupt', including as it does the political, economic and media establishment, which are accused of using the state institutions for their own interests at the expense of the people. The general will necessitates the direct rule of the people, as opposed to the (elitist) representative government, and it is the general will that is used by the populist leader as a justification to attack scapegoats, such as minority groups, or indeed the establishment and the elites. Populist movements in Europe have expanded in the last decade or so mainly because of a widespread sense of distrust towards the EU and the individual national political establishments. Political discourse in Europe has become dominated by the rhetoric of contrast and opposition between the 'people' and the 'elite', two groups that are portrayed "as vehemently opposed to each other, two epistemic communities, one defined as powerful, the other as powerless; one described as good, innocent, and hard-working, the other as bad, corrupt, criminal, lazy and unjustly privileged" (Wodak, 2017, p. 553).

The division between the 'people' and the 'elite' that is typical of populism results in a "simplification of the political space" (Laclau, 2005, p. 18) and as such is the key to understanding populism in its various forms. These two entities are constructed arbitrarily, each version of populism defining their configuration on the basis of specific ideological interests. The concept of the 'people', in particular, who the populist leader claims to speak on behalf of, is central to populist discourse, both lexically and ideologically. This concept, however, is conspicuous for its vagueness (Mudde, 2004, p. 546), as it is a marker of collective identities that can assume different referential value depending on the interests of those who use it. Its meaning is made visible by each version of populism and is expressed as a signifier that is semantically abstract but nevertheless ideologically evocative and cognitively specific (Chilton, 2017). In this sense, 'people' can be seen as a floating signifier, a linguistic sign that can take different meanings and is used to articulate an "ideology of consensus" (Fowler, 1991, p. 49) structured in different discourses.

Populists do not trust the workings of mainstream state institutions, made up of party representation and parliaments, and present them as not conducive to a fair representation of the popular will. Not surprisingly, of the proceedings occasionally used by representative democracies, it is referenda, as a means of expressing plebiscitary democracy, which populists favour most. The increasing number of referenda held in the past two decades bears witness to the rising importance of "anti-establishment political forces", which, in their struggle against mainstream political parties, have transformed referenda "into a strategic instrument for advancing their own profile and issues" (Topaloff, 2017, p. 130). Populists claim that referenda, as a form of direct democracy, allow the true 'voice of the people' to be heard, as the outcome of a referendum can be considered as the authentic expression of the will of the sovereign people (Canovan, 2005, pp. 108–109). As of 2017, more than 35 referenda have been proposed by populist parties and movements all over Europe, the most popular issues being EU membership and refugees (Topaloff, 2017, pp. 133–135).

With the EU referendum, the British people were asked to express their opinion about a matter that, up to that moment, had always been discussed by governments and elected (and unelected) officials. However, while the referendum was called for by the 'elite' (namely by the then Prime Minister David Cameron), it soon became clear that the decision as to whether or not to leave the EU would channel the anger and frustration that many in Britain felt toward Europe's institutions as well as about migrants (see Kopf, Chapter 10 this volume; Miglbauer & Koller, Chapter 6 this volume). Not surprisingly, then, support for Leave was built on an anti-establishment, anti-immigration, anti-politics and ultimately populist platform. Support for the campaign came from UKIP, whose policies were based on hostility to immigration and EU membership (Wodak, 2015, p. 35; Cap, Chapter 5 this volume), plus a coalition that cut across party lines, with both Tories and Labour internally (and sorely) divided on the issue. The deeply populist bias of the Leave campaign was also strengthened by the way the Leave campaign framed the referendum: the Brexit vote was represented as an opportunity for 'real' people to punish the political and economic establishment (Hobolt, 2016, p. 1266). Indeed, in true populist fashion, former London Mayor Boris Johnson (who can hardly be called an outsider to the political establishment) often attacked the privileges bestowed on the elites because of Britain's membership in the EU: in an article in the *Daily Telegraph* he wrote against the "vast clerisy of lobbyists and corporate affairs gurus – all the thousands of Davos men and women who have their jaws firmly clamped around the euro-teat" (Johnson, 2016a), and the headline of another *Telegraph* article was "Of course our city fat cats love the EU – it's why they earn so much" (Johnson, 2016b). These attacks became a distinctive feature of the Leave campaign and fed into the growing suspicion that many members of the British public had long felt towards politics and politicians in general (Evans & Menon, 2017, p. 65).

The Leave victory may be seen as the result of the changing social and political landscape in Britain over the past couple of decades, a landscape in which the growing convergence of the main parties on a set of shared core values left a few groups – mostly the white working class with few education qualifications and low earnings – without political representation within mainstream politics. These "left-behind" groups (Ford & Goodwin, 2017, p. 20) had a more conservative outlook on British society than the better-educated, generally younger and more affluent "winners of globalization" (Hobolt, 2016, p. 1265), and looked at multiculturalism and immigration with profound hostility. The referendum highlighted "a new Cultural cleavage dividing Populists from Cosmopolitan Liberalism" (Inglehart & Norris, 2016, p. 3), or a division between "social conservatives" and "social liberals", with the former feeling threatened by an ethnically and culturally diverse society, whereas the latter are comfortable with it (Curtice, 2016). Social conservatives also felt a strong sense of nostalgia for Great Britain: for them, English nationalism became aligned with Euroscepticism because of "a nostalgic rendering of Britain's past, from a desire to return to the 'golden age' of British history – an age that was defined by British imperialism, even if present-day Eurosceptics do not call the Empire by name" (Grob-Fitzgibbon, 2016, p. 468).

During the referendum campaign Jeremy Corbyn and the Labour party were officially supporting Remain. Corbyn himself, however, had long boasted strong Eurosceptic credentials: he had voted to leave the EU in the 1975 referendum, had opposed the Maastricht and Lisbon treaties and, as a long-time Bennite backbencher,[1] had constantly distanced himself from the official pro-EU line of New Labour, criticising the EU on many occasions. In a parliamentary debate in 1993, for instance, he attacked the Maastricht Treaty:

> If my hon. Friend is now envisaging the establishment of a federal Europe, will he not reflect that the Maastricht treaty does not take us in the direction of the checks and balances contained in the American federal constitution? It takes us in the opposite direction of an unelected legislative body – the Commission – and, in the case of foreign policy, a policy Commission that will be, in effect, imposing foreign policy on nation states that have fought for their own democratic accountability.
>
> *(Hansard, 1993)*

Drawing on an old Eurosceptic strain in Labour history (Evans & Menon, 2017, p. 11), Corbyn's emphasis on the lack of accountability and the unelected nature of the European Commission was an argument that would become very familiar among Leavers. While running for Labour leadership, Corbyn did not hide his own Euroscepticism. On 25 July 2015, during a hustings with other Labour candidates running for the party's leadership, he did not rule out voting Leave in a referendum on Britain's membership of the EU. His words resounded with a Eurosceptic attitude that is typical of the hostility towards the EU at the centre of populist discourse, even though he motivated his hostility with wanting to secure workers' rights and environmental protection, and limit corporations' power:

> No I wouldn't rule it out [. . .] Because Cameron quite clearly follows an agenda which is about trading away workers' rights, is about trading away environmental protection [. . .] The EU also knowingly, deliberately maintains a number of tax havens and tax evasion posts around the continent – Luxembourg, Monaco and a number of others – and has this strange relationship with Switzerland which allows a lot of European companies to outsource their profits to Switzerland where tax rates are very low. I think we should be making demands: universal workers' rights, universal environmental protection, end the race to the bottom on corporate taxation, end the race to the bottom in working wage protection.
>
> *(Final Labour Leadership Hustings, 2015)*

Just after these controversial declarations, Labour's Europe spokesman Pat McFadden mused on the real nature of Corbyn's position on Europe, comparing the Labour leadership contender to both left-wing and right-wing populists:

> There has been some attempt to suggest that Mr Corbyn's campaign is a parallel of the Syriza movement in Greece, but Syriza is a firmly pro-European movement that has fought to keep Greece in the EU and the Eurozone. If Mr Corbyn comes out as anti-EU it will show there is nothing new about his politics – it is simply Bennism from the 1980s reheated. Is he going to fight for Britain as an open, outward-looking country engaged with the world or line up with Nigel Farage on a nationalist nostalgia trip?
>
> *(quoted in Helm & Doward, 2015)*

During the referendum campaign, Corbyn did not fully disperse McFadden's doubts. The Labour leader constantly refused to associate himself with those New Labour leaders who supported Remain by declining invitations to join former Labour Prime Ministers Tony Blair and Gordon Brown on public Remain events (Evans & Menon, 2017, pp. 66–67). Furthermore, according to Corbyn's critics, pro-Remain statements drafted by key Labour officials were deleted or severely watered down by Corbyn's office (Waugh, 2016). He maintained a conspicuously low profile during the referendum campaign: among the politicians appearing in news regarding the referendum on Britain's major TV channels and in the main print media in the period from 6 May to 22 June 2016,[2] Corbyn ranked seventh, appearing in only 6.1 per cent of news items (Loughborough University, 2016).[3]

Right after the Brexit vote, Corbyn's leadership came under attack mainly because of his supposedly non-committal attitude during the campaign. Indeed, Labour rank and file as well as supporters were baffled and during the campaign did not even know what Labour's official position on Brexit was (Ashmore, 2016; Shipman 2017, p. 340). Corbyn was accused by many key Labour figures of not having lent his full weight to the campaign and of not having set his own party on a clear political course: former European Commissioner and Business Secretary Lord Peter Mandelson declared that "[w]e were greatly damaged by Jeremy Corbyn's stance, no doubt at all about that" (quoted in Shipman, 2017, p. 364), and former culture secretary Ben Bradshaw said that Corbyn's "lack of leadership on [the] EU referendum has been abysmal" (quoted in Riley-Smith, 2016).

However, a close reading of Corbyn's speeches and statements prior to the referendum vote show that the Labour leader did support Remain on the basis of a social agenda that would later be developed into the core of his campaign for the General Election.

Corbyn's 'people' and 'the many' vs 'the few'

The analysis presented in the following section is based on a dataset of 98 speeches, public statements and newspaper articles by Corbyn in the period from 1 February 2016 to 31 December 2017. The texts were collected from https://jeremycorbyn.org.uk and https://labourlist.org, currently the most extensive collections of Corbyn's texts. This section will assess the nomination strategies (Fairclough, 2014; Reisigl & Wodak, 2016) employed by Corbyn in the definition of the key collective signifier of populism as identified by most literature on the subject (Mudde, 2004; Canovan, 2005; Laclau, 2005; Mudde & Kaltwasser, 2012): the 'people'. The first part of this section focuses on Corbyn's texts during the referendum campaign, while the second part is devoted to his post-referendum rhetoric, leading up to and following the 2017 General Election. I argue that although Corbyn publicly supported Remain, populist tropes otherwise associated with the discourse of the Leave campaign played a key role in his rhetoric during this two-year period. Specifically, the 'people' vs 'elite' dichotomy, which characterised the populist discourse at the basis of the Brexit campaign, was complemented, in Corbyn's post-referendum discourse, by the 'many' vs the 'few' dichotomy, a Manichean opposition that became the key theme of the Labour campaign for the 2017 General Election.

Corbyn's discourse and the EU referendum: 'people'

In his speeches, Corbyn repeatedly emphasised the central role of the 'people'. 'People' is the second most frequent lexical item used in the dataset under examination, appearing 828 times, while the most frequent, 'Labour', appeared 829 times (see Table 8.1). Uses of 'people' with and without the definite article (as in 'some people' or 'many people') both serve the same purpose in Corbyn's discourse, namely to establish a people vs elite dichotomy.

The word appears throughout the period under examination, with two peaks, June 2016 and May–June 2017, in concomitance with the Brexit vote (23 June 2016) and the General Election (8 June 2017) (Figure 8.1), indicating the strong importance of 'people' as a discourse topic in Corbyn's political campaigns.

TABLE 8.1 Frequency of the top ten lexical items in Corbyn's texts, February 2016–December 2017

Lexical item	*Total frequency*	*Relative frequency*
Labour	829	0.65%
people	828	0.65%
government	656	0.52%
country	435	0.34%
Britain	434	0.34%
rights	334	0.26%
work	296	0.26%
public	293	0.23%
economy	279	0.22%
need	262	0.21%

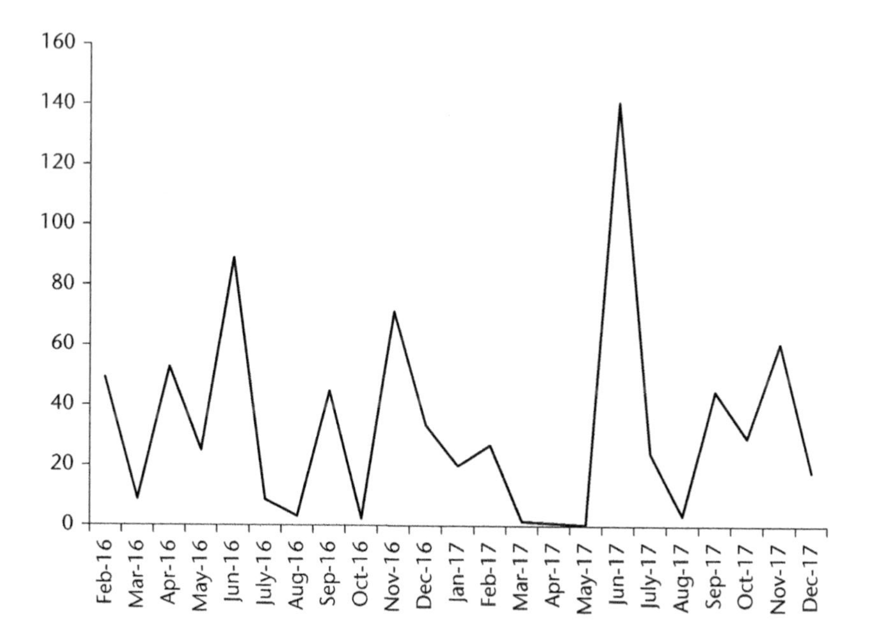

FIGURE 8.1 Occurrences of 'people' in Corbyn's texts, February 2016–December 2017

But how does Corbyn define 'people' in his rhetoric? Corbyn's notion of the 'people' is founded on the assumption that the current Conservative government and, in general, the establishment, are working to undermine individual and social rights. While Corbyn's claims may be associated with socialism, they are worded according to a populist vocabulary. In an article in the *Mirror* called, quite significantly, 'Power to the People' and published on 18 February 2016, he attacked the Conservatives' proposed Trade Union Bill[4]:

(1) They are skewing economic life so that wealth is funnelled towards the 1% and away from working people [. . .] *the party of privilege* is taking us back to the days when the people were locked out of power [. . .] the commitment I give to you is that *a Labour Government will put the people back in power* (18 February 2016).[5]

In true populist fashion, Corbyn assumes that power is not currently in the hands of the people. Indeed, the opposition between the people and the elite, represented here as the '1%', is also one of the key discourse topics used by Leave campaigners in the months leading up to the EU referendum. At the same time, Corbyn's mention of the 1 per cent who own most of the nation's wealth recalls the rhetoric of the most important recent left-wing populist movement in the United States, Occupy Wall Street, whose slogan 'We are the 99 per cent' was constructed in opposition to the wealthiest 1 per cent. The Occupy movement considered the elite, the 1 per cent, as a homogenous entity in which government and finance merged (Mudde & Kaltwasser, 2017, pp. 26–27). However, the movement prided itself on the vagueness of its own (largely populist) categorisations: 1 per cent and 99 per cent could signify different things depending on the different communities and interests involved, the 1 per cent being a "symbolic space rather than a factual identification" (Schneider, 2016). The ultimate political target of the Occupy movement was the fight against economic, social and political inequality.

Just like the Occupy movement, Corbyn's rhetoric of the people vs the elite was based on economic inequality. The sense of an ongoing crisis threatening national unity, which is the ideological core of populism, was attributed by Corbyn to economic and social imbalances. In the months prior to the referendum, the 'people' are continually constructed by Corbyn in direct opposition to the political and financial establishment, which has deprived the majority of their say in the political process:

(2) *For too many people in the UK who aren't the super-rich elite* [. . .] life is wrecked by insecurity, at work and at home, and the Tories are making it worse (20 February 2016).

(3) The first is about a new kind of politics: that aims to democratise our public life from the ground up, *giving people a real say in their communities and workplaces breaking open the closed circle of Westminster and Whitehall* (3 March 2016).

Interestingly, Corbyn rarely used the noun 'elite' to characterise the people's enemies,[6] and when he did, both before and after the referendum, he never associated it with Europe but used it mainly in conjunction with the British elite, namely the 'governing elite', the 'Westminster elite' and 'Britain's ruling elite', as well as the 'tiny corporate elite', who are 'super-rich', 'wealthy', 'small' and 'self-serving' (see example 2).

Europe is described by Corbyn in terms that echo an internationalist urge to share the social and economic benefits of EU membership:

(4) Labour is convinced that a vote to remain is in *the best interests of the people of this country* (14 April 2016).

Corbyn emphasised the advantages that Britain and its people had by staying in the EU, and these advantages, similarly to those promoted by the Remain campaign, were based on the economy more than anything else (see Zappettini, Chapter 4 this volume). During the referendum campaign, Europe was discussed by Corbyn as a political institution that is by no means perfect and needs to be reformed, as can be seen by the Labour leader's frequent use of comparatives, signalling his implicit critique of the way things are:

(5) We need to work with our allies in Europe to achieve *the more progressive reforms* that its people need to build *a more democratic Europe* that delivers jobs, prosperity and security for all its people (3 February 2016).
(6) That is why we need a Labour government [. . .] to work with our allies *to make both Britain and Europe work better for working people* (14 April 2016).
(7) *Europe can and must do far more* to meet the needs of our people [. . .] The way in which Greece was treated by its creditors, including the EU, shows that *Europe has to develop fairer and more effective mechanisms* to manage such crises for the future [. . .] *Europe needs to change* (2 June 2016).
(8) On workers' rights, *we need far stronger action across Europe* (16 June 2016).

Europe was for Corbyn still a powerful guarantee for workers' rights and social guarantees, and he often highlighted the need for cooperation with Britain's and Labour's allies in Europe:

(9) That is the case we are going to be making – it is for a Europe that is socially cohesive, and a Europe that shares the benefits of wealth and prosperity among all its citizens (22 February 2016).
(10) [W]e are also campaigning for reform of the European Union because we are convinced *Europe needs to change to work for all, to become more democratic, strengthen workers' rights, ditch austerity and end the pressure to privatise*. So we have a vision for Europe, and *an agenda for change* (16 June 2016).
(11) On 23 June we are faced with a choice: do we remain to protect jobs and prosperity in Britain that depend on trade with Europe? Or do we step into an unknown future with Leave, where a Tory-led Brexit risks economic recovery and threatens a bonfire of employment rights? (21 June 2016)

Corbyn's arguments for Remain derived, first and foremost, from the economic benefits that 'our people' could reap. Indeed, in many respects, the economic arguments made by Corbyn against the EU when he was not yet Labour leader were later used by him to support Remain. His repeated emphasis on the importance of Britain's interests in the international context mirrors, as a sort of equal and opposite reaction in discourse, the rhetoric of Leave: his campaign for Remain highlighted the need for social justice and better economic conditions by remaining in Europe, not by leaving it. However, while siding with Remain, Corbyn echoed the same populist argument made by Leavers about the legitimising nature of the referendum: he had welcomed the opportunity of having a referendum, as it would allow people to express their own opinion clearly and declared that "[the referendum] is now a crucial democratic opportunity for people to have their say on our country's future, and the future of our continent as a whole" (16 April 2016). Later, despite his declared support for Remain, he was adamant in accepting Brexit, saying that "[a]s far as Labour is concerned, the referendum result delivered a clear message" (10 January 2017).

In fully accepting the result of the referendum, Corbyn was using the same argument made by Leave supporters, namely that the referendum result represented the 'will of the people'. For example, the *Daily Mail* had urged its readers to vote Leave "if you believe in the will of the people and don't want to be ruled by faceless bureaucrats" (*Daily Mail*, 2016); after the referendum, former UKIP leader Nigel Farage famously spoke of the outcome of the referendum as "a victory for real people, a victory for ordinary people, a victory for decent people" (quoted in Saul, 2016), and even as late as June 2018, Prime Minister Theresa May responded to Remain supporters in Parliament by saying that "it's also important that parliament cannot and should not overturn the will of the British people, which was to leave the EU" (quoted in Macwhirter, 2018). After the referendum, Corbyn would still use the populist phrase the 'will of the people', reformulating the core notion of the 'people' by using a quantitative definition of the concept which was no less legitimising politically: the 'many'.

Corbyn's discourse and the 2017 General Election: 'the many' vs 'the few'

The people vs the elite dichotomy, with the latter depriving the former of political and economic power, was the populist basis of the Leave campaign and could also be observed in some of Corbyn's general and referendum-related rhetoric (see examples 2 and 3, and 4 and 5, respectively). However, it would also become the central topic of Corbyn's discourse leading up to the General Election. Indeed, the title of the Labour 2017 General Election manifesto itself became the key element of Corbyn's campaign: 'For the many not the few'. The slogan[7] recalls the final lines of Percy Bysshe Shelley's poem, 'The Masque of Anarchy' ("Rise, like lions after slumber/In unvanquishable number! / Shake your chains to earth like dew / Which in sleep had fallen on you: / Ye are many – they are few!"), written in 1819 after the massacre of Peterloo (Northern England), when the army was sent to crush down the rebellion of non-violent demonstrators who were petitioning for the right to vote (Shelley, 1832). The poem has been widely celebrated by the British left and its last four lines were also recited by anti-Poll Tax[8] protesters in the early 1990s (Chakelian, 2017). Additionally, the slogan 'For the many not the few' had already been used by Tony Blair in the opening statement of the Labour General Election Manifesto of 1997:

(12) I want a Britain that is one nation, with shared values and purpose, where merit comes before privilege, run for the many not the few, strong and sure of itself at home and abroad.

Published at a time of similar distrust in politics and the establishment, Blair's words caught the mood of the British electorate at the time, and Labour returned to power with a landslide victory on 1 May 2017, after 18 years of Conservative rule. However, according to Mouffe (2018, p. 38), Corbyn used the dichotomy in a stark ideological departure from Blair, as Corbyn, following a typical populist strategy, "re-signified it in an agonistic way as constructing a political frontier between 'we' and 'they'".

Corbyn used the 'many vs few' dichotomy for the first time during a speech at the Welsh Labour Conference on 20 February 2016:

(13) [T]he Tories [implement] [t]ax cuts for the few, the super-rich and big business public service cuts and welfare cuts for the many (20 February 2016).

The 'many vs few' contrast was used by Corbyn only once during the referendum campaign ("What we have instead is an economy that works for the few, not for the many", 21 May 2016), and it only became a ritual element in the Labour leader's discourse during the General Election campaign (see Figure 8.2). Corbyn turned the 'many vs few' dichotomy into the key discourse topic of his campaign for the General Election of 2017 and, thereby, employed the same quantitative basis of social relations used by the Occupy movement and even Tony Blair before him.

The two areas that Corbyn's opposition between the many and the few revolves around are government and the economy. The connection between these two areas is made explicit in the following example:

(14) Our Westminster system [. . .] and our economy [. . .] *are run in the interests of the few* (9 May 2017).

The 'few' are identified as those groups that are reaping benefits from their privileged social and economic position at the expense of the 'many':

(15) A way for the public really to take back control so that our key utilities and our railways are taken into public ownership and are *run in the interests of the many; not to pay the dividends of the few* (23 June 2017).

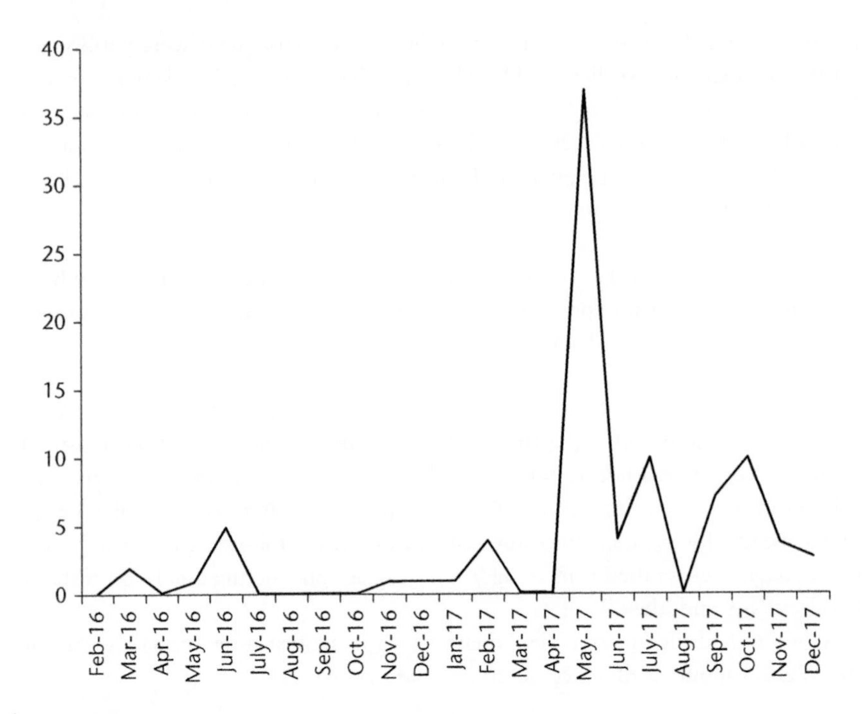

FIGURE 8.2 Occurrences of 'many' as part of the 'many vs few' dichotomy in Corbyn's texts, February 2016–December 2017

(17) We already know that the Tory way of running the economy has dramatically widened regional inequalities, sharply increased the wealth gap, *with tax breaks for the few* and *public services cuts for the many* (24 June 2016).

(16) *People want a country run for the many not the few.* That is because for the last seven years our people have lived through the opposite; a Britain run for *the rich, the elite and the vested interest* (16 May 2017).

The imbalance in economic power is reflected in who, according to Corbyn, the government represents:

(17) Only Labour stands for *the many against government by, of and for the few* (20 May 2017).

(18) We can stop a Conservative Government that wants to pit the old against the young. And replace it with a Labour Government that offers hope and unity. *A government for the many not the few and a government that ensures culture is for the many not the few* (22 May 2017).

(19) But beyond that transition, our task is a different one. It is to unite everyone in our country around a progressive vision of what Britain could be, but *with a government that stands for the many not the few* (27 September 2017).

The 'many vs few' dichotomy not only became a distinctive trait of the campaign leading to the General Election, but was used by Corbyn several times afterwards as well. The 'many' are those social actors who have been marginalised by the global economy and who receive very few benefits from the elite in power. In commenting on the result of the Stoke and Copeland by-elections in February 2017, Corbyn justified Labour's mixed results by using arguments that would not be out of place in Leave rhetoric:

(20) Both these areas [. . .] have been *left behind by globalisation and lost out from a rigged economy* [. . .] they rejected the status quo by voting to leave in the EU referendum. That's why it was important for Labour to respect the result and vote for Article 50 (25 February 2017).

During the campaign for the General Election, Corbyn would be very specific in his identification of the marginalised classes in British society:

(21) [W]e can transform Britain for the many not the few. When we win, *the British people win. The nurse, the teacher, the small trader, the carer, the builder, the office worker win* (9 May 2017).

(22) Right across our country, *too many people are trapped in precarious, low paid work* while a few at the top get richer (1 June 2017).

Corbyn's separation of the many from the few is where populism builds up its discursive space, made of social conflict and polarisation, and the 'unvanquishable number' represented by the 'people' engaging in a fight against the privileges of the 'few'. Thus, Corbyn constructs a polarised view of society, in which the elite, the few, go against the interest of the many. The disadvantaged 'many' are those who were the preferred audience of populist discourse and who mostly voted for Brexit (Goodwin & Heath, 2016). The 'few' or the 'elite', on the other hand, are exactly those who were also attacked by Leave campaigners (see Koller & Ryan, forthcoming). This polarised construction of the people vs the elite, or the many vs the few, reflects the anti-elitism typical of populist rhetoric, as argued by Mudde and Kaltwasser (2012, p. 8).

Corbyn shared with other contemporary populists a strong anti-establishment rhetoric and attacked corporations, banks and the political and economic elite who he represented as going against the needs of the 'real' people. Indeed, Corbyn appealed to the same large pool of the 'left behind' who were convinced by the populist message of the Leave campaign, and he did so by appealing to their quantitative strength ('for most people','for the majority').

Conclusions

The analysis of Corbyn's language has revealed that the Labour leader tapped into some of the discourse structures that were at the centre of the populist appeal of

Brexit. The EU referendum was indeed an influential factor in the way Corbyn structured his discourse in the 2017 General Election. The polarised framework that is a natural feature of referenda, with their inevitable Manichean schemata (Yes/No or, in the case of the EU referendum, Leave/Remain), is replicated by Corbyn in the run-up to the General Election: his contrast between the 'many' vs the 'few' can be seen as a further development of the populist 'people' vs the 'elite' dichotomy and became the discourse topic that most clearly expressed his ideology. Indeed, referenda are considered by many as the most evident example of direct democracy and the oppositional nature of populist politics finds a fertile ground in them: the clear choice between two alternatives has often provided populists with the opportunity to use referenda as a way to fight the political establishment. Despite his campaigning for Remain, Corbyn's schema of the 'many' vs the 'few' replicated the populist opposition between the people and the elite that was also employed by Leave supporters associating the interests of the British people with Leave, and the EU (and Remain) with the interests of the elites.

Given the centrality of the dichotomy of the 'people' vs the 'elite', or of its later formulation of the 'many' vs the 'few' in Corbyn's texts, the role of the 'people' may be interpreted as the nodal point of Corbyn's discourse and the key element in an antagonistic representation of the political space that is typical of left-wing populism (Stavrakakis, 2014). Corbyn's use of 'people', or the 'many', is instrumental in the representation of social and political relations as conflictual because these relations are dominated by the disparity in social and economic opportunities between the two segments of society. Indeed, the discursive logic offered by Corbyn's populism is one in which society is represented as split between two blocs, the establishment, which holds the power, and the people, the underdog, who have been deprived of their rights by the establishment.

Notes

1 Bennites were those of the left of Labour who supported Tony Benn and his democratic socialism. They became increasingly marginalised within the Labour party after Benn's failed bid to the party's leadership in 1981 and during the age of New Labour.
2 The report, led by the Centre for Research in Communication and Culture at Loughborough University, was based on a survey of the news coverage on the referendum by Britain's major television news programs (*Channel 4 News*, 7 pm; *Channel 5 News Tonight*, 6.30 pm; *BBC1 News at 10, ITV1 News at 10, Sky News*, 8–8.30pm) and print media (the *Guardian, The Times, Daily Telegraph, Financial Times, Daily Mail, Daily Express, Daily Mirror, Sun, Star* and the *i*).
3 Prime Minister David Cameron featured most prominently during this period, appearing in 24.9 per cent of news items.
4 The original Trade Union Bill would have severely curtailed the right to strike and take collective action. The amended Trade Union Act received Royal assent on 4 May 2016.
5 Italics in examples from Corbyn's texts are mine.
6 In the dataset under examination, 'elite' and 'elites' appear only 30 times.
7 James Schneider, Corbyn's election adviser, denies that the slogan was taken directly from Shelley's poem (quoted in the *Evening Standard*, 2017).

8 The Community Charge, or Poll Tax, was introduced by the Conservative government led by Margaret Thatcher in 1990. It was deeply unpopular and caused a wave of protests across Britain.

References

Ashmore, J. (2016, 31 May). Labour voters remain unsure of party's EU referendum position. *Politics Home*. Available at www.politicshome.com/news/europe/eu-policy-agenda/brexit/news/75574/labour-voters-remain-unsure-partys-eu-referendum, accessed 12 April 2018.

Canovan, M. (2005). *The People*. Cambridge: Polity.

Chakelian, A. (2017, 27 June). 'Rise like lions after slumber': Why do Jeremy Corbyn and co. keep reciting a 19th-century poem? *New Statesman*. Available at www.newstatesman.com/politics/uk/2017/06/rise-lions-after-slumber-why-do-jeremy-corbyn-and-co-keep-reciting-19th-century, accessed 9 December 2017.

Chilton, P. (2017). 'The people' in populist discourse. *Journal of Language and Politics, 16*(4), 582–594. https://doi.org/10.1075/jlp.17031.chi

Curtice, J. (2016, 28 June). Brexit reflections: How the polls got it wrong again. Centre on Constitutional Change. Available at www.centreonconstitutionalchange.ac.uk/blog/brexit-reflections-how-polls-got-it-wrong-again, accessed 13 November 2017.

Daily Mail (2016, 21 June). If you believe in Britain, vote Leave. Lies, greedy elites and a divided, dying Europe – why we could have a great future outside a broken EU. Available at www.dailymail.co.uk/debate/article-3653385/Lies-greedy-elites-divided-dying-Europe-Britain-great-future-outside-broken-EU.html, accessed 6 May 2018.

Evans, G., & Menon, A. (2017). *Brexit and British politics*. Cambridge: Polity.

Evening Standard (2017, 17 May). Londoner's diary: Jeremy Corbyn's romantic notions traced back to Percy Shelley. Available at www.standard.co.uk/news/londoners-diary/londoners-diary-jeremy-corbyns-romantic-notions-traced-back-to-percy-shelley-a3541276.html, accessed 11 November 2017.

Fairclough, N. (2014). *Language and power*. 3rd ed. London: Routledge.

Final Labour Leadership Hustings (2015, 25 July). *HuffPostUK*. Available at www.youtube.com/watch?v=E2K8qM1lEhk, accessed 10 November 2017.

Ford, R., & Goodwin, M. (2017). Britain after Brexit: A nation divided. *Journal of Democracy, 28*(January), 17–30.

Fowler, R. (1991). *Language in the news: Discourse and ideology in the press*. London: Routledge.

Goodwin, M., & Heath, O. (2016). Brexit vote explained: Poverty, low skills and lack of opportunities. Joseph Rowntree Foundation. Available at www.jrf.org.uk/report/brexit-vote-explained-poverty-low-skills-and-lack-opportunities?gclid=CjwKCAjws8vaBRBFEiwAQfhs-MrZ08DNZzbPk26jQ5Nf2hyT8KFkjj6lCdl75Grxrs8wv0_unbEsSxoCEq8QAvD_BwE, accessed 21 July 2018.

Grob-Fitzgibbon, B. (2016). *Continental drift: Britain and Europe from the end of empire to the rise of euroscepticism*. Cambridge: Cambridge University Press.

Hansard (1993, 30 March). Treaty on European Union. Available at https://api.parliament.uk/historic-hansard/commons/1993/mar/30/treaty-on-european-union, accessed 21 July 2018.

Helm, T., & Doward, J. (2015, 25 July). Jeremy Corbyn draws fire for position on Britain's EU future. *Observer*. Available at www.theguardian.com/politics/2015/jul/25/jeremy-corbyn-draws-fire-position-future-britain-eu-membership, accessed 13 November 2017.

Hobolt, S. B. (2016). The Brexit vote: A divided nation, a divided continent. *Journal of European Public Policy, 23*(9), 1259–1277. doi: 10.1080/13501763.2016.1225785

Inglehart, R. F., & Norris, P. (2016). Trump, Brexit, and the rise of populism: Economic have-nots and cultural backlash. Harvard Kennedy School, Faculty Research Working Paper Series. Available at https://research.hks.harvard.edu/publications/getFile.aspx?Id=1401, accessed 2 April 2018.

Johnson, B. (2016a, 24 April). Do Bremainers really think voters will be cowed by the likes of Obama? *Daily Telegraph*. Available at www.telegraph.co.uk/news/2016/04/24/do-bremainers-really-think-voters-will-be-cowed-by-the-likes-of, accessed 6 June 2018.

Johnson, B. (2016b, 15 May). Of course our city fat cats love the EU – it's why they earn so much. *Daily Telegraph*. Available at www.telegraph.co.uk/news/2016/05/15/of-course-our-city-fat-cats-love-the-eu--its-why-they-earn-so-mu, accessed 21 July 2018.

Koller, V., & Ryan, J. (forthcoming). 'A nation divided': Metaphors and scenarios in the media coverage of the 2016 British EU referendum. In C. Hart (Ed.), *Cognitive linguistic approaches to discourse: From poetics to politics*. Edinburgh: Edinburgh University Press.

Laclau, E. (2005). *On populist reason*. London: Verso.

Loughborough University (2016). Media coverage of the EU referendum (Report 5), Loughborough University Centre for Research in Communication and Culture. Available at https://blog.lboro.ac.uk/crcc/eu-referendum/uk-news-coverage-2016-eu-referendum-report-5-6-may-22-june-2016, accessed 13 November 2017.

Macwhirter, J. (2018, 18 June). 'You can't overturn the will of the people!' Theresa May hits back at rebel Remainer MPs. *Express*. Available at www.express.co.uk/news/uk/975459/Brexit-news-Theresa-May-rebel-Remainer-MPs-binding-vote-Dominic-Grieve-EU, accessed 6 July 2018.

Mouffe, C. (2018). *For a Left populiism*. London: Verso.

Mudde, C. (2004). The populist zeitgeist. *Government and Opposition, 39*(4), 541–563. https://doi.org/10.1111/j.1477-7053.2004.00135.x

Mudde, C., & Kaltwasser, C. R. (2012). Populism and (liberal) democracy: A framework for analysis. In C. Mudde & C. R. Kaltwasser (Eds), *Populism in Europe and the Americas: Threat or corrective for democracy?* (pp. 1–26). Cambridge: Cambridge University Press.

Mudde, C., & Kaltwasser, C. R. (2017). *Populism: A very short introduction*. Oxford: Oxford University Press.

Reisigl, M., & Wodak, R. (2016). The discourse-historical approach (DHA). In R. Wodak & M. Meyer (Eds), *Methods of critical discourse studies*. 3rd ed. (pp. 23–61). London: Sage.

Riley-Smith, B. (2016, 24 June). Jeremy Corbyn could face leadership challenge within days as Labour MPs submit no confidence motion after Brexit. *Daily Telegraph*. Available at www.telegraph.co.uk/news/2016/06/24/jeremy-corbyn-calls-for-brexit-process-to-begin-urgently-as-labo, accessed 19 February 2018.

Saul, H. (2016, 24 June). Brexit: Nigel Farage branded shameful for claiming victory without a single bullet being fired. *Independent*. Available at www.independent.co.uk/news/people/eu-referendum-nigel-farage-branded-shameful-for-claiming-victory-without-a-single-bullet-being-fired-a7099211.html, accessed 14 November 2017.

Schneider, N. (2016). The Occupy movement and its legacy: Populism, networks and institutions. An interview with journalist and activist Nathan Schneider. *Populismus*, Interventions, no. 5. Available at www.populismus.gr/wp-content/uploads/2016/05/intervention5-schneider.pdf, accessed 18 May 2018.

Shelley, P. B. (1832). *The masque of anarchy: A poem*. London: Edward Moxon.

Shipman, T. (2017). *All out war: The full story of Brexit*. 2nd ed. London: William Collins.

Stavrakakis, Y. (2014). The European populist challenge. *Annals of the Croatian Political Science Association: Political Science Journal, 10*(1), 25–39.

Topaloff, L. (2017). The rise of referendums: Elite strategy or populist weapon? *Journal of Democracy, 28*(3), 127–140.

Waugh, P. (2016, 25 June). Jeremy Corbyn allies 'sabotaged' Labour's In campaign on the EU referendum, critics claim. *Huffington Post.* Available at www.huffingtonpost.co.uk/entry/jeremy-corbyn-allies-sabotaged-labour-in-campaign-and-fuelled-brexit_uk_576eb1b5e4b0d2571149bb1f, accessed 13 November 2017.

Wodak, R. (2015). *The politics of fear: What right-wing populist discourses mean.* Los Angeles, CA: Sage.

Wodak, R. (2017). The 'establishment', the 'élites', and the 'people': Who's who? *Journal of Language and Politics, 16*(4), 551–565. doi 10.1075/jlp.17030.wod

9

THE OFFICIAL VISION FOR 'GLOBAL BRITAIN'

Brexit as rupture and continuity between free trade, liberal internationalism and 'values'

Franco Zappettini

Introduction

While at the time of writing (June 2017) the exact nature of Britain leaving the EU is still unclear, one cannot escape the fact that institutional and public discourses since the referendum result have primarily boiled down to a debate over the UK's future organisation of its economic activities. Striking the best possible free trade agreements with the EU and the rest of the world has become common currency in Brexit parlance. Likewise, imagined new 'global' economic and political roles for Britain – which were among the key drivers of the Leave campaign (Zappettini, forthcoming) – have escalated into institutional discourses legitimising Brexit as 'a new era for Britain' and its place in the world. As Prime Minister Theresa May put it in a key talk given just before triggering Article 50:

(1) A little over 6 months ago, the British people voted [. . .] to leave the European Union and embrace the world [. . .] June the 23rd was not the moment Britain chose to step back from the world. It was the moment we chose to build a truly global Britain (May, 2017).

This chapter aims to show how the institutional discursive productions of 'global Britain' have been sustained by the ideological vision of a new liberal (inter)national order that has been one of the key legitimising tools in the 'critical juncture' of Brexit (Zappettini & Krzyżanowski, forthcoming). Internationalism, like many other broad concepts, is laden with different, sometimes opposed, ideologies. For example, what Marx meant by internationalism – solidarity across borders that would unite workers under a common socialist cause – is different from, say, how the American idea of internationalism (as opposed to isolationism) has shaped post-war involvement in world affairs. This chapter draws on two interrelated dimensions of internationalism:

international liberalism as a political economic theory of inter-state governance that has defined most world economic policies in the last few decades, and liberal internationalism as an international relations theory emphasising interdependence and cooperation between states (see for example Moravcsik, 1997 and 2008 for both definitions). Trading on these perspectives, this chapter examines a corpus of official documents in which the British government sets out its vision for a new partnership with the European Union, aiming to foster a 'global Britain' that trades freely with the world. This data is analysed through argumentation theory (Fairclough & Fairclough, 2012) to identify how specific representations of internationalism and global free trade act as legitimising tools for post-Brexit Britain. From this standpoint, the chapter addresses the following questions: (i) What kind of internationalism is pursued by the British government? (ii) Which specific meanings of 'global Britain' have been discursively constructed and used to legitimise Brexit? (iii) Given that EU membership grants the UK access to the world's largest free trade area, how can one understand the seeming paradox of Britain wanting to leave the EU to expand its trade by pursuing new international trade arrangements?

This chapter argues that the official vision of a new, global, and out-of-the-EU Britain imagined in the texts draws on discourses of Brexit as both rupturing and continuing international narratives. From an economic perspective, the internationalism advocated by the British government indulges in post-imperial nostalgia and is predicated on mercantile logics. While it rhetorically supports a social liberal vision of Britain's economy 'that works for all', it remains unclear how that could be concretely achieved through Brexit. Furthermore this chapter analyses the rhetoric of Brexit, its discursive logics and its underlying values, arguing that while the institutional vision of a new international Britain conveniently shifts between national, European and global imaginaries, any actual economic policies that would follow Brexit still remain underdeveloped.

The rest of this chapter is organised as follows: the next section introduces international liberalism and discusses discourses of free trade and liberal policies as the backdrop of the Brexit referendum. Data sources, theoretical and methodological considerations are unpacked in the subsequent section. Key findings are discussed in the penultimate section and a critical discussion of these is offered in the concluding section.

Key discursive logics of (inter)nationalism, liberalism and Brexit

Different political and economic rationales have historically underpinned the case for free trade, i.e. trans-border trade conducted without the application of restrictions such as tariffs and quotas. For example, according to the classic doctrine of economic liberalism that emerged at the height of British mercantile power and was notably expounded in the work of Adam Smith (1776/1993) and David Ricardo (1821/1951), nations will benefit from opening up to international trade and reducing barriers. According to this line of thinking, this is because, while they compete with each other and focus on the specialised production of goods, the market for selling those goods will expand and so will national wealth. In this sense, free trade has also been a political corollary of the liberal tenet that cooperation between states helps the development of democratic institutions and ultimately benefits individuals as they prosper in a cosmopolitan peaceful society (Moravisck, 1997). Most liberal internationalists assume that two countries with trading arrangements are less likely to engage in war as any gains from fighting is greatly outweighed by the economic losses they would incur. This rationale was a key driver of the early European Coal and Steel Community, which in the aftermath of the Second World War attempted to pool French and German resources in the hope that their interdependence would prevent conflict occurring again.

Since 1960, liberal internationalist ideology has sustained an accelerating worldwide pattern of trade liberalisation through the proliferation of Free Trade Agreements – especially via multilateral agreements under the World Trade Organisation (WTO) – resulting in an overall exponential growth of inter-state trade (Ortiz-Ospina & Roser, 2018). While market democracies have often legitimised the introduction of free trade policies through the ideological premises that wealth production would lead to democratic and peaceful domestic and foreign societies, it is in fact market rationalities that have prevailed, exposing a disjuncture between the theory of liberal internationalism and its practice (Jahn, 2013). Since the 1980s the expansion of liberal internationalism has been especially fuelled by neoliberal approaches to economic policies, primarily – but not exclusively – promoted by Anglo-Saxon governments on both sides of the political spectrum (notably Reagan and Bush in the United States, Thatcher and Blair in the UK). This has resulted in policies that emphasise competition, financial deregulation and privatisation. Aspects of the neoliberal economic model have also filtered down to the EU's single market project, of which the UK has been a keen promoter (Menon & Salter, 2016), especially as financial liberalisation greatly benefitted the British service industry and "British trade shifted away from the Commonwealth towards the EU" (Thompson, 2017, p. 436).

In the wake of this liberal economic surge, goods – as well as capital and labour – have become freer to move transnationally and economies have become ever more closely integrated. However, the benefits of free trade have also increasingly been questioned vis-à-vis growing national and global patterns of social inequalities exacerbated by major global and European financial crises and austerity policies. These dynamics have resulted in different political and economic responses from most national governments. In broad terms, there has been a notable tendency to decelerate or even revert transnational agreements and a shift back to bilateralism (for example with the US decision to pull out of the Transpacific Partnership, to renegotiate the North America Free Trade Agreement and to introduce 'trade war' policies). These attitudes have tallied with various forms of economic populism and national protectionism (instantiated for example in slogans such as 'America first') which have overtly opposed global trade as the perceived cause of falling economic standards (Hopkin, 2017). Economic nationalism has thus (re)emerged as a powerful discourse in many political quarters resulting in some states adopting different protectionist measures in the name of economic nationalism. Rather than isolationism and economic retreat from global markets, however, these economic policies have primarily advocated national independence by focusing on competition for resource among countries and by emphasising the zero-sum logic of one nation's gain vis-à-vis others within the international economic system (*The Economist*, 2016).

It is within this complex social, economic and political conjuncture that different discursive nexuses of international economic policies conflated into the polarising 'in' and 'out' opinions of the EU referendum campaigns. In those campaigns, economic and political arguments were frequently invoked by both Leave and Remain sides to (de)legitimise Brexit. While the Remain camp legitimised the status quo through arguments about the benefits of the single market and the risk of leaving it (Hughes, 2016), the Leave choice rested on a set of contradictory arguments. On the one hand, the single market (and the whole EU project) was seen by a minority of Labour voters as too skewed towards a free market ideology and thus preventing any progress towards a true social democracy (see Demata, Chapter 8 this volume), while, on the other hand, the same EU set-up was deemed as not business-friendly enough by a large cohort of neoliberal advocates who resented the 'red tape' and 'chains' imposed by Brussels to British business (Buckledee, 2018, pp. 79–84; Zappettini, forthcoming). Further polarisation around the in/out split was constructed in a large section of the media, especially in the tabloid press (Zappettini, 2018; Koller & Ryan, forthcoming), which typically represented Brexit as an opportunity for the 'British people' to reassert economic nationalism and to withstand political interference from the economic and international political and economic elite (variously identified as Brussels, the IMF and President Obama). The different argumentative positions that validated the two referendum choices also cut across political parties and members of the Cabinet, highlighting deep ideological divides and a shift from traditional Left/Right partisan affiliations towards the in/out split (Wenzl, Chapter 3 this volume; Zappettini & Krzyżanowski, forthcoming). These divisions notwithstanding, and despite the lack of consensus – or preparation – among politicians and the public on how exactly Brexit 'should be done' (Allen, 2018, p. 106), the British government took the referendum outcome as a mandate for a 'hard Brexit' (that is ruling out any possible British membership of the single market or any customs union) and committed to execute the 'will of the people' by triggering Article 50 to leave the EU in March 2019. In the run-up to the negotiations that will eventually define the nature of such a hard Brexit, the institutional rhetoric has focused on a narrative of national unity and on constructing a new imaginary for an 'EU-free' Britain on the world's political and economic stage. As discussed in the following sections, it is on the discursive manifestations of this soul-searching process – in particular on the official vision(s) of 'global' Britain constructed in a corpus of governmental positioning papers – that the analysis in this chapter has focused.

Data, theoretical and methodological approach

Data

The corpus analysed in this chapter consists of a collection of public documents that the newly created Department for Exiting the European Union (DExEU) published on the official UK government website.[1] Those documents comprise White Papers, position papers, PM and Cabinet Ministers' official speeches, statements and press releases in which the Government provides "[i]nformation about the Article 50 process and our negotiations for a new partnership with the European Union" (British Government, 2017). These documents belong to a discursive genre strategically aimed at communicating the Government's view and obtaining public support for the proposed actions (which are necessarily conditional on the actual negotiation with the EU). The context of production is also crucial. Papers were released ahead of each negotiation round and conceivably reflect early negotiating positions rather than actual detailed implementation plans. In fact, in the phrasing of these documents one must assume a degree of rhetorical spin and "calculated ambivalence" (Wodak, 2015, p. 20), which would allow the Government some room for manoeuvre around their proposed strategies while 'sounding out' the other negotiating party. Finally, it must be noted that, as discussed above, even as the official British Government standpoint, these documents only voice selected Cabinet views rather than the gamut of contradictory opinions within the Conservative Party or, indeed, the devolved national parliaments of Scotland, Wales or Northern Ireland.

Due to space constraints and the balance between breadth and depth of analysis, this chapter focuses on the analysis of two position papers that are highly representative of the macro-discursive themes that characterise the corpus. These documents are: the Department for International Trade's 'Preparing for Our Future UK Trade Policy' (42 pages) and the Government's 'Foreign Policy, Defence and Development: A Future Partnership Paper' (24 pages).[2] As they focus on how post-Brexit economic and intergovernmental relations are envisaged through new trade deals and through cooperation on security with the EU and third countries, respectively, these documents were also selected because they relate to the key dimensions of internationalism discussed earlier.

Theoretical and methodological approach

The general theoretical approach to the analysis has been informed by the post-structuralist view of (political) discourse as constitutive – rather than simply descriptive – of social reality and social action (Critchley & Mouffe, 1997). In this sense, discourses represent powerful – albeit not the only – forms of action available to political actors to achieve certain goals. More specifically, as argued by Fairclough and Fairclough (2012), political discourse can be seen as a form of practical reasoning aimed at directing change from one current state of affairs ('the way things are now') to an imagined future state of affairs ('how things ought, should, must or will be in the future'). The analytical operationalisation of this theoretical approach has followed Fairclough and Fairclough's (2012) systematic identification of argumentative schemes and their typical constituents. This analytical taxonomy sees arguments as typically constructed around:

(i) a claim for action carried out by certain means (what should/will be done and how) in order to achieve
(ii) the desired goal (a future state of affairs) in accordance with
(iii) certain values (e.g. ideological stances on individual and social prosperity, equality, etc.) and warranted by
(iv) certain circumstantial premises (i.e. representations of the 'problem' that the action is trying to resolve).

For Fairclough and Fairclough (2012), representations – or "imaginaries" (Jessop, 2010) – of current and future states of affairs and/or of values underpinning the goal are key to how political agents are able to frame an argument and increase its rhetorical effectiveness. Thus, in addition to other components, the argumentative analysis has also focused on imaginaries as discursive representations of present realities (or circumstantial premises) and future states of affairs (or intended goals) as meaning-making frames that organise the discursive field in which the argument is developed (e.g. the understanding of economic issues at stake). Finally, following Fairclough and Fairclough (2012), the analysis was not simply concerned with the structure of an argument per se but it also involved a critical evaluation of its intended goals (i.e. a normative critique). This was achieved for example by addressing questions such as: are the values underlying the proposed action morally acceptable? Is the action proposed to achieve the desired goal effective? What other possible consequences could the proposed action have? Are there any other means whereby the action could be achieved in an equally or more effective manner? Of course, the limitation of such normative critique is that no universal moral standards can be applied and ultimately the evaluation of arguments rests on my own personal belief that social progress is achieved better through the transnational rather than (inter)national organisation of economic and political activities (Zappettini, 2019).

Key arguments and imaginaries of 'global Britain'

Different clusters of arguments and different internationalist visions emerged from the documents' analysis, which portrayed Brexit as both rupturing and continuing international narratives and related discursive logics as they were discussed above. While arguments relating to trade policy were oriented towards a legitimisation of Brexit as a macro-means to further liberalisation of the UK's economy and its independence from the EU institutional framework, in relation to foreign policy the institutional discourse portrayed Brexit as a form of continuity of the international state of affairs and the current balance of powers. Three key discursive constructs associated with these visions are discussed in detail below: (i) arguments for further trade liberalisation and the imaginaries of 'British influence' and the 'great trading nation'; (ii) arguments of wealth (distribution) and protection from competition; and (iii) arguments of shared European values.

The argument for further trade liberalisation and the imaginaries of 'British influence' and the 'great trading nation'

One of the key themes articulated in the texts is the UK's desire to expand its trade activities outside the European area while maintaining a 'deep' relation with the EU (these future trading partners are represented as 'new allies' and 'old friends'). The overarching discourse on a future economic partnership with the EU is thus driven by arguments of both closeness with and independence from the EU. The imagery of the 'trading nation' is invoked as a historical premise for the implementation of an ambitious trade policy that would enable the UK to trade freely and independently with other countries after Brexit:

(1) The United Kingdom has a long and proud history as a great trading nation and champion of free trade with all parts of the world. We want to maximise our trade opportunities globally and across all countries – both by boosting our trading relationships with old friends and new allies, and by seeking a deep and special partnership with the EU (Preparing For Our Future UK Trade Policy, p. 5).
(2) The Prime Minister also underlined that the people of the UK have decided to be a global, free-trading nation, able to chart our own way in the world (Preparing for Our Future UK Trade Policy, p. 5).

Example (1) constructs the circumstantial premises around the imaginary of the proud British trading tradition, a historical discourse that links with Adam Smith's *Wealth of Nations* and the British Empire. This argument sets out the primary goal of increasing worldwide trade (with the significant implicit assumption that achieving this goal is incompatible with remaining in the EU) and puts forward the means to achieve the goal, i.e. negotiating independent trade policies with the EU and other countries (note the expression 'deep and special partnership', introduced into the Government's discourses since the triggering of Article 50). Example (2) presents a similar goal based on a circumstantial premise that equates the referendum outcome with a deliberation on the free-trading nation imaginary. The latter is linguistically expressed via a realisation of the maritime metaphor NATIONS ARE SHIPS ('chart our own way'). In addition to representations of the 'great trading nation', the imaginary of British influence was often invoked in the corpus analysed as the means to future trade policies of an 'independent' Britain. For example, one of the frequent argumentative schemes that legitimised Brexit as a means to a 'global' Britain pivoted around the ostensive benefits of the UK's future membership of the WTO, as exemplified by example (3):

(3) When we leave the EU we will regain our independent seat at the WTO. As an independent member and one of the largest economies in the world, we will be in a position to intensify our support for robust, free and open international trade rules which work for all, and to help to rebuild global momentum for trade liberalisation [. . .] we will continue to work within the WTO to promote global action to cut red tape across borders, phase out distortive subsidies, scrap tariffs on trillions of dollars' worth of trade, and work to ensure the rule book stays relevant as patterns of trade change and technological innovations develop. We will do this all firmly in the belief that the WTO should remain central to the liberalisation and governance of international trade. Already a champion of multilateral trade from within the EU, the UK is preparing to take on an even greater role in the WTO outside the EU, but still firmly alongside our partners (Preparing for Our Future UK Trade Policy, p. 7).

The goal discussed in this argument is to promote further liberalisation and is associated with the circumstantial premises that Brexit will enable the UK (which, as all EU member states, is currently represented at the WTO table by the EU) to be a single independent actor and, as such, to exercise greater influence on WTO policies. This argument echoes prominent discourses of the Leave campaign on the burden of Brussel's red tape and the need for better influencing WTO rules which were used to delegitimise the EU as an inefficient actor and the single market as a static and distorted economic system (Zappettini, forthcoming). The presupposition that the UK will be able to shift its trade away from the EU and at the same time to significantly shape WTO rules rests here on the imaginary of British influence. While this representation constitutes an effective rhetorical device as it nostalgically appeals to an 'imagined' powerful nation, it represents a much more problematic factual warrant for a number of reasons. First, as the influence that a party is able to exert in a Free Trade Agreement negotiation is normally a function of the size of its internal market and its output, the British government would not conceivably be able to exert the same influence as the EU, of which the UK is only one of the 28 members. Second, the representation of British influence backgrounds the fact that considerable financial and time resources would be required in any future reorganisation of the UK's trade. For example, shifting the UK's trade pattern from the EU to, say BRICS countries (Brazil, Russia, India, China and South Africa) – which currently represent about 44% and 8% of UK exports respectively (Full Fact, 2016) – could not happen without significant economic damage, as acknowledged by the Government itself in a recently leaked paper (Fox, 2018). Similarly, considerable resources would be needed to renegotiate anew the trade deals that currently give Britain access to 53 countries under the EU membership. Third, EU membership has not prevented the UK from benefitting from various tariff-free deals negotiated by the EU. As acknowledged in the document containing example (3) above, the statement on scrapping 'tariffs on trillions of dollars' worth of trade' refers to a trade deal reached in 2015 by 24 WTO members (including the EU and therefore the UK) that guarantees that no tariffs will be paid on 201 high-tech products. Fourth, representations of the UK as enjoying the highest degree of free trade outside the EU are also problematic since WTO rules in fact exist to promote fair competition and result in most countries applying some tariffs to foreign trade unless such countries are part of a customs union such as the EU, whose internal market is tariff-free (while EU external trade is still subject to different tariffs).

Arguments of wealth (distribution) and protection from competition

The positioning paper 'Preparing for Our Future UK Trade Policy' also makes the case for free trade through arguments of wealth, growth and social prosperity. Typically, these arguments restated the classic economic theory of international trade and specialisation of labour as key drivers of one country's growth and prosperity (as discussed above). For example, page 6 of the paper discusses international trade and its impact on business efficiency, innovation and job creation, which, in turn, are said to result in wider choice of cheaper goods for consumers. Along with arguments for international trade as beneficial to the wider society, the paper raises the question of the uneven distribution of such benefits (euphemistically referred to as 'adjustment effects of trade'). As discussed above, such unevenness is increasingly being seen as the counterargument against further liberalisation. The issue of the 'left behind', however, is only sketchily addressed by the Government's ambitious vision of free trade post-Brexit. For example, the following argument is developed under the heading 'Making trade work for everyone':

(4) Free and open trade has had, and continues to have, an overwhelmingly positive impact on prosperity around the world and has taken more people out of abject poverty in the last 25 years. However, we recognise that some areas and sectors may benefit from trade liberalisation more than others, while some people feel left behind. Likewise there is a feeling that increased openness to trade may threaten our protections, including consumer safety standards and public services. The proper response to these concerns is not to turn our backs on international trade. The challenge is clear: to make sure the whole of the UK is able to take full advantage of the opportunities that trade offers. It is for this reason that the Government has committed to building a global economy that works for everyone. We will ensure the way we develop our own trade policy is transparent and inclusive so that concerns are heard and understood, and the right facts are available. [. . .] Through our trade remedies measures [. . .] we will ensure that our domestic industries do not suffer harm as a result of distortions of international trade caused by dumping or subsidy (Preparing for Our Future UK Trade Policy, p. 19).

The circumstantial premises represent free trade as having both positive and negative effects. A rather convoluted response (means) is proposed to address the latter.

This consists of: (i) a non-action ('not to turn our backs on it'); (ii) a restatement of the 'challenge'; and (iii) a generic intertextual reference to the more recent slogan of the Conservative party 'a country that works for everyone'. Further, while openness to dialogue with stakeholders is discussed, the argument does not provide an explanation of whether and how redistribution under the new trade policy would operate differently from the current EU's principle of funding poorer regions – a principle that has benefitted some parts of the UK (Di Cataldo, 2017) and might no longer be available after Brexit. Similarly, recognising the potential negative impact of free trade on domestic industries that might be adversely exposed to deregulated worldwide competition, 'trade remedies' are proposed as a means to prevent dumping and subsidy practices. These proposed solutions would, however, simply replicate measures that are already extant under the single market rules and that, paradoxically, in the intention of the Leave voters, would be scrapped through Brexit. Moreover, under these provisions, in a post-Brexit global economy British manufacturers might be somewhat protected against import of foreign cheap goods but they would still have to pay tariffs to export to the single market (unless the EU agreed to remove its tariffs). Additionally, a free trade approach opens up potential risks not only for domestic manufacturers but also for sources of production that, in a competitive and deregulated market, become more exposed to the risk of exploiting cheap labour and suppressing workers' rights. While these issues are acknowledged in the Government's papers, the argument for equal benefits and protection from competition is discussed from the higher moral ground of national values and their diffusion:

(5) After we leave the EU, the UK intends to pursue new trade negotiations to secure greater access to overseas markets for UK goods exports as well as push for greater liberalisation of global services, investment and procurement markets [. . .] The Government is fully committed to ensuring the maintenance of high standards of consumer, worker and environmental protection in trade agreements. [. . .] Our standards can also ensure that consumers are able to have confidence in choosing products which conform to UK values, whatever their budget. Trade agreements with single countries or groups of countries can promote and support labour protections, the environment, human rights, anti-corruption, animal welfare and other important factors which support sustainable trade and development across the world. We want to ensure economic growth, development and environmental protection go hand in hand, and it is in everyone's interest to avoid any 'race to the bottom'. We will have the opportunity to promote our values around the globe in the areas that are of greatest importance to us as a United Kingdom (Preparing for Our Future UK Trade Policy, p. 30).

In this case the argument reiterates the vision of Brexit as an opportunity for increasing international free trade and market liberalisation. This argument represents Brexit as a win-win situation that can provide the maximum benefits to all members of society and is realised through the neoliberal *topos* of the 'trickle-down effect' (see Zappettini & Unerman, 2016 for the use of this *topos* in corporate discourse). Along with these representations of Brexit that were driven by a mix of (inter)national economic and social logics, representations of 'British values' represented another powerful discursive imaginary deployed in the documents analysed. In example (5) the term 'British values' was used to construct two future scenarios in relation to Brexit. In one case 'British values' can be inferred as quality standards that, in a post-Brexit price-driven economy, consumers would still able to expect (and that could quite possibly replicate existing EU standard requirements). The second scenario constructed around 'British values' draws on the imaginary of British influence and independence (as discussed above). In this case Brexit appears legitimised through the goal of international trade policies that would clearly benefit the imagined national community (such meanings are conveyed by the deictics 'our' and 'us').

Representations of 'values' were key discursive drivers underpinning imaginaries of Brexit that went beyond the trade argument. For example, they were at the core of the framework for future foreign policies, which is discussed in the following subsection.

Arguments of closeness and the imaginary of shared (European) values

In contrast to the trade policy paper discussed in the previous section, which emphasises economic, political and cultural independence from the EU, the Government's paper titled 'Foreign Policy, Defence and Development: A Future Partnership Paper' portrays Britain as highly committed to upholding shared 'European values' with its partners (see also Bennett, Chapter 2 this volume). The vast majority of arguments in this paper rely on imaginaries of British closeness and unity with Europe. These imaginaries sustain a characterisation of Britain as deeply rooted in a continental tradition of democratic values and legitimise Brexit as not disrupting the continuity of a 'deep and special' relationship that would preserve such values in the face of common threats. This is illustrated by the following passage:

(6) The UK will remain a committed partner and ally to its friends across the continent, not simply because UK and EU citizens face the same threats and as it is in both our interests to do so, but because the UK has a deep, historic belief in the same values that Europe stands for: peace, democracy, freedom and the rule of law, in our continent and beyond. Promoting our shared values, tackling our shared threats, and maintaining a strong and prosperous Europe will require a deep and special partnership, including on foreign [*sic*], defence and security, and development engagement (Foreign Policy, Defence and Development: A Future Partnership Paper, p. 2).

Significantly, in opposition to economic discourses making the case for free trade, argumentative schemes in the area of defence and international relations were aimed at recognising the importance of European rather than British influence on a global stage. The imaginary of international Britain in this case is constructed around a de-antagonisation of the UK–EU relationship and on the premise that Britain will contribute to European prosperity. However, an overall controversial representation of antinomic interests and values driving Brexit was also constructed: in example (7) the discourse shifts between different representations of global, European and national interests being pursued by the Government:

(7) The UK supports a strong, secure and successful EU with global reach and influence. UK priorities after it leaves the EU will continue to be based on a European outlook and these shared values. The UK is exiting the EU, not withdrawing from Europe. As the UK leaves the EU, the UK is committed to a 'global Britain': a country actively engaged in Europe and the world in the interests of the British people, and playing a leading role in advancing European and international security and an international rules-based system (Foreign Policy, Defence and Development: A Future Partnership Paper, p. 3).

In this extract, the overall imaginary state of affairs portrayed by the Government is once again a positive representation of international relations and of close cooperation with the EU. In particular, the claim that the UK supports a successful and influential EU plays into a narrative of 'nested hierarchies' in which national interests are embedded in European and, in turn, global interests (this meaning is supported by the expression 'UK priorities based on a European outlook'). This premise also appears to contradict the delegitimisation of the EU institutions working 'against British interests' that frequently characterised arguments of trade and sovereignty invoked by Leavers during the referendum campaign (Zappettini, forthcoming). At the same time, however, while 'global Britain' is imagined through a vision of international engagement it also portrays Brexit along the discursive split EU/Europe. In this sense the claim that 'Britain leaves the EU but not Europe' reinforces the imaginary of Brexit as rupture and continuity. While claiming the continuation of a 'deep relationship' with European values, the institutional discourse also reproduces historical discourses of 'British exceptionalism', which makes the European social and political project incompatible with British aspirations. Global Britain thus shows the tension of these two discourses: wanting to support the EU while distancing itself from it.

Conclusions

This chapter has adopted the lens of internationalism to analyse the arguments and imaginaries through which post-Brexit Britain was envisaged in a corpus of positioning papers published by the Government ahead of the UK's official departure from the EU. The analysis has suggested that Brexit is legitimised through different argumentative schemes and different discursive constructions of internationalism. Economic visions of 'Global Britain' and the push for further international trade are key discursive drivers and rest on arguments that represent closeness with the EU framework and its benefits but, at the same time, independence from it. In turn, within this discursive scenario, the means of Brexit as the opportunity to trade freely with the world appeals to the imaginary of the 'great trading nation' and the influence that an 'EU-free' UK would be able to exercise in a new international liberal order. The analysis has highlighted how these arguments are warranted by a set of premises that represent the UK as able to effortlessly re-route its current EU trade to other partner countries and the trade-offs of this shift as economically worthwhile.

While the rhetorical appeal to the nation underpins several argumentative schemes in the corpus of papers, the analysis has also shown how such values often shift between global, European and national discursive frames and imaginaries of British influence. For example, unlike the case for free trade made in the economic policy positioning papes, discourses related to foreign policy, defence and international development legitimised European rather than British influence and represent Brexit as continuing narratives of shared European values rather than rupturing the current institutional system. The duality of these discourses of rupture and continuity is, for example, encapsulated in the Prime Minister's assertion that 'Britain leaves the EU but not Europe'. Ironically, however, promoting European values and maintaining a 'prosperous Europe' seems hardly what Brexit was set in motion to achieve in the first place. Despite the widespread use of the phrase 'value sharing', the discursive focus of the Government's Brexit discourse zeros in on a convenient and strictly economic form of neoliberal internationalism. This vision of 'global Britain' decouples economic elements of the single market framework from any political and social implications attached to the EU project such as freedom of movement and redistribution of resources at a European level (an attitude that has often been described as 'having its cake and eating it too'; see Musolff, Chapter 13 this volume). It also reproduces historical discourses of English/British exceptionalism and its incompatibility with the European project, assuming that successful trade is only possible outside the EU and that British influence is dampened rather than boosted by current membership. By contrast, in spite of imaginaries of independence, the policy documents analysed indicate that most economic arrangements post-Brexit would reproduce current provisions existing under the EU institutional framework. While this would effectively normalise 'trade minus political engagement' as the new international 'business as usual', it also raises the critical question of who will ultimately benefit from Brexit.

Answers to this question can only be speculative at this stage. However, the analysis has suggested that the argument of Brexit as 'levelling the social playing field' through a mix of liberalisation (e.g. free trade) and restrictions (e.g. freedom of movement) is – ambiguously and perhaps intentionally – not fully developed: the institutional vision does not explain how an out-of-the-EU and further liberalised Britain might foster equal benefits in an inclusive society that 'works for all'. In this sense, 'global Britain' embodies the potential paradox of Brexit as the imaginary of escaping from the negative consequences of global liberalism only to aim for more of the same. Adding to the uncertainty of future scenarios is the unknown quantity of immigration as a topic that was instrumental in the legitimisation of Brexit in the Leave referendum campaign but was absent in the papers. It is not clear how immigrant labour – which is needed by an international supply chain and might no longer be available under new immigration rules after Brexit – will be part of the 'society that works for all'. Most discourses of Brexit in the documents analysed consist of future promises of a better and more prosperous society. Ascertaining whether these promises will be delivered is beyond the scope of this chapter, but it is certainly an open critical question that must be addressed by future research.

Notes

1 www.gov.uk/government/collections/article-50-and-negotiations-with-the-eu
2 These two documents are available at https://assets.publishing.service.gov.uk/government/uploads/system/uploads/attachment_data/file/654714/Preparing_for_our_future_UK_trade_policy_Report_Web_Accessible.pdf and https://assets.publishing.service.gov.uk/government/uploads/system/uploads/attachment_data/file/643924/Foreign_policy__defence_and_development_paper.pdf, respectively, both accessed 17 August 2018. They contain public sector information licensed under the Open Government Licence v3.0.

References

Allen, N. (2018). 'Brexit means Brexit': Theresa May and post-referendum British politics. *British Politics, 13*(1), 105–120. https://doi.org/10.1057/s41293-017-0067-3

British Government (2017). Department for Exiting the European Union. *Article 50 process and negotiations with the EU*. Available at www.gov.uk/government/collections/article-50-and-negotiations-with-the-eu, accessed 22 January 2018.

Buckledee, S. (2018). *The language of Brexit: How Britain talked its way out of the European Union*. London: Bloomsbury.

Critchley, S., & Mouffe, C. (1997). *Deconstruction and pragmatism*. London: Routledge.

DiCataldo M. (2017). The impact of EU objective 1 funds on regional development: Evidence from the UK and the prospect of Brexit. *Journal of Regional Science, 57*, 814–839. https://doi.org/10.1111/jors.12337

Economist, The (2016, 19 November). The new nationalism. Available at www.economist.com/leaders/2016/11/19/the-new-nationalism, accessed 28 August 2018.

Fairclough, I., & Fairclough, N. (2012). *Political discourse analysis: A method for advanced students*. London: Routledge.

Fox, B. (2018). Lost trade will nullify Brexit dividend, UK government admits. Available at www.euractiv.com/section/uk-europe/news/lost-trade-will-nullify-brexit-dividend-uk-government-admits, accessed 9 March 2018.

Full Fact website (2016). Available at https://fullfact.org/europe/uk-eu-trade, accessed 7 December 2017.

Hopkin, J. (2017). When Polanyi met Farage: Market fundamentalism, economic nationalism, and Britain's exit from the European Union. *British Journal of Politics and International Relations, 19*(3), 465–478. https://doi.org/10.1177/1369148117710894

Hughes, K. (2016). Neither tackling lies nor making the case: The Remain side. In D. Jackson, E. Thorsen, & D. Wring (Eds), *EU referendum analysis: Media, voters and the campaign* (p. 65). Poole: The Centre for the Study of Journalism, Culture and Community, Bournemouth University. Available at www.referendumanalysis.eu, accessed 9 March 2018.

Jahn, B.(2013). *Liberal internationalism: Theory, history, practice.* Basingstoke: Palgrave Macmillan.

Jessop, B. (2010). Cultural political economy and critical policy studies. *Critical Policy Studies, 3*(3–4), 336–356. https://doi.org/10.1080/19460171003619741

Koller, V., & Ryan, J. (forthcoming). 'A nation divided': Metaphors and scenarios in the media coverage of the 2016 British EU referendum. In C. Hart (Ed.), *Cognitive linguistic and textual analysis: From poetics to politics.* Edinburgh: Edinburgh University Press.

May, T. (2017). *Full transcript of the speech given at Lancaster House on 18 January 2017.* Available at www.bbc.co.uk/news/uk-politics-38662998, accessed 20 January 2017.

Menon, A., & Salter, J.-P. (2016). Brexit: Initial reflections. *International Affairs, 92*(6), 1297–1318. https://doi.org/10.1111/1468-2346.12745

Moravcsik, A. (1997). Taking preferences seriously: A liberal theory of international politics. *International Organization, 51*(4), 513–553. https://doi.org/10.1162/002081897550447

Moravcsik, A. (2008). The new liberalism. In C. Reus-Smit & D. Snidal (Eds), *The Oxford handbook of international relations* (pp. 234–254). Oxford: Oxford University Press.

Ortiz-Ospina, E., & Roser, M. (2018). *International trade.* Available at https://ourworld indata.org/international-trade, accessed 17 January 2018.

Ricardo, D. [1821] (1951). *On the principles of political economy and taxation.* Cambridge: Cambridge University Press.

Smith, A. [1776] (1993). *Inquiry into the nature and causes of the wealth of nations.* Oxford: Oxford University Press.

Thompson, H. (2017). Inevitability and contingency: The political economy of Brexit. *British Journal of Politics and International Relations, 19*(3), 434–449. https://doi.org/ 10.1177/1369148117710431

Wodak R. (2015). *The politics of fear: What right-wing populist discourses mean.* London: Sage.

Zappettini, F. (2018). The tabloidization of the Brexit campaign: Power to the (British) people? Paper presented at the conference *Political discourse – multidisciplinary approaches #2: New discourses of populism and nationalism* 21–22 June, Edinburgh Napier University.

Zappettini, F. (2019). *European identities in discourse: A transnational citizens' perspective.* London: Bloomsbury.

Zappettini, F. (forthcoming) The Brexit referendum: How trade and immigration in the discourses of the official campaigns have legitimised a toxic (inter)national logic. *Critical Discourse Studies.*

Zappettini, F., & Krzyżanowski, M. (forthcoming). 'Brexit' in media and political discourses: From national populist imaginary to cross-national social and political crisis. *Critical Discourse Studies.*

Zappettini, F., & Unerman, J. (2016). 'Mixing' and 'bending': The recontextualisation of discourses of sustainability in integrated reporting. *Discourse & Communication, 10*(5), 521–542. https://doi.org/10.1177/1750481316659175

10

'GET YOUR SHYTE TOGETHER BRITAIN'

Wikipedians' treatment of Brexit

Susanne Kopf

Introduction

The well-known platform Wikipedia is usually associated with collaboratively created encyclopaedic articles. However, as the quotation in the title of this chapter suggests, the Wikipedia community's engagement with Brexit exceeds authoring such an encyclopaedic article on the topic. Indeed, to facilitate collaboration, Wikipedia also provides spaces for informal opinion and knowledge exchange for any Wikipedia user interested in going beyond reading Wikipedia articles. This chapter homes in on two such Wikipedia discussion sites where Wikipedia contributors debated Brexit. On the one hand, there is the talk page (TP) accompanying the Wikipedia article called 'Brexit'. This site serves to allow Wikipedia editors (so-called 'Wikipedians') to discuss controversial issues connected to the article in question (Wikipedia, 2016d). On the other hand, the Wikipedia reference desk (RD) permits Wikipedians to ask any additional questions about Brexit and have these answered by other editors who feel equipped to do so (Wikipedia, 2017).

As an ongoing process with many specifics still unknown, (a possible) Brexit has been debated among Wikipedians since before the referendum in 2016. These discussions have continued through the invocation of the Lisbon Treaty's Article 50 in March 2017 and are still ongoing at the time of writing this chapter (March 2018). Therefore, this chapter addresses Wikipedians' treatment of Brexit on the discussion sites from the first entry on Wikipedia – which was made in May 2016 – to January 2018. Using a corpus that consists of both talk page and reference desk data, this study examines what the Wikipedia community's debates have focused on in connection with the UK's withdrawal from the EU. In particular, this chapter presents findings on the community's treatment of possible Brexit repercussions, shows how, in this context, the role of experts and academics is questioned and, finally, explores how the Wikipedia community has addressed possible reasons for the outcome of the referendum. This examination of Wikipedians' debates complements this book's kaleidoscopic perspective on Brexit by shedding light on how a transnational community of private individuals has grappled with Brexit and what aspects of Brexit have been most controversial and unclear enough to warrant debate.

Wikipedia discourse and Brexit

Discourse, here understood as language use as social practice, is both a mode of action as well as a mode of representation (Fairclough 1992, p. 63). That is, on the one hand, Wikipedia discourse about Brexit is a means of representing the issue in certain ways. On the other hand, discourse as a mode of action refers to the understanding that – using language – Wikipedia editors act "upon the world and especially upon each other" (ibid.).

Concerning discourse as a mode of representation, the question arises whose voices and views are represented on Wikipedia. Principally, Wikipedia as a collaboratively created website with "free content that anyone can use, edit, and distribute" (Wikipedia, 2016b) exemplifies the "participatory internet", where users are not mere recipients of top-down communication but can also engage in content creation (KhosraviNik & Unger, 2016, p. 207). That is, in contrast to traditional news media, where an elite group disseminates information and certain perspectives on events, Wikipedia allows the inclusion and representation of a multitude of non-elite voices from various backgrounds, as any Wikipedia visitor can also edit the website, i.e. become a Wikipedian. Consequently, the examination of discourse material taken from the encyclopaedia permits a glimpse into how private individuals from a variety of backgrounds co-construct and conceive of certain world events such as Brexit. Moreover, as Wikipedia pages are not limited nationally but are open to contributions from anybody with internet access and a degree of (digital) literacy, the exploration of Wikipedia sites allows an insight into how Brexit has been negotiated on a transnational plane. However, before prematurely celebrating the apparent democratisation and diversification of content creation on Wikipedia, it is worth noting that there are limitations to this. One caveat is Wikipedia's self-selecting bias concerning contributor demographics as the website is skewed towards college-educated males from Europe and the United States (Wikimedia Foundation, 2011). That is, an already powerful and influential social group is overrepresented on Wikipedia and is likely to have its views of Brexit disproportionately represented and proliferated on the site. In addition to this, there are certain gatekeeping mechanisms that may be used to prevent Wikipedia users from editing Wikipedia. These mechanisms aim to forestall vandalism of Wikipedia by equipping particular Wikipedians with the means to lock articles or block editor groups from contributing to the website (see Kostakis, 2010; Kopf, 2018 for more detail). Still, contributing to Wikipedia *discussion* pages is usually not restricted and, indeed, the Wikipedia discussions on Brexit were not protected in this manner at any time (Wikipedia, 2016c, 2018).

Apart from whose views are represented on Wikipedia, the purpose of Wikipedia talk pages (TP) and the reference desk (RD) is worth noting as it impacts on what, specifically, is represented on these pages. The TP and the RD allow Wikipedians to grapple with problematic or unclear aspects with respect to the topic at hand, here Brexit. Therefore, an examination of TP and RD data on Brexit provides an insight not merely into Wikipedians' general conception(s) of Brexit but, in particular, into aspects that they have found controversial or difficult to grasp over the past few years. What is more, Wikipedia policy mandates that editors engage with and build on outside sources when contributing to the encyclopaedia (Wikipedia, 2015b). That is, the contributors' discussions of Brexit synthesise and reflect a variety of outside sources from academia to various national news media, which makes an examination of Wikipedia discussion data particularly worthwhile.

In addition to these considerations concerning discourse as representation, it is important to understand Wikipedia discourse as a mode of action, e.g. in the form of Wikipedians shaping Wikipedia readers' understanding of Brexit. This is particularly the case in light of the English Wikipedia's global impact: the website consistently ranks among the top six most visited websites (Alexa, 2016) and was found to be consulted frequently especially in Europe (Zachte, 2017). While Wikipedia discussion sites are not consulted as regularly as Wikipedia articles, the debates on these sites directly impact and feed into the Wikipedia articles, which are then received by and, arguably, affect a considerable number of people. Furthermore, Wikipedia discussion sites are spaces that allow Wikipedians to debate Brexit – to argue for or against certain views, to persuade and convince each other – in short, to shape each other's perspectives on Brexit. Altogether then, Wikipedia discussion pages, on the one hand, reflect and synthesise controversial or unclear aspects of Brexit. On the other hand, these platforms serve to harmonise, disseminate and reinforce the contributors' views concerning Brexit.

Although Wikipedia constitutes an attractive venue of study, the encyclopaedia has hitherto received relatively little research attention in linguistics and discourse studies: Myers (2010) gives an overview of the English Wikipedia's structure and possible aspects of investigation, while Mederake (2016) provides a comprehensive discussion of the German Wikipedia and likewise highlights potential areas for linguistic study. By comparison, Emigh and Herring (2005) assess different language versions of Wikipedia for cultural biases, whereas Page (2014), focusing on a particular article in the English and Italian versions of Wikipedia, tracks how a particular controversial event is represented in a Wikipedia article over a period of time. Still, so far there is very little research that focuses on the treatment of particular issues on Wikipedia discussion sites. Apart from this lack of research on Wikipedia, the UK's decision to leave the EU is a fairly recent development and, therefore, linguists and discourse analysts are only just delving into explorations of associated linguistic phenomena and discourses. In this context, research has, understandably, focused on the events leading to the 2016 referendum rather than addressed post-referendum developments (e.g. Buckledee, 2018; Kelly, 2018).

Data and method of analysis

The corpus, consisting of both the TP and RD data, amounts to 80,898 tokens. The TP constitutes the majority of data – it encompasses 74,850 tokens organised into 145 threads, that is, conversations that consist of a "hierarchically organized collection of notes in which all notes but one (the note that started the thread) are written as 'replies' to earlier notes" (Black et al., 2011, pp. 625–626; see also Hewitt, 2005, p. 568). All relevant TP data – from the first entry on Brexit in May 2016 to January 2018 – were sampled. In this context, it is worth noting that only seven conversations took place before the referendum results were published on 24 June 2016 and none of these could be called heated debates – only one conversation consists of more than two postings, i.e. more than two conversation turns.[1] The RD entries complement the TP discussions with 6,048 tokens in nine threads that were predominantly produced after the referendum in June 2016. A caveat concerning the RD data is that only entries containing the word 'Brexit' in the query were sampled. Therefore, the data sample does not include conversations that use references to Brexit by another name or that only refer to Brexit within a conversation thread.

Using the concordance programme AntConc (Anthony, 2015), I took a qualitatively oriented, corpus-assisted approach to the data. Since the corpus is small, each occurrence of 'brexit' was examined in a wide-angle co-text view, i.e. concordance lines of the node word 'brexit' including at least 40 words to the left and to the right of the node were examined (cf. Partington et al., 2013, p. 18). Alphabetical sorting to the left and the right of the node further facilitated the recognition of patterns of Wikipedians' references to the UK's withdrawal from the EU, e.g. a focus on the possible effects of Brexit versus speculations about the reasons for Brexit. In addition to this purely qualitative perspective on the data, I investigated the collocational profile of 'brexit' to glean an insight into statistically significant co-occurrences of items with the node. In accordance with Stubbs' recommendations, t-score with a cut-off point of 2.0 was used for the collocation calculation seeing as t-score takes into account corpus size and indicates certainty of co-occurrence (Stubbs, 1995, p. 34; Gatto, 2014, p. 27). The top collocates of 'brexit' were then also examined in the qualitatively oriented, wide-angle concordance view.

Data discussion

An expanded view of all 674 concordance lines of 'brexit' shows that the Wikipedia community debates three issues in particular. First, the most heatedly debated element is the potential effects of Brexit. Second, in these debates on the repercussions of Brexit, the Wikipedia community touches upon the role of experts and academics. Finally, the involved Wikipedians discuss possible reasons for the outcome of the UK's referendum on European Union membership. The following sections will analyse these three aspects in more detail.

Effects of Brexit

The alphabetically sorted concordance lines of 'brexit' already permit a glimpse into the focus of the Wikipedia community's discussions (e.g. 'explain what a Brexit effect is') and this is confirmed by the collocation list of the item 'brexit' – collocates are 'effects' (t-score 5.7), 'effect' (4.2), 'impact' (3.05) and 'consequences' (2.5). Table 10.1 provides an overview of what the concordance lines of these co-occurrences discuss, namely economic effects, uncertainty, social and political effects.

Economic effects and uncertainty

A notable collocate with 'brexit' is 'economic' at a t-score of 2.8. Indeed, of the 161 concordance lines that incorporate 'effect*', 'consequence*' or 'impact*' in addressing Brexit repercussions, 48 per cent (78 concordance lines) focus on economic effects of Brexit. The discussed aspects can be classified into four broader categories. First, the community focuses on concrete industries (12 lines), such as the UK's housing market, e.g. 'consequences/London mortages [*sic*] Shouldn't we mention, how devastating the Brexit was at the London housing market?' Second, the editors refer to key indicators used to measure economic success or lack thereof (18 concordance lines), e.g. 'Research on effects that have already materialised since the referendum show that the rise in inflation [. . .] amount[s] to annual losses of £404 for the average British household'. Third, international trade relations with focus on the EU's single market are cited in 7 lines, e.g. 'we lose access to our European markets, that will be an instant effect'. Finally, the Wikipedia editors make reference to vague and unspecified economic consequences (41 lines), e.g. 'the long term effect of Brexit on the British economy will be negative'. The above examples taken from these four kinds of economic effects already give an inkling of a noteworthy phenomenon – the Wikipedia community's focus is almost exclusively on Brexit effects on the United Kingdom rather than on the EU.

TABLE 10.1 The effects of Brexit – 161 concordance lines

78 lines: economic effects (35 of these also refer to uncertainty)	12 lines: concrete industries 18 lines: key figures to measure economic success 7 lines: international trade 41 lines: unspecified
64 lines: uncertainty regarding effects (35 of these also debate economic consequences)	
28 lines: social effects	22 lines: effects on academia 6 lines: general social effects
26 lines: political effects	24 lines: political effects – UK and EU 2 lines: connection to Trump presidency

Indeed, of all concordance lines on economic effects, only two lines that reference unspecified economic consequences, refer to repercussions for the EU as well as the UK, e.g. 'economic uncertainty and anticipation effects will impact the economies of the United Kingdom or the European Union'.

Another notable element in this context is the fact that the Wikipedia community overwhelmingly focuses on Brexit as having disadvantageous consequences for the UK, which is, incidentally, already indicated by the fact that 'brexit' collocates with 'negative' at a t-score of 2.7. The concordance lines on economic impact consistently refer to the Brexit effects in negatively connoted words such as 'devastating' or 'loss', to the UK as 'burdened', and to developments concerning the pound sterling as 'frightening', expecting it to 'weaken' and 'fall'. Only three concordance lines entertain the idea of consequences being not as negative as anticipated, for instance, an editor claims that, while the 'effects of Brexit [will be] better than most had predicted [. . .], most economists say the ultimate impact [. . .] appears likely to be more negative than positive'.

Wikipedians also repeatedly and consistently refer to the uncertainty with which predictions about Brexit effects can be made. In a total of 64 concordance lines, that is in 40 per cent overall, Wikipedians make reference to the certainty – or lack thereof – with which the repercussions of Brexit can be known already. Of these, 39 lines give a clear indication concerning whether the editor in question believes that Brexit consequences can or cannot be accurately predicted before the actual Brexit set to occur in March 2019: on the one hand, 23 lines argue that the 'effects of Brexit on the UK and the EU are, as yet, unknown' and 'it's difficult to know what the effect of the UK being outside the EU is going to be'. On the other hand, 16 concordance lines counter this view, e.g. 'There is overwhelming agreement on what the effect on the UK economy is' and '"commonly discussed and analysed but remain uncertain" is just bullshit when it comes to the economic impact'. All in all, the dominant view is that Brexit effects cannot be known with certainty yet, although there is a marked counter-stance to this perspective as the latter two examples demonstrate.

These last two examples also illustrate another remarkable aspect, namely that there is considerable overlap of reference to economic consequences and (un)certainty (see also Lutzky & Kehoe, Chapter 7 this volume) – of all 78 lines making reference to economic consequences and all 64 lines focusing on (un)certainty, there is an overlap of 35 concordance lines that refer to both issues. In this context, another aspect can also be observed: where posters concede that there is uncertainty regarding Brexit consequences on the UK's economy, they argue that this uncertainty in itself will lead to negative consequences. To give an example, one poster argues that Brexit cannot have had negative effects to date as it has not occurred yet and the particularities of Brexit are as such uncertain and unknown. However, this posting is met with '[t]here's somebody who needs a primer on the effects of uncertainty in economics': using an *ad hominem* attack on the preceding poster, the responding editor points out that the uncertainty connected to Brexit has in itself already had a negative impact, namely, as they then claim, a 'recession in 2017/2018'.

Social and political effects

In addition to the focus on economics and uncertainty, social and political effects are mentioned. Social repercussions of Brexit are mentioned in 28 lines. Six concordance lines merely stress that the Wikipedia article on Brexit ought to feature information on the social impact of Brexit, e.g. 'I think including the social impact its extremely important as well', which is not contested. The remaining 22 concordance lines home in on academia, again with a focus on the UK's academic future and not the EU's.

The Wikipedia community debates two issues in this context: initially, Wikipedians briefly refer to the potential loss of EU funding but then focus their debate on the impact of Brexit on academic staff.[2] The first posting addressing Brexit effects on academia was produced in February 2017 – a poster argues that the effects of Brexit on academia will be more far-reaching than described in the Wikipedia article on the issue at that time. In fact, they propose an expansion of the Wikipedia article in this regard based on the view that 'Brexit will not only affect funding but also research personnel'. The subsequent discussions focus on academic staff, e.g. 'Brexit will affect the non-British research community in the UK but, if the non-British scientists leave post-Brexit, it will also penalize British science' and 'The best scientists would be tempted to leave the UK for EU countries'. These examples referring to 'penalising' and 'best scientists leaving the UK' also demonstrate another point, namely that – comparable to the discussions on economic effects – the Wikipedia community predominantly views the repercussions of Brexit as disadvantageous for the UK.

Regarding political effects, another 26 concordance lines address issues that affect nation states in their entirety. Interestingly, the only Wikipedia discussion on effects that took place before the 2016 referendum focuses on this very aspect. In this discussion thread, a Wikipedia contributor asks whether the Wikipedia article should 'also cover the consequences of a LEAVE vote? Such as the breakup of the Union with Scotland choosing to REMAIN'. The responding editors agree that such a discussion of effects is worthwhile. In this context, it is important to draw attention to the fact that in this debate, the Wikipedia community implicitly equates the effects of a Leave vote with Brexit effects, that is, the referendum is implicitly represented as binding and a Leave vote as inevitably leading to Brexit.

Post-referendum debates also refer to the UK's continued existence in its current form and connected border issues with Scotland and Ireland. One editor proposes that the Wikipedia article on Brexit ought to background possible Brexit effects concerning Scotland's secession and highlight issues concerning the Irish border instead: 'The Scottish thing is realistically a non-issue, while the Irish border has proven to be far more weighty and problematic during the Brexit process'. They base this claim on the outcome of the Scottish independence referendum of 2014: 'The Scots bottled it when they had an opportunity to vote for independence in 2014 and since that time the SNP has actually lost ground massively'. Other Wikipedians agree that the border between Northern Ireland (UK) and Ireland

(EU) is problematic but argue that 'Irish "concerns" on the border are right now being politely pushed aside by the UK and the EU26 [*sic*]'. The community implies that this stems from the perceived lack of importance of Ireland and one poster even suggests 'that is what needs improving in the EU: small fry like Ireland must have the same weight as the bigger fish, otherwise the EU is in danger of disintegrating'.

The discussion of the Irish border also contains a complaint by an editor who takes note of the UK-centric discussion of Brexit effects already mentioned above: 'all we get is British navel-gazing in the Wikipedia article'. This editor argues for a shift of focus on Brexit effects on the EU and supports this with their view of a particular EU member – Germany – as particularly powerful: 'But I have news for you: Germany, not Britain, is writing the rulebook'. Interestingly, the community indeed refocuses its discussion and, in 11 concordance lines on political repercussions, addresses consequences for the EU. These consequences cluster around Germany's position in the European Union, e.g. 'the major effect for the EU is the loss of Germany's political ally (the UK) which regularly upheld liberal economic principles' and 'effect on the EU: Germany and her remaining northern EU allies will lose their blocking minority of 35% in the EU Council, enabling the other EU countries to enforce specific proposals'. That is, the Wikipedia community connects the UK's withdrawal from the EU to a loss of political power of Germany within the EU.

Finally, of the 26 lines on political repercussions, two lines are especially noteworthy as they give an insight into a conversation thread on the connection between the outcome of the EU referendum and the election of Donald Trump as US president (or 'Trumpit', as one Wikipedian calls it; see Lalić-Krstin & Silaški, Chapter 14 this volume, on Brexit-induced neologisms). The original posting was made before Trump's election – using an argument from authority, an editor proposes that there is a connection between Brexit and Trump's success in an interrogative, i.e. mitigated, form: 'Trump has repeatedly ascribed his success to the Brexit effect. Does this not deserve a mention in the Wikipedia article?' The idea is rejected, first because at that time, it was still in doubt whether Trump would actually be successful and gain the presidency ('we won't know if there will even be a President Trump'). Later, the idea is rejected since Trump is not accepted as a reliable authority that can speak to this alleged causal connection between Brexit and his election: 'wikipedia has to stick to bare facts (so unfashionable nowadays, I know, but there you are)'.

The latter rejection hinges on the perceived lack of factuality of such a causal connection and the comment in brackets, in particular, leads to another issue debated among Wikipedians, namely the idea of reliable sources and the role of experts and academics.

Brexit effects and reliable sources

Within these conversation threads about possible Brexit effects, the Wikipedia community devotes some discussion to challenging the status of recognised experts and debating the reliability of academics in the context of Brexit (see Zappavigna,

Chapter 4 this volume). An examination of the concordance lines of 'expert*' and 'academi*' shows that this phenomenon constitutes a non-dominant part of the debates (see Tables 10.2 and 10.3 for more details on the number of challenges with regard to 'expert*' and 'academi*'). However, it is a remarkable trend in light of Wikipedia's policy on reliable source material and might be indicative of a broader societal shift towards a post-truth/post-fact discourse.

Generally, Wikipedia aims to incorporate "all of the significant views that have been published by reliable sources on a topic" (Wikipedia, 2015a). The Wikipedia page on reliable sourcing adds that "recognized experts" and "academic and peer-reviewed publications, scholarly monographs, and textbooks are usually the most reliable sources" (Wikipedia, 2016a). In addition to hedging the reliability of academia ("usually"), the encyclopaedia does not clarify what precisely constitutes an expert but emphasises the social element that makes an expert an expert, i.e. expert legitimation and recognition by society ("recognized"). This definition does not prevent discussion about whether a particular source is reliable or expert enough.[3] Although the policy still suggests that, generally, academia and recognised experts ought to be accepted as reliable, this was doubted in the context of Wikipedians' discussions of Brexit effects, particularly economic effects.

With respect to 'expert*', there are 11 lines that take a critical perspective on the role of experts in the context of Brexit. That is, these lines do not merely challenge whether a particular group/source has sufficient expert status and thereby engage in expected debates on reliable sourcing. Rather, they comment and pass judgement on the genericised group 'expert(s)' as such. These lines challenge the identifying feature of the group 'experts' and reframe experts as non-experts.

Ten of these lines limit their criticism to the field of *economic* forecasting concerning Brexit effects. These lines either reject the existence of experts in this area altogether or cast doubt on the expert status of the entire group of recognised experts in economic forecasting. References to allegedly erroneous past economic predictions (without any detail on how these were flawed) are used to do so, e.g. 'there are no experts in the field of economic forecasting. High-quality scientific research on economic forecasts? Are you not aware of the crap record these clowns have?' This posting illustrates the underlying assumption that 'experts' are to be correct in their assessments in order to remain accepted as experts. In fact, alleged past errors ('crap record') lead this editor to redefine experts as 'clowns'. Another example is 'the [economic] predictions are generally about as accurate as flipping a

TABLE 10.2 Uses of 'expert*' – 49 concordance lines

14 lines: debate a critical perspective on experts	11 lines: (economic) experts as reliable sources challenged 3 lines: experts as reliable sources defended
38 lines: other	Non-critical uses: cite and refer to experts

coin [. . .] [anonymised]'s naive search for authority fails because the experts ain't expert'. This statement mistakes lack of accuracy of predictions for chance ('flipping a coin') and then proceeds to reject the expert status of the group 'experts'.

Beyond economic experts, one line of 'expert*' moves to a profound challenge concerning experts in general: '[y]our touching faith in "experts" belongs in the field of theology'. Drawing on the domain of religion to evoke the idea of worship and unquestioning belief, this posting questions another editor's alleged blind trust in experts and thereby calls into question the reliability of the whole group defined as 'experts'. Only three concordance lines defend 'experts' – possibly the community did not see cause to respond more extensively because the overall number of critical voices on 'expert*' is still relatively low. To give an example of a reaction, one poster dismisses the challenge of experts in the form of an *ab absurdo* argument and ironically draws on a comparison to climate change to make their point: 'expert forecasts of what will happen under conditions XYZ are just a silly debate and the guy who predicts an annual −10 °C cooling is just as right as the consensus of climate scientists, right?'

Generally, the Wikipedia community connects experts and academia – this is succinctly illustrated in one posting that incorporates both 'expert*' and 'academi*': '[t]here is a persistent and biased belief that there are experts in this field [economic forecasting]; that these experts are clustered in academia; and that their expertise constitutes WP:RS'.[4] Indeed, examining the 91 concordance lines of 'academi* shows that (19 + 24 =) 43 lines (see Table 10.3) , i.e. 47 per cent, address similar issues as the lines featuring 'expert*', namely the issue of academics as experts (and academia as a metaphorical container hosting experts) and reliable sources.

In 12 lines of 'academi*', the focus is again on economics. For example, the community debates whether academia and/or the genericised group of 'academics' is an adequate source of information with respect to this area: '[b]ringing an undue respect for academia, which is appropriate in many other circumstances and fields, into economic forecasting, is plain daft'. An example that passes less extreme judgements on academia but points out that it is not the only reliable source on economic matters is: '[anonymised]'s fetishistic worship of academia as the sole source of information is, in the field of economics, unwarranted'.

TABLE 10.3 Uses of 'academi*' – 91 concordance lines

19 lines: critical view	12 lines: academi* as reliable source in economic context challenged
	7 lines: general challenge of academi* as reliable source
24 lines: defend 'academi*' as reliable source	10 lines: reference to Wikipedia policy 14 lines: dismissive metacomments
48 lines: other	Non-critical uses: cite academi*, discuss Brexit effect on academia

Apart from the concordance lines that question academic expertise with respect to the field of economics, seven concordance lines go beyond this limited criticism. These lines cast doubt on the reliability of academia in general, e.g. '[t]he robustness of academic claims is also exaggerated' and 'we can see the scale of mumbo jumbo the mainstream, academic, so-called "reliable" sources are spouting at us'. In connection with this perspective, two lines draw on Wikipedia policy on reliable source material: '[t]here's nothing in [Wikipedia] policy that requires something to be academic or gives any privilege to academic sources'. This statement is immediately countered and rejected by ten concordance lines that cite Wikipedia policy: 'But reliable source policy does privilege academic sources: "If available, academic and peer-reviewed publications are usually the most reliable sources"' and 'Really? You gonna try to Wikilawyer this too? Look, it says right there "academic and peer-reviewed publications are usually the most reliable source". You can try to pretend it doesn't, but . . . it does' and finally, '[a]cademic research is considered reliable on Wikipedia. Indeed, it is generally seen as the "'reliablest of the reliable"'.

Another 14 lines also react to the critical assessment of academics as unreliable, for instance, 'a pathetic attempt by editors who are hostile towards academia to keep academic content from readers', 'it's just [anonymised] and [anonymised], whose sole edits to this Wikipedia article have been to try to remove academic assessments of Brexit because of spurious non-Wiki policy reasons, namely a disdain for academia' and '[anonymised] has made his hostility towards academia and economics clear'. These strongly worded comments ('pathetic', accusation of non-compliance with Wikipedia policy) serve to dismiss the debate on the reliability of experts and academia/academics as valid and reliable sources in the context of Wikipedia.

On the whole, while the number of concordance lines that take a critical stance towards experts and/or academics as reliable sources of information is still relatively low, this critical attitude might be indicative of a potential and disconcerting social shift towards what Mihailidis and Viotty (2017) call a 'post-fact' approach to information "that is hostile toward any claim of expertise" (p. 448), at least in the context of Brexit effects. What is more, this phenomenon is remarkable as it occurs in spite of Wikipedia policy; in fact, it directly challenges site policy, which emphasises the reliability of experts and academics/academia.

Reasons for the Brexit vote

The Wikipedia community repeatedly debates possible reasons for the referendum's outcome as indicated by 'reason*' collocating with 'brexit' at a t-score of 2.8. Generally, the Wikipedians involved in the debates acknowledge the difficulty of identifying a clear reason for the outcome of the referendum. This reaches from short postings such as 'It's complicated' to discussions of how Remain and Leave voters cannot be easily divided into left- or right-wing supporters, e.g. '[t]he belief that this is a left/right issue is not just simplified, it is wrong'. Yet, despite this principal awareness concerning the complexity of the situation, Wikipedians primarily focus on one reason for the outcome in their discussions – migration to the UK (see Cap, Chapter 5 this volume). The collocation calculation for 'brexit' already suggests that (im)migration constitutes an important part of the Wikipedians' debates, as the word 'immigration' collocates with 'brexit' at a t-score of 2.1.

Before discussing the co-text of the term in more detail, some preliminary observations deserve mention. First, the use of 'immigration' already illustrates that immigration as a social phenomenon is at the centre of attention and not the people who immigrate. The term '*migrant*' is only used 12 times and – because of its rare usage – does not have collocates beyond the threshold of 2.0. However, the item is notable as it is used in reference to people's (negative) attitudes towards immigrants: 'fear immigrants' (twice), 'anti-immigrant voters' and, in reference to possible positive Brexit effects, the 'declining number of immigrants'. In addition, the absence of the items 'refugee*' or 'asylum seeker*' throughout the corpus is notable as it hides that there is a subgroup of immigrants displaced by war or other calamities. Avoiding direct reference to individuals who require or even have the legal right to protection might serve to avoid the (moral) dilemma of representing negative attitudes towards such individuals.

Expanding the concordance lines of '*migration' shows that 19 out of 39 lines refer to immigration into the UK as a potential reason for the referendum result, e.g. 'the principal reason for Brexit was immigration concerns'. It is notable that only 5 of these 19 lines use the term 'migration' instead of 'immigration'. That is, the Wikipedians predominantly use a term that refers to spatially oriented movement, which is, again, indicative of posters' focus on the UK – an alphabetical sort to the right of the node confirms that immigration 'to the UK' is the focus of discussion. Interestingly, the point of origin is not a major aspect of the debate on immigration as a reason for the referendum result. Unsurprisingly, an alphabetical sort to the left of '*migration' reveals that 'limiting', 'controlling' or even 'stopping' immigration is another pattern in the debate, e.g. 'one of the reasons for the Brexit vote is concern over the lack of control over immigration into the UK' and 'interpretation of the referendum result is relevant, because it's been taken into consideration in the subsequent UK negotiation positions (e.g. control of immigration is taken to be important)'.

Interestingly, the Wikipedia community never questions whether the matter of controlling and limiting immigration to the UK was in fact a deciding factor in the 2016 referendum. To give but one example, in a thread called 'Immigration caused the turnout of the referendum?' a poster states that '[t]he immigration issue is mentioned in the [English Wikipedia] article' but argues that even 'more could be added to the immigration part and what it meant for the [Leave] voters and perhaps also in what way, they had began to fear immigrants'. Neither this nor any responding posters question the underlying assumption that Leave supporters indeed 'fear' immigrants and that the matter of controlling and limiting immigration to the UK was a deciding factor in the 2016 referendum.

In addition to immigration, nationalism is discussed as motivating the referendum outcome – 'brexit' and 'nationalism' collocate at a t-score of 2.6. Of 34 uses of 'national*', 18 concordance lines permit an insight into how nationalism is discussed as a potential reason for the referendum outcome. Moreover, there is a notable overlap of discussions about immigration and nationalism, i.e. 17 of the 18 relevant lines of 'national*' co-occur with '*migration*'. Interestingly, this overlap of occurrences illustrates how the idea of nationalism as a reason for the referendum outcome is rejected: whenever editors propose nationalism as a reason, this is met with the idea that immigration is the actual issue worth noting. For example, in an *argumentum ad populum*, the poster quoted below claims that nationalism ought to be mentioned as possible reason for the referendum outcome since

> [m]any triumphant supporters are drawing parallels between Brexit and the ascendance of National Socialism in Germany in the 1930s. I have often heard these interesting individuals calling Brexit 'the fourth reich' and claiming 'We have taken our country back from the Arabs, Browns, Negros, and Jews'.

Another editor does not reject this idea as such but argues that the presented issue actually belongs to the article section already dedicated to dealing with 'sentiments regarding immigration'. To give another example, one editor argues that '[t]here should be some coverage of English nationalism in the article as that seems to be the almost unspoken driver' behind the Brexit vote. This proposition is dismissed, however: '[y]our proposal makes little sense to me [. . .] the principal reason for Brexit was immigration concerns'.

Conclusion

The findings presented in this chapter reflect a plethora of voices (with the limitations discussed in the second section of this chapter) and shed light on what elements of Brexit a transnational and influential community of private citizens grappled with when discussing Brexit before and, in particular, after the referendum in June 2016. As this study focuses on private individuals' debates about Brexit, it complements studies of traditional top-down media and elite contexts, e.g. newspapers, political speeches and official documents. Examining Wikipedians' debates sheds light on what reasons for the Brexit vote private citizens identified and, generally, what aspects connected to Brexit they grappled with – this investigation allows a glimpse of what aspects of Brexit are recontextualised by individuals who had been recipients of top-down communication, such as news media reporting and political campaigns, about Brexit.

The most heated debates among Wikipedians involved in the discussions on Brexit are on potential Brexit effects, which recalls Lutzky and Kehoe's (Chapter 7 this volume) findings in a newspaper corpus and might be indicative of the sources the Wikipedia community consulted. In this context, the Wikipedians focus their debates on anticipated repercussions for the UK rather than for the

European Union – from expressing uncertainty to making or at least citing bleak predictions about the UK's (economic) future, the general outlook present in these Wikipedia debates is rather pessimistic. In addition, the Wikipedia community debates reasons for the referendum outcome. Without notable controversy in order to reach consensus, the Wikipedians identify immigration into the UK, and concerns about stopping, controlling or limiting it, as the main reason for the referendum result – a finding that echoes Cap's claim as immigration as deciding factor (Chapter 5 this volume).

Finally, in the context of debates on the repercussions of Brexit, some Wikipedians' view of experts and academia is notable (see also Zappavigna, Chapter 4 this volume). On the one hand, editors express critical attitudes towards an unspecified group of 'experts', that is, the reliability of this group of experts (in economics) is doubted. On the other hand, editors also question whether the group 'academics' and the field 'academia' constitute a reliable source, again in particular with respect to economics. While a substantial part of these critical postings focus on the area of economics, there are also postings that cast more general doubt on experts and academics/the field of academia as reliable sources of information. This trend is notable as it challenges Wikipedia policy concerning reliable source material. What is more, and despite the fact that this critical attitude was met with rejection by the majority of the Wikipedia community, it might be indicative of a more general tendency to distrusting and rejecting expert insights at least with regard to Brexit and Brexit effects.

Notes

1 The low number of turns indicates that potential interlocutors did not find the matter sufficiently important to warrant a response.
2 The reason for this focus on academia might be that academics are overrepresented among Wikipedia editors (see above).
3 Some of these debates have garnered public attention (e.g. Adams, 2017; Jackson, 2017).
4 This is an abbreviated reference to Wikipedia's policy of reliable sourcing.

References

Adams, G. (2017, 4 March). The making of a Wiki-Lie: Chilling story of one twisted oddball and a handful of anonymous activists who appointed themselves as censors to promote their own warped agenda on a website that's a byword for inaccuracy. *Mail Online*. Available at www.dailymail.co.uk/news/article-4280502/Anonymous-Wikipedia-activists-promote-warped-agenda.html, accessed 18 August 2018.

Alexa (2016). The top 500 sites on the web. Available at www.alexa.com/topsites, accessed 18 August 2018.

Anthony, L. (2015). AntConc. Available at www.laurenceanthony.net/software.html, accessed 18 August 2018.

Black, L., Welser, H., Cosley, D., & DeGroot, J. M. (2011). Self-governance through group discussion in Wikipedia: Measuring deliberation in online groups. *Small Group Research*, *42*(5), 595–634. https://doi.org/10.1177/1046496411406137

Buckledee, S. (2018). *The language of Brexit: How Britain talked its way out of the European Union*. London: Bloomsbury.

Emigh, W., & Herring, S. (2005). Collaborative authoring on the web: A genre analysis of online encyclopedias. *Proceedings of the 38th Annual Hawaii International Conference on System Sciences*, 1–11.

Fairclough, N. (1992). *Discourse and social change*. Cambridge: Polity Press.

Gatto, M. (2014). *The web as corpus: Theory and practice*. London: Bloomsbury.

Hewitt, J. (2005). Toward an understanding of how threads die in asynchronous computer conferences. *Journal of the Learning Sciences*, *14*(4), 567–589. https://doi.org/10.1207/s15327809jls1404_4

Jackson, J. (2017, 8 February). Wikipedia bans *Daily Mail* as 'unreliable' source. *Guardian*. Available at www.theguardian.com/technology/2017/feb/08/wikipedia-bans-daily-mail-as-unreliable-source-for-website, accessed 18 August 2018.

Kelly, M. (2018). *Languages after Brexit: How the UK speaks to the world*. Basingstoke: Palgrave Macmillan.

KhosraviNik, M., & Unger, J. (2016). Critical discourse studies and social media: Power, resistance and critique in changing media ecologies. In R. Wodak & M. Meyer (Eds), *Methods of critical discourse studies*. 3rd ed. (pp. 205–233). London: Sage.

Kopf, S. (2018). Debating the European Union transnationally: Wikipedians' construction of the EU on a Wikipedia talk page (2001–2015). PhD thesis, Lancaster University.

Kostakis, V. (2010). Peer governance and Wikipedia: Identifying and understanding the problems of Wikipedia's governance. *First Monday*, *15*(3). https://doi.org/10.5210/fm.v15i3.2613

Mederake, N. (2016). *Wikipedia: Palimpseste der Gegenwart: Text- und Wissensverfahren im kollaborativen Hypertext* [*Wikipedia: Present-day palimpsest: Text and knowledge creation in collaborative hypertext*]. Frankfurt am Main: Peter Lang.

Mihailidis, P., & Viotty, S. (2017). Spreadable spectacle in digital culture: Civic expression, fake news, and the role of media literacies in 'post-fact' society. *American Behavioral Scientist*, *61*(4), 441–454. https://doi.org/10.1177/0002764217701217

Myers, G. (2010). *The discourse of blogs and wikis*. London: Continuum.

Page, R. (2014). Counter-narratives and controversial crimes: The Wikipedia article for the 'Murder of Meredith Kercher'. *Language and Literature*, *23*(1), 61–76. https://doi.org/10.1177/0963947013510648

Partington, A., Duguid, A., & Taylor, C. (2013). *Patterns and meanings in discourse: Theory and practice in corpus-assisted discourse studies*. Amsterdam: Benjamins.

Stubbs, M. (1995). Collocations and semantic profiles: On the cause of the trouble with quantitative studies. *Functions of Language*, *2*(1), 23–55. https://doi.org/10.1075/fol.2.1.03stu

Wikimedia Foundation. (2011). *Wikipedia editors study: Results from the editor survey, April 2011*. Available at https://upload.wikimedia.org/wikipedia/commons/7/76/Editor_Survey_Report_-_April_2011.pdf, accessed 18 August 2018.

Wikipedia (2015a). Neutral point of view. Available at https://en.wikipedia.org/wiki/Wikipedia:Neutral_point_of_view, accessed 18 August 2018.

Wikipedia (2015b). Verifiability. Available at https://en.wikipedia.org/wiki/Wikipedia:Verifiability, accessed 18 August 2018.

Wikipedia (2016a). Identifying reliable sources. Available at https://en.wikipedia.org/wiki/Wikipedia:Identifying_reliable_sources, accessed 18 August 2018.

Wikipedia (2016b). List of policies and guidelines. Available at https://en.wikipedia.org/wiki/Wikipedia:List_of_policies_and_guidelines, accessed 18 August 2018

Wikipedia (2016c). Protection policy. Available at https://en.wikipedia.org/wiki/Wikipedia:Protection_policy#extended, accessed 18 August 2018.

Wikipedia (2016d). Talk page guidelines. Available at https://en.wikipedia.org/wiki/Wikipedia:Talk_page_guidelines, accessed 18 August 2018.

Wikipedia (2017). Reference desk. Available at https://en.wikipedia.org/wiki/Wikipedia:Reference_desk, accessed 18 August 2018.

Wikipedia (2018). All public logs – Talk: Brexit. Available at https://en.wikipedia.org/wiki/Special:Log?page=Talk:Brexit, accessed 18 August 2018.

Zachte, E. (2017). Wikimedia traffic analysis report: Wikipedia page views per country – overview. Available at https://stats.wikimedia.org/wikimedia/squids/SquidReportPageViewsPerCountryOverview.htm, accessed 2018.

11

CITIZENS' REACTIONS TO BREXIT ON TWITTER

A content and discourse analysis

Catherine Bouko and David Garcia

Introduction

On 24 June 2016, the day the results of the British referendum on EU membership were announced, more than 4 million posts including the hashtag #Brexit were posted worldwide on Twitter within a matter of hours. This abundance of tweets is a gold mine for analysts, who can examine how individuals position themselves in relation to event-related debates. Supplementing computer-supported studies, which focus on general patterns of content emerging in the wake of the Brexit vote on Twitter, our quantitative-qualitative research seeks to provide fine-grained insights related to citizens' reactions to the vote on Twitter. Given that including visual content in tweets is a widely adopted practice, we sought to examine some features of tweets in which citizens make use of images when they react on Twitter in the aftermath of the EU referendum. In particular, we sought to analyse to what extent and how multimodal post-result tweets covered issues similar to the ones in traditional and social media during the campaign.

The chapter is structured as follows: in the following section, we outline the topics that were brought to the fore during the referendum campaign, on both traditional and social media, and we highlight that the tweets composing our corpus illustrate practices of civic involvement. In the following two sections, we present how we collected the tweets, removed those written by bots and analysed our corpus based on a quantitative methodological framework inspired by the Hallidayan ideational and interpersonal functions of language. The results are summarised in the subsequent section. In the penultimate section, we outline our qualitative discourse analysis of the subjective presence or absence of the tweet's authors in their tweets, which has an impact on monoglossia or heteroglossia. Lastly, we discuss our results in the final section.

Background and context

Coverage of the EU referendum campaign in traditional media

The media industry is considered to partly deserve blame or credit for the Brexit vote (Mair et al., 2017). A major claim concerns the coverage of immigration during the campaign, both quantitatively and qualitatively. The various content analyses of the Brexit media coverage outline to what extent immigration and other topics were covered. The insights provided in the different studies are summarised in Table 11.1.

Commentators also point out the particularly negative, sometimes even discriminatory, tones of immigration-related news items (Clark, 2017, p. 93; Gerard, 2017; Moore & Ramsay, 2017, p. 137). Such items and other reporting on Brexit were sometimes misleading or even simply inaccurate, e.g. "Queen backs Brexit" on the *Sun*'s front page (Dixon, 2017).

Observers also noted the media's failure in educating British citizens about the EU, by mostly covering EU-related news in negative ways for years and by not providing information that was particularly needed (Lewis & Cushion, 2017, p. 209). As we will see in the following section, the main topics discussed in traditional media were also prevalent on social media.

Topics about the EU referendum discussed on social media

The *Independent*'s analysis of the words used most in the Facebook posts and tweets of the two official EU campaigns between 20 February and 20 April 2016 reveals that 'job', 'trade' and 'businesses' were most used by the Remain camp, in contrast to 'controlled', 'NHS' and 'money', which were used by the Leave camp (Lavoie, 2016). The Centre for Analysis of Social Media DEMOS analysed 100,000 EU referendum-related tweets sent to UK MPs between 20 May and 2 June 2016 and points out a narrowing focus in both groups, given that most tweets centred around three issues, but in different order: 24 per cent of Leave supporters' tweets were immigration related, 40 per cent were about the economy and 36 per cent about sovereignty, while the Remain backers focused first on the economy (58 per cent), then on sovereignty (26.5 per cent) and lastly on immigration (15.5 per cent) (Krasodomski-Jones, 2016).

Most published research focuses on messages on social media posted during the campaign until the day of the referendum. Some studies, however, are based on a timespan that reaches well beyond 23 June 2016: researchers at the University of Sheffield analysed the tweets posted by around 40,000 Leave supporters and 40,000 Remain backers between June and November 2016. Their study reveals that immigration dwarfed every issue except economic concerns (especially in the run-up to referendum day). It appears that immigration was the key issue in Leave supporters' tweets and outweighed issues such as sovereignty and the NHS (Ball & Applegate, 2016). Another DEMOS study highlights the prominence

TABLE 11.1 Content analyses of the UK media coverage of the 2016 EU referendum campaign

Authors	*Corpus*	*Time frame*	*Top issues in Brexit-related news items*
Deacon et al. (2016)	5 broadcasters, 10 newspapers	6 May to 22 June 2016	The referendum campaigns (30.9%) Economy/business (18.9%) Immigration (13.2%)
Levy et al. (2016)	9 newspapers	20 February to 23 June 2016	The vote and the campaign (49%) Arguments (42%) Economy/business (45%) UK sovereignty (25%) Migration/mobility (16%)
Moore & Ramsay (2017)	4 broadcasters, 10 newspapers, 3 newsmagazines, 3 digital-only news media	20 February to 23 June 2016	Economy (48%) Immigration (30%) Health (11%)
Cushion & Lewis (2016)	5 broadcasters	20 February to 23 June 2016	The process of the referendum (roughly 50%) Economy (over 20%) Immigration (over 10%)

of immigration as a topic after the referendum, given that 28 per cent of EU referendum-related tweets posted by Leave supporters were about this very issue (Miller et al., 2016).

Our corpus is composed of tweets exclusively posted after the results of the referendum. In our opinion, they illustrate civic involvement, as we will see in the next section.

Civic involvement in tweets

Our research sought to identify the content patterns through which individuals perform their citizenship in reaction to the Brexit referendum. The tweets of our corpus are not designed to play a role in setting the political agenda. Rather, they are written as private reactions to a societal event and not as political mobilisation of "citizen marketers" (Penney, 2017) who wish to influence other citizens' votes during a campaign. Such post-referendum practices seem to be "democratic but not democratizing" (Papacharissi, 2010, p. 144), to the extent that they do not belong to citizens' movements that call for societal changes. Rather, they take the form of 'ambient communities':

> The connections are "ambient" in the sense that other users are potentially present within the social network, but not necessarily linked together through connections between user accounts, or by direct conversational exchanges. Instead, social affiliation may be enacted via participation in large-scale practices such as internet memes (e.g. viral catchphrases or captioned images) and social tagging.
>
> *(Zappavigna, 2015, p. 1)*

In our corpus of post-referendum posts, Twitter is used as a public space rather than as a public sphere: the first one enhances discussion while the second one aims to promote democratic progress (Papacharissi, 2010, p. 124). That being said, the fact that the posters do not explicitly position their activities as civic engagement does not diminish these activities' civic relevance (Burgess et al., 2006, p. 6). This statement is in line with Ekman and Amnå's (2012) typology of political participation and civic engagement, in which they emphasise the importance of taking *latent* forms of participation into account. Their model differentiates between involvement and engagement. Involvement concerns individual forms of attentiveness to politics and societal issues, while engagement is related to concrete individual and collective actions that citizens engage in to help others, to improve the living conditions in their community, etc. We consider reacting to the Brexit vote in tweets as such involvement in political issues, and therefore see it as civic participation in its own right.

In the next two sections, we outline how we collected the tweets, removed those written by bots and analysed our corpus.

Data collection

We randomly collected 9,631 tweets that included 'Brexit' as a hashtag or search word, contained some visual content and were posted between 24 June and 23 July 2016. We then filtered the tweets for the 6,612 that were written in English. To gain meaningful insights from tweets, we conducted preliminary steps to refine our corpus and take "context collapse" (Marwick & Boyd, 2011) into account: as social media collapse multiple audiences into single contexts, individuals who, when offline, present themselves according to the context of the interactions, tend to write for 'imagined audiences' in virtual public spaces. This collapsed context on social media is true for the production of posts but also for their reception by other users and indeed researchers. The best alternative to deal with this collapse would be to complement the research with interviews with users (Barton, 2015; Breiter & Hepp, 2018); however, those are impractical to conduct for large corpora. Instead, we ensured the relevance of our corpus through the following steps.

Bot detection

Twitter is famous for containing many bots, i.e. software that performs certain tasks, here running a Twitter account: Varol et al. (2017) estimate that between 9 and 15 per cent of Twitter accounts are bots. Tweets from bots are likely to be present in our corpus, as around 39,000 tweets were spread by Russian bots the day after the referendum (Lomas, 2017). In order to eliminate bots from our corpus, we used the bot detection system Botometer in addition to Twitter's own bot detection system. Botometer's algorithm organises its insights into three categories that classify the probability of facing bots: tweets that yield a score between 0 and 40 per cent are considered to have been posted by humans while tweets above 60 per cent are considered to be coming from bots. The system allows for a grey area and cannot determine whether a tweet is made by a bot or by a human with certainty between 40 per cent and 60 per cent. To exclude as many bots as possible from our corpus, we only selected tweets with a score between 0 and 40 per cent. In doing so, we accepted that tweets from humans that yielded a score above 40 per cent would disappear from our corpus, but we chose to work on a corpus that was as bot-free as possible. Among the 6,612 tweets, 3,744 tweets were posted by an account that scored higher than 40 per cent and 672 tweets came from accounts that no longer existed when we performed the bot detection (usually deleted bot accounts). After using the bot filter, our corpus shrank from 6,612 to 2,196 tweets.

Analysis of Twitter profiles

Twitter users are not socio-demographically representative but "tend to be highly motivated (with an axe to grind), younger than average (though not exclusively young) and are likely more often men when engaged in political debate.

WSo any insights are partial" (Llewellyn & Cram, 2016, p. 90). This is particularly problematic for Twitter analyses that seek to provide representative insights that complement traditional polls (Miller et al., 2016).

Our research does not so much seek to be socio-demographically representative of the British people but rather aims to identify Brexit-related reaction patterns among the citizens who express their opinions on Twitter. To do so, it is essential to distinguish citizens' profiles from other types of profiles. Only a few studies have focused on Twitter profiles (Vainio & Holmberg, 2017). To categorise profiles, Semertzidis et al. (2013) analysed the most frequent keywords by relating them to categories (occupation, interests, etc.). For our part, we conducted a manual analysis of all profiles to look not only at search words, but also at thematic units and personal pronouns (especially 'I' and 'we') with a view to drawing a distinction between tweets written by individual or by collective profiles (1,822 and 374, respectively).

Among the 1,822 tweets by individuals, we differentiated tweets written by politicians (7) and journalists (131) from those authored by citizens (1,684) who are not professionally involved in the EU referendum. In our research, a profile is considered a private citizen's profile when it does not mention any professional journalistic or political position or affiliation. On the basis of this profile analysis, we kept 1,684 of the 1,822 tweets. During this first level of detailed tweet analysis, we also removed 142 tweets that were replies. At that stage, our corpus comprised 1,542 tweets.

Methods for a multimodal analysis of tweets

Our method is inspired by Halliday's (1985) systemic functional approach to language. His is a model for thinking about general social and semiotic processes; it is not limited to linguistic signs and can be applied to visual signs as well, which explains its predominance in research on multimodality (see e.g. Kress & van Leeuwen, 2006; Bateman, 2014). Our analysis focuses on Halliday's ideational and interpersonal metafunctions of language:

> While construing, language is always also enacting: enacting our personal and social relationships with the other people around us. The clause of the grammar is not only a figure, representing some process [. . .] with its various participants and circumstances [i.e. the ideational function]; it is also a proposition, or a proposal, whereby we inform or question, give an order or make an offer, and express our appraisal of and attitude towards whoever we are addressing and what we are talking about. [. . .] We call it the interpersonal metafunction, to suggest that it is both interactive and personal.
>
> *(Halliday & Matthiessen, 2004, pp. 29–30)*

We previously used this methodology to analyse Brexit-related posts shared on Flickr during the same timespan (see Bouko et al., 2018).

We analysed the ideational function on four levels by answering the questions below:

(a) *Do the posts contain a direct, an indirect or no connection with Brexit?* We removed from our corpus the few posts that were not connected with Brexit in their visual content or their text, despite the use of 'Brexit' as a hashtag or keyword, like a picture of the Rocky Mountains without Brexit-related text, for example. A post was considered indirectly connected if Brexit was mentioned as a general context for another topic. A picture of London bikes available for hire by the public entitled 'Brexit bikes' illustrates such indirect posts. In this example, 'Brexit' only denotes a time frame.

(b) *Is the point of view on Brexit positive, negative or undetermined?* Again, the point of view was reflected in the image and/or in the text. In order to avoid any haphazard interpretation, our analysis took only manifest and explicit content into account. Consequently, we did not aim to determine what the tweet's author might *think*, but what they *show*: for example, a message without any political comment containing a picture of an anti-Brexit march was considered negatively oriented, independent of the author's personal opinion, to which we did not have access. One might argue that this person is against Brexit as they shared a picture and thereby endorsed the march, but we cannot be certain. By contrast, a picture of a cake with icing saying 'Independence Day! We did it!' and the text in the tweet 'Cake for #BrexitTheParty' is an example of positive evaluation. Undetermined tweets are tweets in which we could not identify the presence or predominance of positive or negative markers, neither in the image nor in the text.

(c) *What types of visual content did citizens use in the posts?* Contrary to the two preceding research questions, this question only concerns the visual components of the tweets. We distinguished between the following mutually exclusive types:

1. Visuals from linked content where the images were automatically uploaded in the tweets. In such cases, the Twitter users refer to the content of the link in their tweets and the picture seems to be only included by default.
2. Graphics about financial markets.
3. Brexit-related indexical photographs (e.g. pictures of anti-Brexit marches or political leaflets).
4. Brexit-unrelated indexical photographs (e.g. a photo of someone's breakfast in a tweet to express how they feel about Brexit in the morning).
5. Symbolic and metaphoric images (e.g. images of flags or fences).
6. Narrative images (e.g. cartoons).
7. User-generated content typical of social media (e.g. memes, texts embedded in images).
8. Catch-all media images (e.g. standard images of banknotes, portraits of politicians that do not refer to any particular context).
9. Journalistic content (e.g. pictures of articles, screenshots of political TV programmes).

10 Cultural artefacts (e.g. a picture of Mel Gibson in *Braveheart* in a tweet mentioning 'This is how I feel today' or the CD cover of the Sex Pistols' *Anarchy in the UK*). In such cases, cultural artefacts are visually presented in unmodified images. The comment is written in the tweet and not merged with the image. Such posts differ from memes that share characteristics of content, form and/or stance (Shifman, 2014, p. 41). In our category of cultural artefacts, the images are deprived of units of imitation that people may replicate.
11 Messages from other social media.
12 Historical pictures (e.g. pictures of Thatcher and Reagan).
13 Plain texts (plain texts written on white background, without any references).
14 Other.

(d) What are the different subtopics addressed in the tweets? We identified the following non-mutually exclusive possible subtopics:

1 No subtopic.
2 National sovereignty.
3 Economy.
4 Mobility I.
5 Mobility II.
6 Criticisms of the opposing side (Leave vs Remain supporters).
7 Politics and politicians (e.g. political post-referendum developments).
8 The future of the UK (e.g. independence for Scotland).
9 The future of Europe.
10 Europe as a value (e.g. specific components of the European project like peace or liberty).
11 Other.

Contrary to previous content analyses of media coverage in which immigration was analysed as a whole (see above), we distinguished two types of mobility: the first type refers to short-term or long-term mobility of highly skilled workers, who offer a "high level of human capital" to the host country and who are therefore welcomed as part of a strategy of economic growth and competitiveness (Ruhs & Anderson, 2010, p. 2). To a lesser extent, tourists and students also belong in this category. The second type of mobility refers to people who do not answer to this strategy of highly skilled human capital. These people could be refugees looking for international protection as well as migrants looking for living conditions that will enable them to live in dignity. The citizens' representations of these two types of mobility obviously differ: while the first one is rather accepted, the second type fuels populist political beliefs, which, in turn, nourish negative stereotypes and feelings of rejection. Questions about multi-ethnicity (in hate posts as well as in posts advocating multicultural richness) were subsumed under this second type.

In order to analyse the interpersonal function, we coded the types of social relations that the visual content and/or the text of the posts might enhance between the message's author and potential readers. We categorised the tweets into establishing six types of social relations, which are again not mutually exclusive:

1 information sharing (journalistic or personal information);
2 eye-witnessing (e.g. sharing pictures of observed events, in private or public spaces);
3 sharing personal moments (e.g. personal moments like eating a post-Brexit consolation cake);
4 play;
5 self-expression (personal points of view and/or personal analyses, e.g. 'IMO the main winner for Leave vote in #Brexit is Putin');
6 call for action (e.g. call for signing a petition for a second referendum) – this category was added during the analysis inductively and given our hypothesis that the tweets of our corpus were reactions to Brexit rather than real cases of political mobilisation, we did not expect to encounter calls for action. This category turned out to be marginal however (see results), which confirms our hypothesis.

Quick! Bring a shovel.
I've found where Boris is hiding!
#Brexit

2:59 AM - 27 Jun 2016

FIGURE 11.1 Tweet that illustrates the social relation of playing

Our category of 'play' is based on incongruity theory: According to Koestler (1964), incongruity involves the juxtaposition of two incongruous frames of reference, that is, the simultaneous presence of two contradictory meanings. Following this theory, the violation of an expected pattern may provoke humour in the observer (Parovel & Guidi, 2015, p. 22).

In the tweet in Figure 11.1, for example, incongruity is created by comparing Boris Johnson's haircut to yellow grass.

It is important to note that our category of play focuses on the production strategies of incongruity and excludes the analysis of the potential effects on recipients, given that those are subjective and variable. Therefore, whether tweets coded as play are perceived as humorous or not is not taken into consideration. Moreover, incongruity is not a sufficient condition to create comic effects (Parovel & Guidi, 2015, p. 22): "While incongruity is a component of all comedy, not all comedy is incongruity" (O'Shannon, 2012, p. 11). For these reasons, in our model of categories, play cannot be conflated with comedy, fun or humour.

Tweets containing only one type of social relation are expected to be quite rare, as it is possible to play around with visual content and express one's point of view in the comment, for instance.

To address the issue of single-coding reliability, the total corpus was coded twice with an interval of one month in between the coding sessions (Kouper, 2010). The second coding generated identical results, which confirmed the stability of the categories. Our results are presented in the following section.

Results

Connections with Brexit

Our analysis of the posts' connections with Brexit reveals that the vast majority of the tweets have a direct connection with Brexit (88 per cent). Some 10 per cent of the tweets have an indirect connection with Brexit and 2 per cent have no identified connection with it, neither through image nor through text. These results indicate that while most individuals focus on Brexit, one out of ten shares content in which Brexit is a secondary topic and is most often included as a spatio-temporal context for another topic, like holidays.

The points of view on Brexit

Figure 11.2 reveals that in general, 50 per cent of the tweets share negative content about Brexit and 38 per cent are undetermined. Some 12 per cent of the tweets contain content in favour of Brexit. These general insights hide discrepancies among the types of social relations encountered in tweets. Indeed, on the one hand, the tweets in which individuals express their opinions are

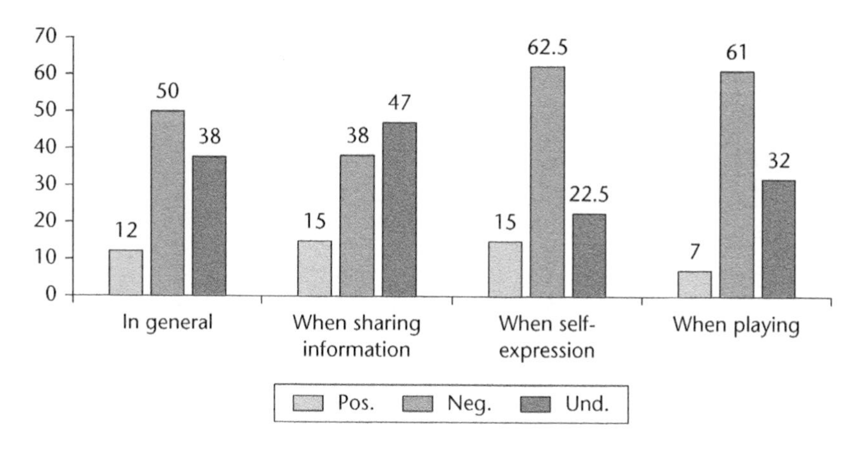

FIGURE 11.2 Points of view on Brexit (%)

more polarised: 62.5 per cent of the tweets contain a negative point of view on Brexit, 22.5 per cent are undetermined and only 15 per cent are positive about Brexit. On the other hand, tweets in which individuals share information about Brexit are less polarised: 38 per cent are negative, 47 per cent are undetermined and 15 per cent are positive. When individuals engage in play about Brexit, tweets with a positive point of view diminish (7 per cent) while negative points of view prevail (61 per cent) and undetermined points of view rank second with 32 per cent.

Types of visual content

Figure 11.3 shows the large diversity of types of visual content used: with 21 per cent, only information sharing reaches more than 20 per cent. User-generated content (19 per cent) is the second most prevalent category. A second set of categories ranges from 6 to 10 per cent: images from linked content (10 per cent), Brexit-unrelated indexical pictures (9 per cent), graphics about financial markets and catch-all media images (7 per cent each) and symbolic images (6 per cent). Three categories reach 5 per cent: Brexit-related indexical pictures, narrative images and images of cultural artefacts.

Quite surprisingly, the low proportion of Brexit-related indexical pictures shows that only a few Tweeters used the platform to share content they saw in public spaces (such as anti-Brexit events, messages written in the streets or visual evidence of the campaigns). The same number of Tweeters shared quite a specific type of tweets, in which they used an unmodified picture of a cultural artefact and made interdiscursive connections between this and their view on Brexit in the text. A fourth set, consisting of four categories, brings up the rear, each of them remaining under 4 per cent.

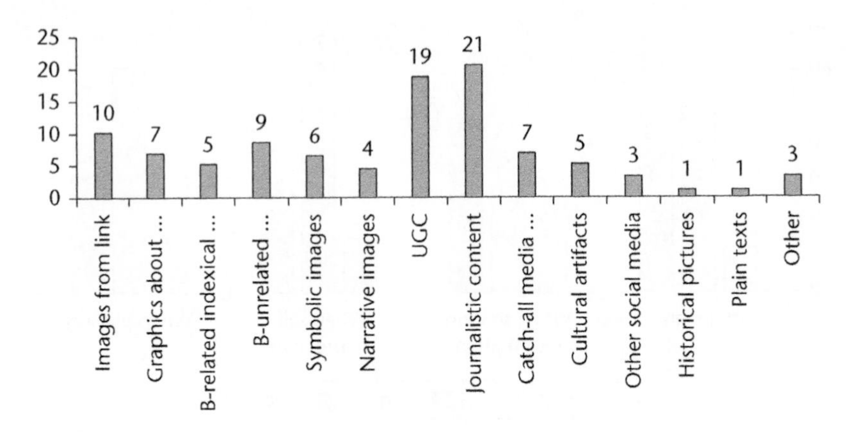

FIGURE 11.3 Types of visual content (%)

Types of social relations

Figure 11.4 highlights to what extent the function of self-expression is important (in 61 per cent of the tweets), followed by information sharing (48 per cent) and playing (31 per cent). Let us bear in mind that the types of social relations are not mutually exclusive. When we subdivide the category of information sharing, it becomes apparent that 25 per cent of all the tweets exclusively fall under the function of information sharing while 9 per cent of the tweets fulfil this function through sharing links to online journalistic content. These results highlight that while Twitter is used to spread information, this function is not as predominant as one would imagine. The mere function of sharing links in particular is less prevalent than expected. The other four social relations are rarely used by the citizens, even eye-witnessing is under 6 per cent.

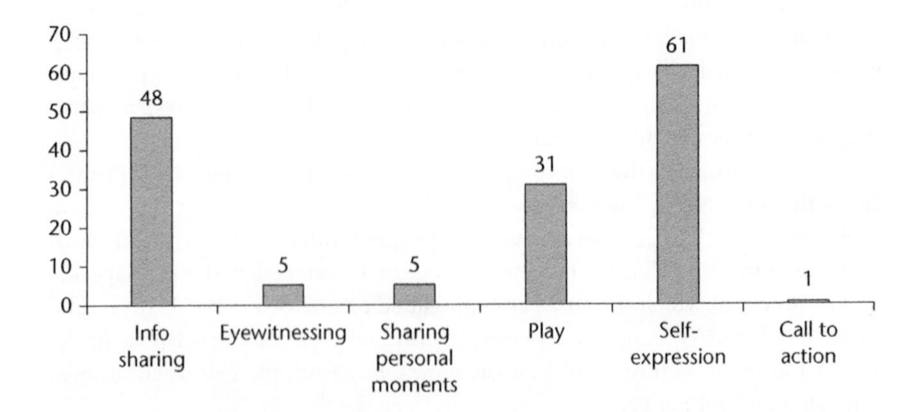

FIGURE 11.4 Types of social relations (%)

More generally, personal pictures are quite rare in our corpus, whether they are private pictures or snapshots in public spaces. Most of the time, pictures of private moments are shared in tweets in which Brexit is a peripheral topic (e.g. holiday pictures).

Subtopics

In Figure 11.5 (below), we can see that three categories are predominant: one tweet out of three does not contain any subtopic but focuses on Brexit in a general way. The economy/finance is a recurrent subtopic (22 per cent), neck and neck with politics (23 per cent). In a second set of categories, 8 per cent of the tweets contain content about the vote and the results while 9 per cent of the tweets focus on the opposing side's votes. In these tweets, the older generation in particular is blamed for voting in favour of Brexit. The other categories never reach 5 per cent of the corpus, not even national sovereignty, which was central during the campaign.

Qualitative analysis of the emotional dimension of self-expression

In order to complement our quantitative results, we performed a qualitative discourse analysis of all the tweets comprising emotion(s). We decided to focus on these types of tweets because they fall within the scope of social relation of self-expression, which is the most prominent one in our corpus (822 tweets). Some 16 per cent of this subcorpus was coded as emotional and our qualitative analysis concerns these 130 tweets.

We analysed 'emotion talk', which comprises the linguistic occurrences that denote emotion (Bednarek, 2008, p. 11) and focused on the following linguistic markers, inscribed in nouns, verbs, adjectives and adverbs:

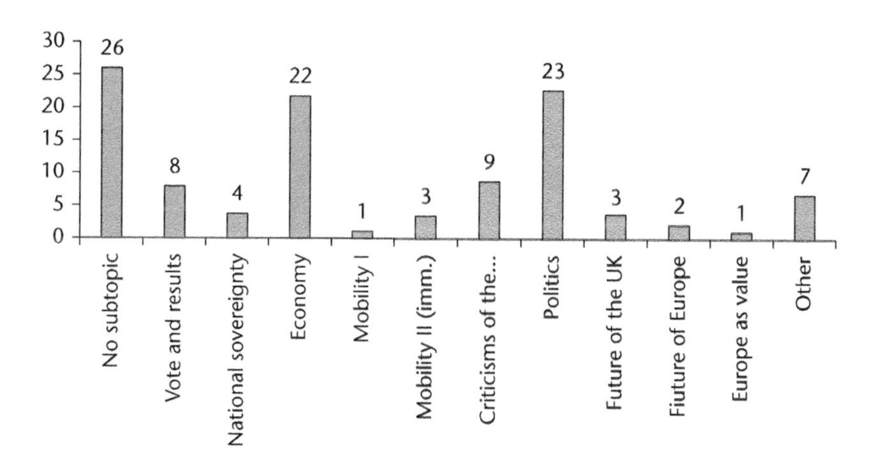

FIGURE 11.5 Types of subtopics (%)

TABLE 11.2 Intensity of the subjective presence of the authors in emotional tweets

Degrees	*Patterns*	*Examples*
	Absent emoter	
1	General statements or thoughts	Sometimes you just have to laugh or you'll cry. #Brexit #EURef (undirected and overt affect)
2	Non-authorial emotional responses	The Iron Lady is smiling down tonight . . . #Brexit (+ portrait of M. Thatcher with the quote 'liberty is fundamental') (undirected and overt affect)
		Good news, If you're upset over #Brexitresult you're a greedy slimy globalist animal, if you're happy your a human (directed and overt affect)
3	Affirmative imperatives	Stay strong #out #brexit (undirected and overt affect)
		Keep calm and drink Darjeeling. #EURefResults #Brexit (undirected and overt affect)
4	Negative imperatives	Guys no need to worry about Brexit look at my pleasingly tesselated waffles. Share if you agree (+ image of waffles) (directed and overt affect)
		Not to worry. A huge rise in the market for Union Jack emblazoned shite will save us. #Brexit (undirected and overt affect)
5	Arguments	Those who voted #Brexit in UK's #EUReferendum have effectively authored the break-up of the United Kingdom. #sadday (undirected and covert affect)
		Maybe there is hope, individuals are learning that decentralisation is conducive to a more free society. #Brexit #EU (directed and overt affect)
6	Emotional lexis	#Brexit #disappointment (undirected and overt affect)
		This is so sad #Brexit (undirected and covert affect)

(continued)

TABLE 11.2 *(continued)*

Degrees	*Patterns*	*Examples*
7	Emotional responses through inferred personal life	Comfort eating for #PostBrexit ontological insecurity (+ image of home-made sweets) (directed and overt affect)
	Present emoter	
8	Non-authorial emotional responses	This is partly why my son's generation (18-year-old Scots) feel specially betrayed by Brexit . . . (+ table of a survey showing how age groups voted) (undirected and overt affect)
9	General personal emotional responses	I can't believe it. #Brexit So Sad. Goodbye UK (undirected and covert or overt affect)
		The consistent emotion for me through all the coverage: sadness. #Brexit (undirected and overt affect)
		Never felt prouder than this, we did it #Brexit (+ image of 'UK votes out') (undirected and overt affect)
		Me right now #Brexit (+ picture of person in tears) (undirected, overt affect in image)
10	Personal emotional responses through personal life	OK I think we all need cheering up a bit so here is a picture of my new Bengal kitten Dave! #Brexit (+ picture of kitten) (undirected and overt affect)
		I won a drink from my friend! I'm happy. #Brexit (undirected and overt affect)
		I can sleep soundly tonight because my kids know this was #notmyvote but I am heartbroken for them. #Brexitfail (directed and overt affect)

- mental disposition terms (e.g. 'sad', 'happiness', 'hopefully');
- fixed figurative expressions (e.g. 'my heart sank');
- psycho-physiological descriptions of emotional experiences (e.g. 'my voice trembled').

We sought to determine how Brexit-related emotions were framed in emotional patterns and how these patterns might align or disalign people, notably through the subjective presence of the tweets' authors. To do so, we analysed the tweets using Bednarek's (2008) three factors that allow to classify affect patterns: "(1) is an emoter present or absent (emoted versus unemoted affect); (2) is a trigger present or absent (directed versus undirected affect); and (3) is an emotional response implied or directly expressed (covert vs. overt affect)?" (p. 95). However, we slightly modified Bednarek's approach to the distinction between present or absent emoter. In Bednarek's (2008) model, the emoter is absent in occurrences in which emotions appear as abstract entities rather than emotional responses to triggers by individuals, like in "[b]ooks: [t]he sorrows of love and the joys of political hate" (p. 72). The emoter is also referred to as absent in occurrences in which it is the context that allows the reader to identify the emoter. In line with this, we consider it relevant to distinguish between three types of emoters rather than two: no emoter (e.g. in abstract and general statements), absent emoter (inferred through co-text or context) and present emoter (inscribed in the occurrence). In our corpus, there is always an emoter, either inscribed or inferred; tweets are always interpersonal instead of abstract statements and the emoter can always be easily identified (through their Twitter profile). We analysed the presence or absence of the emoter and of the trigger as well as the implied or direct expression of an emotional response. This methodology allowed us to provide the categories below. Generally, the tweets belong to only one category but these categories are not mutually exclusive by definition; a tweet might contain segments that fall under different categories. In this typology, the subjective presence of the tweet's author is graded for intensity, from low to high subjective presence.

In non-authorial occurrences, emoters attribute the emotion to others, while it is self-attributed in authorial instances (Bednarek, 2008, p. 85). For Martin and White (2005), "the imperative is monoglossic in that it neither references, nor allows for the possibility of, alternative actions" (p. 111). However, we made the distinction between affirmative and negative imperatives: if the first type is indeed monoglossic, the second type is constructed as an alternative to another behaviour (e.g. 'to worry' in our corpus), which makes it more heteroglossic than its affirmative counterpart. The category labelled 'emotional lexis' concerns the occurrences that are nearly only composed of affect terms. In this pattern, many tweets contain phrases like 'so sad'. This is a subject-verb omission of either 'It is (so sad)' or 'I'm (so sad)'. The complete occurrences indicate covert and overt affect, respectively. Omissions are typical of language strategies in tweets (which used to contain only 140 characters until November 2017). In such cases, it is impossible to determine whether the tweet's author expresses a monoglossic point of view ('It is so sad') or a more personal, and hence more heteroglossic, emotion ('I'm so sad'). Such absence of the subjective presence of the tweet's author reinforces the monoglossic dimension of the tweet.

In a similar vein, in our last category with an absent emoter, the tweet's author omits subject and verb and by doing so, avoids any linguistic subjective presence; the personal dimension is only inferred through the image (and cannot be warranted). The emoter can be present though a pronoun, like in degree 8 in Table 11.2. Her subjective presence is reinforced when she anchors her reaction to Brexit in slices of her personal life (often with personal pictures). This latter pattern corresponds to the highest level of subjective presence in our cline.

Discussion and conclusion

Messages left on social media are written by individuals who feel passionate enough about an issue to take the time to post about it, which explains why public spaces on social media are often particularly polarised (Miller et al., 2016). However, our analysis of Brexit-related corpora of Flickr posts (Bouko et al., 2018) and this analysis of Twitter reveal that undetermined points of view on Brexit are more prevalent on Flickr (over 50 per cent) than on Twitter (38 per cent). Besides, the Leave supporters are less present in our corpus than in analyses of the campaigns (see above). This is not exceptional. Indeed, Thelwall et al. (2011) observed that events, even positive or comparatively less controversial ones like the Oscars, often generate an increase in negative sentiments in tweets.

Our analysis of the subtopics suggests that while the economy and immigration were the two most frequently covered themes in the media during the referendum campaign, only the economy occupies an important place in our corpus. The two types of mobility that we distinguished hardly reach 3 per cent of the corpus. So, the concerns expressed on Twitter after the referendum results do not coincide with the main topics developed throughout the campaign. Besides, the topics related to Europe are completely marginal: they barely reach 1 per cent of the corpus and seem to reflect the lack of interest in the EU, for which journalists are claimed to be partly responsible.

Self-expression is the most predominant social relation in our corpus. Our qualitative analysis of the subjective presence of the tweets' authors outlines the richness in emotional patterns, especially to express monoglossic emotional reactions to the referendum. Surprisingly, only a few tweets share visual records of personal moments or events that take place in public space. This contrasts with our Flickr analysis, in which these two social functions are central (Bouko et al., 2018).

By way of conclusion, we would like to insist that, from a qualitative perspective, the categorisation of human artefacts like tweets will always remain an operation that reduces complex phenomena to approximate categories. Therefore, even if our high Cohen's kappas testify our rigorous methodology (Bouko et al., 2018), the percentages we obtained are, in our view, primarily relevant in the trends they reveal, rather than in the exact figures they deliver. Nevertheless, we are confident that the fine-grained methodology for a multimodal analysis of social media posts presented here not only allows for deeper insights than automated methods can deliver, but also illustrates the roles images play in these messages and the various forms of civic involvement they illustrate.

References

Ball, J., & Applegate, C. (2016, 9 December). How Britain talked Brexit. Buzzfeed. Available at www.buzzfeed.com/jamesball/3-million-brexit-tweets-reveal-leave-voters-talked-about-imm?utm_term=.bmw9xWAGBK#.qmD3rVAd6G, accessed 23 August 2018.

Barton, D. (2015). Tagging on Flickr as a social practice. In R. Jones, A. Chik, & C. A. Hafner (Eds), *Discourse and digital practices: Doing discourse analysis in the digital age* (pp. 48–65). Abingdon: Routledge.

Bateman, J. (2014). *Text and image: A critical introduction to the visual/verbal divide*. London: Routledge.

Bednarek, M. (2008). *Emotion talk across corpora*. Basingstoke: Palgrave Macmillan.

Bouko, C., De Wilde, J., Decock, S., Manchia, V., De Clercq, O., & Garcia, D. (2018). Reactions to Brexit in images: A multimodal content analysis of shared visual content on Flickr. *Visual Communication*. https://doi.org/10.1177/1470357218780530

Breiter, A., & Hepp, A. (2018). The complexity of datafication: Putting digital traces in context. In A. Breiter, A. Hepp, & U. Hasebrink (Eds), *Communicative figurations* (pp. 387–405). Basingstoke: Palgrave Macmillan.

Burgess, J., Foth, M., & Klaebe, H. (2006). Everyday creativity as civic engagement: A cultural citizenship view of new media. *Proceedings of the Communications Policy & Research Forum*. Available at https://eprints.qut.edu.au/5056, accessed 23 August 2018.

Clark, T. (2017). Just how much influence did the press have over the Brexit vote? In J. Mair, N. Fowler, R. Snoddy, R. Tait, & T. Clark (Eds), *Brexit, Trump and the media* (pp. 91–95). Bury St Edmunds: Abramis Academic.

Cushion, S., & Lewis, J. (2016). The narrow agenda: How the news media covered the referendum. In D. Jackson, E. Thorsen, & D. Wring (Eds), *Scrutinising statistical claims and constructing balance: Television news coverage of the 2016 EU Referendum* (pp. 40–41). Poole: The Centre for the Study of Journalism, Culture and Community, Bournemouth University. Available at www.referendumanalysis.eu, accessed 23 August 2018.

Deacon, D., Harmer, E., Wring, D., Downey, J., & Stanyer, J. (2016). The narrow agenda: How the news media covered the Referendum. In D. Jackson, E. Thorsen, & D. Wring (Eds), *EU referendum analysis 2016: Media, voters and the campaign* (pp. 34–35). Poole: The Centre for the Study of Journalism, Culture and Community, Bournemouth University. Available at www.referendumanalysis.eu, accessed 23 August 2018.

Dixon, H. (2017). Facts as newspapers saw them, Ipso's role – and a weak BBC. In J. Mair, N. Fowler, R. Snoddy, R. Tait, & T. Clark (Eds), *Brexit, Trump and the media* (pp. 107–122). Bury St Edmunds: Abramis academic.

Ekman, J., & Amnå, E. (2012). Political participation and civic engagement: Towards a new typology. *Human Affairs*, *22*(3), 283–300. https://doi.org/10.2478/s13374-012-0024-1

Gerard, L. (2017). The match is over, but the winners won't leave the pitch. In J. Mair, N. Fowler, R. Snoddy, R. Tait, & T. Clark (Eds), *Brexit, Trump and the media* (pp. 101–106). Bury St Edmunds: Abramis academic.

Halliday, M. (1985). *An introduction to functional grammar*. London: Edward Arnold.

Halliday, M., & Matthiessen, C. (2004). *An introduction to functional grammar*. 3rd ed. London: Routledge.

Koestler, A. (1964). *The act of creation*. London: Hutchinson.

Kouper, I. (2010). The pragmatics of peer advice in a LiveJournal community. *Language@Internet*, 7. Available at www.languageatinternet.org/articles/2010/2464, accessed 23 August 2018.

Krasodomski-Jones, A. (2016). Brexiteers shout the loudest on Twitter. DEMOS. Available at www.demos.co.uk/blog/brexiteers-shout-the-loudest-on-twitter-2, accessed 23 August 2018.

Kress, G., & van Leeuwen, T. (2006). *Reading images: The grammar of visual design*. 2nd ed. London: Routledge.

Lavoie, J. (2016, 31 May). EU referendum: The words used most by Brexit and Remain camps – and what they say about the campaigns. *Independent*. Available at www.independent.co.uk/news/uk/politics/eu-referendum-brexit-remain-camps-britain-stronger-in-europe-vote-leave-a7057826.html, accessed 23 August 2018.

Levy, D., Aslan Ozgul, B., & Bironzo, D. (2016). UK press coverage of the EU referendum. Reuters Institute for the Study of Journalism. Available at https://reutersinstitute.politics.ox.ac.uk/our-research/uk-press-coverage-eu-referendum, accessed 23 August 2018.

Lewis, J., & Cushion, S. (2017). Broadcasting, balance and Brexit: The role of impartiality in an age of confusion. In J. Mair, N. Fowler, R. Snoddy, R. Tait, & T. Clark (Eds), *Brexit, Trump and the media* (pp. 209–218). Bury St Edmunds: Abramis academic.

Llewellyn, C., & Cram, L. (2016). The results are in and the UK will #Brexit: What did social media tell us about the UK's EU referendum? In D. Jackson, E. Thorsen, & D. Wring (Eds), *EU referendum analysis 2016: Media, voters and the campaign* (pp. 90–91). Poole: The Centre for the Study of Journalism, Culture and Community, Bournemouth University. Available at www.referendumanalysis.eu, accessed 23 August 2018.

Lomas, N. (2017, 15 November). *Study: Russian Twitter bots sent 45k Brexit tweets close to vote*. Available at https://techcrunch.com/2017/11/15/study-russian-twitter-bots-sent-45k-brexit-tweets-close-to-vote, accessed 2 March 2018.

Mair, J., Fowler, N., Snoddy, R., Tait, R., & Clark, J. (Eds) (2017). *Brexit, Trump and the media*. Bury St. Edmunds: Abramis academic.

Martin, J. R., & White, P. R. R. (2005). *The language of evaluation: Appraisal in English*. Basingstoke: Palgrave Macmillan.

Marwick, A. E., & Boyd, D. (2011). I tweet honestly, I tweet passionately: Twitter users, context collapse, and the imagined audience. *New Media & Society*, *13*(1), 114–133. https://doi.org/10.1177/1461444810365313

Miller, C., Arcostanzo, F., Josh, S., Krasodomski-Jones, A., Wiedlitzka, S., Jamali, R., & Dale, J. (2016). *From Brussels to Brexit: Islamophobia, xenophobia, racism and reports of hateful incidents on Twitter*. DEMOS. Available at www.demos.co.uk/wp-content/uploads/2016/07/From-Brussels-to-Brexit_-Islamophobia-Xenophobia-Racism-and-Reports-of-Hateful-Incidents-on-Twitter-Research-Prepared-for-Channel-4-Dispatches-%E2%80%98Racist-Britain%E2%80%99-.pdf, accessed 23 August 2018.

Moore, M., & Ramsay, G. (2017). *UK media coverage of the 2016 EU referendum campaign*. Centre for the Study of Media, Communication and Power. King's College London. Available at www.kcl.ac.uk/sspp/policy-institute/CMCP/UK-media-coverage-of-the-2016-EU-Referendum-campaign.pdf, accessed 23 August 2018.

O'Shannon, D. (2012). *What are you laughing at? A comprehensive guide to the comedic event*. London: Bloomsbury.

Papacharissi, Z. (2010). *A private sphere: Democracy in a digital age*. Cambridge: Polity Press.

Parovel, G., & Guidi, S. (2015). The psychophysics of comic: Effects of incongruity in causality and animacy. *Acta Psychologica*, *159*, 22–32. https://doi.org/10.1016/j.actpsy.2015.05.002

Penney, J. (2017). *The citizen marketer: Promoting political opinion in the social media age*. Oxford: Oxford University Press.

Ruhs, M., & Anderson, B. (2010). *Who needs migrant workers? Labour shortages, immigration, and public policy*. Oxford: Oxford University Press.

Semertzidis, K., Pitoura, E., & Tsaparas, P. (2013). How people describe themselves on Twitter. *Proceedings of the ACM SIGMOD Workshop on Databases and Social Networks* (pp. 25–30). New York: ACM. https://doi.org/10.1145/2484702.2484708

Shifman, L. (2014). *Memes in digital culture*. Cambridge, MA: MIT Press.

Thelwall, M., Buckley, K., & Paltoglou, G. (2011). Sentiment in Twitter events. *Journal of the American Society for Information Science and Technology*, *62*(2), 406–418. https://doi.org/10.1002/asi.21462

Vainio, J., & Holmberg, K. (2017). Highly tweeted science articles: Who tweets them? An analysis of Twitter user profile descriptions. *Scientometrics*, *112*(1), 345–366. https://doi.org/10.1007/s11192-017-2368-0

Varol, O., Ferrara, E., Davis, C., Menczer, F., & Flammini, A. (2017). Online human-bot interactions: Detection, estimation, and characterization. *Eleventh International AAAI Conference on Web and Social Media*. Available at https://aaai.org/ocs/index.php/ICWSM/ICWSM17/paper/view/15587, accessed 23 August 2018.

Zappavigna, M. (2015). Searchable talk: The linguistic functions of hashtags. *Social Semiotics*, *25*(3), 274–291. doi:10.1080/10350330.2014.996948

12

BREXIT AND BLAME AVOIDANCE

Officeholders' discursive strategies of self-preservation

Sten Hansson

Introduction

In modern democracies, governments increasingly engage in blame avoiding behaviour when they initiate loss-imposing policies that hurt the interests of some groups (Weaver, 1986). The decision of the British government to leave the European Union is a case in point. As nearly half of the 2016 EU referendum voters said they wanted to remain, and millions of people were left deeply concerned about possible adverse effects of leaving, the government had to deal with an acute blame risk.

In this chapter, I make a linguistically informed contribution to the study of blame games in government. I identify the discursive strategies by which the so-called Brexiteers – the officeholders who led the United Kingdom's exit from the European Union – tried to advance their divisive policy without sanction. I refer to concrete textual examples from their public statements to illustrate how they used language to minimise the perceived agency of the government, downplay the contentious and potentially harmful nature of their policy, present the UK in a positive and the EU in a negative light and deal with potential charges of inconsistency.

Working within the tradition of discourse-historical studies of political communication (Reisigl & Wodak, 2001, 2015; Wodak, 2011), I seek to uncover the particular ways of arguing, framing, denying, representing social actors and actions, legitimising and manipulating that officeholders exploit when attempting to evade accountability for their actions. A detailed context-sensitive analysis of discursive blame avoidance supports an emancipatory goal: it helps us cut through officeholders' defensive text and talk, thereby enhancing the quality of democratic debate in society.

I will present my argument as follows. First, to contextualise the study, I review some of the main blame risks that the Brexiteers were facing. Second, I outline the analytical categories for a linguistically informed study of bureaucratic self-preservation: the discursive strategies of blame avoidance. I then analyse concrete textual examples from my UK government communication data set to illustrate the particular ways in which top officeholders – such as Prime Minister Theresa May and the Secretary of State for Exiting the EU David Davis – tried to deal with the Brexit-related blame risk. In conclusion, I suggest that critical analysts should seek to better understand the 'language of self-preservation' and explore this further in other contexts of political conflict in which people who occupy leadership positions struggle to hold on to power.

Context: Brexit and blame risks

Political scientists have long claimed that policymakers and civil servants at all levels of government are often motivated by self-preservation in the face of various blame risks, and hence engage in blame avoidance behaviour (Weaver, 1986; Hood, 2011; Hood et al., 2016; Vis, 2016; Hinterleitner, 2017; Leong & Howlett, 2017). Government officeholders make their policy choices, structure their organisations and present their work in particular ways to reduce the likelihood of suffering public blame attacks that could put their credibility and power in jeopardy. Blame avoidance behaviour is particularly salient when officeholders initiate loss-imposing policies that hurt the interests of some groups (e.g. pension cuts) and when facing various crises (e.g. economic recession) or scandals (e.g. public allegations of moral transgressions).

The 2017 decision of the Conservative government in the UK to start negotiating the country's exit from the European Union was a highly contentious one and involved the risk of blame generation from at least four perspectives:

1 Brexit was perceived by many as a loss-imposing policy – an instance of the "politics of pain" (Pal & Weaver, 2003), whereby those adversely affected by the decision were seen as the 'victims of Brexit', destined to be worse off in terms of household incomes, free movement rights, trade opportunities and so forth.[1]
2 The government attracted charges of poor planning and execution of the Brexit negotiations (Smith, 2018). Opponents claimed that the government had not put forward a coherent and credible vision for post-Brexit Britain and lacked the capacity to proceed swiftly with the exit talks. The perception of the government as 'not being on top of things' was exacerbated by the long-running government-internal (or more precisely, Conservative party-internal) strife over the idea of Brexit (Bulmer & Qualiga, 2018).
3 The government was vulnerable to accusations of inconsistency. In 2016, the Conservative government, then led by David Cameron, campaigned in support of the Remain vote and published official reports that highlighted serious downsides of leaving the EU. In 2017, under Prime Minister Theresa May's leadership, the Conservative government went ahead with leaving the Union, claiming that Brexit could be made 'a success' (May, 2017). Especially in the

light of Theresa May's own pre-referendum pro-Remain stance (May, 2016), the positive representation of Brexit by her government risked coming across as inconsistent and insincere.

4 The government also ran the risk of alienating EU leaders who criticised Britain for its hard-line approach to Brexit.

Therefore, Brexiteers' post-referendum communicative behaviour deserves close critical analysis: How did they use language to avoid or minimise these blame risks? To find an answer, I start by looking at specific discursive strategies.

Analytical categories: discursive strategies of blame avoidance

In text and talk, the perception of blameworthiness for (potentially) negative deeds or outcomes can be shaped by using a variety of discursive strategies (Hansson, 2015, 2017, 2018a, 2018b, 2018c):

- *Argumentation*: using argumentation schemes to support the standpoint that the negative event or outcome has been brought about either unintentionally, unknowingly, involuntarily, or by someone else (Hansson, 2018b).
- *Framing/positioning*: representing oneself metaphorically/narratively as a hero, a helper of a hero, or a victim, and/or representing someone else as a villain, to escape being assigned the role of the villain by a blame maker (such formulaic narrative frames have been described and discussed by Propp, 1928/1968 and Lakoff, 2008, among others); positioning oneself as someone belonging to an in-group ('us') together with the audience, presuming that 'being on the same side' would curb their blame making desire.
- *Denial*: rejecting agency (via act-denial, control-denial, intention-denial) and negative consequences (via mitigations, downtoning) in response to accusations (see van Dijk, 1992).
- *Social actor and action representation*: exclusion, suppression and backgrounding (e.g., by impersonalisation or nominalisation) of harmful actions, victims and/or those actors who could possibly attract blame (see van Leeuwen, 2008); adding positively connotated attributions/evaluations to these actions and/or actors.
- *Legitimation*: providing explanations and justifications of possibly blameworthy actions by using references to authority, moral evaluation, rationalisation and mythopoesis (see van Leeuwen, 2007).
- *Manipulation*: attempts by (potential) blame takers to impair or bias the understanding of blame-related information, and to control the formation of mental models in a way that is not in the best interest of the recipients, usually involving extensive use of discursive group polarisation, violations of conversational maxims and other discursive strategies focused on potential vulnerabilities of recipients (see van Dijk, 2006).

These strategies can be employed either in response to specific accusations or pre-emptively: an analytic distinction can be made between reactive and anticipative forms of discursive blame avoidance (Sulitzeanu-Kenan, 2006; Hansson, 2017; Hinterleitner & Sager, 2017).

Officeholders seeking to avert blame risk may come up with various excuses, justifications or apologies. Alternatively, they may try to shift public attention away from particular problems that invite criticism, or restrict access to incriminating information and keep a low profile (Hood, 2011). At times, they may also engage in scapegoating – attempts at redirecting blame to other parties (Mortensen, 2012, 2016; Moynihan, 2012). Although I seek to identify the specific discursive moves that are characteristic of blame avoidance behaviour among Brexiteers, I do *not* do so with the goal of measuring their 'effectiveness'. Instead, my aim is to draw attention to the possible abuses of these strategies: government insiders' self-serving attempts to hold on to power by blocking or derailing reasonable discussions over complex policy issues – such as a country's membership in the European Union.

Analysis: dissecting the Brexiteers' rhetoric of self-preservation

In their public statements on Brexit, the top officeholders applied (combinations of) various discursive strategies to modify the perception of blame in at least five ways. They tried to (1) minimise the perceived agency of the government, (2) downplay the contentious and possibly harmful nature of their policy, (3) present themselves and the UK in a positive light, (4) present the EU in a negative light and (5) deal with potential charges of inconsistency. In what follows, I will offer a selection of textual examples from statements by the Prime Minister, the Foreign Secretary, the Secretary of State for International Trade, and the Secretary of State for Exiting the EU from 2017–2018 and discuss how their self-defensive discursive moves can be deconstructed.

Minimising the perceived agency of the government

Social actors are more likely to attract blame when they are perceived as having caused a negative event while having both the obligation and the capacity to prevent the (potentially) harmful behaviour or outcome from occurring (Malle et al., 2014). Hence, politicians who wish to avoid blame for introducing or implementing untoward policies may try to give an impression that their capacity to make different policy choices is necessarily limited. I use an excerpt from a key speech by Prime Minister Theresa May to illustrate this.

Example 1: 'will of the people'

On 29 March 2017, Prime Minister Theresa May gave a statement in Parliament on her letter notifying the European Council President of the UK's intention to leave the EU. Justifying the UK's withdrawal from the single market, she said:

(1) European leaders have said many times that we cannot 'cherry pick' and remain members of the single market without accepting the four freedoms that are indivisible. We respect that position. And as accepting those freedoms is incompatible with the democratically expressed will of the British people, we will no longer be members of the single market (May, 2017).

In the first sentence, May frames 'European leaders' as actors who necessarily try to limit her government's freedom to act ('European leaders have said many times that we cannot "cherry pick"'). Notably, by juxtaposing 'European leaders' with the UK and its government ('we') she depicts 'European leaders' as a collective actor that does not include herself – even though she is a leader of an EU member state. Moreover, she backgrounds the idea that over the years the UK government has been involved in establishing the rules for the European single market and the four freedoms – the free movement of goods, capital, services and labour – within the EU. In the third sentence, May uses a populist reference to the 'will of the people' (see Wodak, 2017) to support the standpoint that the UK's withdrawal from the single market is inevitable, thereby diminishing the perceived involvement of her government in bringing about the loss of the four freedoms. The phrase 'the democratically expressed will of the British people' alludes to the results of the 2016 EU referendum, which Leavers won with a very small margin: 72 per cent of the electorate turned out to vote and 52 per cent of the votes were cast in support of leaving the EU. Therefore, while using a populist argument, May in effect excludes 48 per cent of those who voted in the referendum from her definition of 'the British people'.

Downplaying the contentious and possibly harmful nature of the policy

The degree of blame attributed to offenders may be affected by the perceived seriousness of the norm violation and harmfulness of the behaviour or outcome (Malle et al., 2014). Therefore, when facing criticism for their policies, officeholders may try to mask norm violations and downplay the potential negativity of the outcomes in their text and talk. I analyse two instances of this kind of strategic communicative behaviour below.

Example 2: 'that works for us all'

Besides representing the Brexit-related losses of freedoms as a seemingly consensual 'will of the people', Prime Minister May tried to minimise the perception of a conflict of interest between the UK and the European Union. She said:

(2) Our vote to leave the EU was no rejection of the values that we share as fellow Europeans [. . .] So there should be no reason why we should not agree a new deep and special partnership between the UK and the EU that works for us all (May, 2017).

In the first sentence, May uses a form of intention-denial to minimise the perception of conflict between the UK and the European Union member states. By doing so, May promotes a particular strategic interpretation of the referendum results: those who voted Leave support 'European values' (see Bennett, Chapter 2 this volume) – even though the question of values was not posed to the electorate. From the perspective of blame avoidance, the reference to shared values functions here as a rhetorical device for eliciting feelings of unity, thereby possibly reducing the blame-generating desire among those who identify as 'Europeans'. An attempt to create similar in-group feelings is also evident in the second sentence, where May uses the personal pronoun 'us' inclusively so that it encompasses both the UK and the EU ('partnership between the UK and the EU that works for us all'). This is notable because in the rest of her statement the pronoun 'we' stands for the UK only (e.g. 'we will no longer be members of the single market').[2]

Example 3: 'the sky has not fallen in'

On 15 September 2017, the Foreign Secretary Boris Johnson, one of the leading figures in the 2016 Leave campaign, published an article titled 'My Vision for a Bold, Thriving Britain Enabled by Brexit' in the *Telegraph*. He wrote:

> (3) [T]he sky has not fallen in since June 23. We have not seen the prophesied 500,000 increase in unemployment and the Treasury has not so far sought to punish the British people with an emergency budget. On the contrary: unemployment is at record lows, and manufacturing is booming "in spite of Brexit", as the BBC would put it (Johnson, 2017).

Here, Johnson constructs a rather narrow definition of what could count as Brexit-related harm. He refers to two types of possible loss: increase in unemployment and decrease in government spending ('emergency budget') due to economic recession in the UK. Thereby he suppresses the idea that there may be other, non-economic kinds of losses related to leaving the EU. Moreover, he only refers to current data and does not mention long-term effects of the Brexit policy, many of which may not have occurred right after the 23 June 2016 referendum but may emerge after Britain's actual departure from the EU several years later. By doing so, Johnson denies possible risks – for example, potential restrictions to free movement of people and goods – simply by excluding these from his representation of Brexit.

In addition, Johnson uses framing devices to ridicule anyone who points out possible negative implications of leaving the EU. 'The sky is falling in' is a common idiom indicating an overly anxious, mistaken belief that disaster is imminent: by saying 'the sky has not fallen in', he casts the critics of Brexit as panicking without cause. He contrasts some of the pre-referendum predictions regarding two selected variables – unemployment and economic recession – with current assessments not only to suggest that the former were false, but to foreground the general idea that taking a negative stance towards the implications of Brexit may be misguided. Finally, the phrase '"in spite of Brexit", as the BBC would put it' seems to allude that the reporters at the influential public broadcaster BBC tend to treat Brexit – mistakenly, from Johnson's perspective – as an essentially negative event.

Presenting the 'in-group' and the self in a positive light

Instead of manipulating the perception of agency or loss in relation to an event or outcome, blame takers may try to quench the blame-making desire of the disaffected groups by pleasing and complimenting them as well as by presenting themselves in a positive light. These communicative moves are based on the assumption that people are less likely to blame someone who says good things about them and who is seen as virtuous in character. Paying a compliment – giving high value to another person's qualities – serves the social goal of maintaining good communicative relations with them (Leech, 2014). And people who are generally seen as virtuous and exhibiting goodwill are less likely to be suspected of committing intentional acts of harm. In politicians' text and talk, positive presentation of self and others is often combined: they position themselves discursively as members of the audience's in-group ('us'), such as a nation, and attribute positive characteristics and feelings to the whole in-group. In-group loyalty is seen as an important factor affecting moral judgements (Graham et al., 2009). Below, I bring two examples of the ways in which these principles are realised in Brexiteers' strategic language use.

Example 4: 'a proud history and a bright future'

In Prime Minister May's statement, references to concrete Brexit-related losses that could attract blame are backgrounded and abstract positive evaluations of the UK are repeatedly foregrounded instead. This often takes the form of self-affirming utterances that contain clusters of positive adjectives like 'great', 'proud' and 'bright'. For instance, she said:

(4) We are one great union of people and nations with a proud history and a bright future (May, 2017).

Here, the pronoun 'we' refers exclusively to the UK as an in-group as the speaker appeals to any nationalist sentiment among her audience. References to national strength and pride are also used in combination with casting Britain metaphorically as a building/home and talking of 'our children' as if Britain was a family:

(5) And we are going to take this opportunity to build a stronger, fairer Britain – a country that our children and grandchildren are proud to call home (May, 2017).

Example 5: 'I am ambitious for Britain'

In her statement, Prime Minister May made several claims about her personal hopes and intentions in relation to Brexit. Here are some examples:

(6) I choose to believe in Britain and that our best days lie ahead (May, 2017).
(7) I want the United Kingdom to emerge from this period of change stronger, fairer, more united and more outward-looking than ever before (May, 2017).
(8) I am ambitious for Britain (May, 2017).
(9) It is my fierce determination to get the right deal for every single person in this country (May, 2017).

From the perspective of anticipative blame avoidance, the strategic task of these utterances is to make potential accusations of wrongdoing or failure targeted at her appear less credible by signalling goodwill towards the British audience ('I choose to believe in Britain', 'I am ambitious for Britain') and giving an impression of a strong personal character ('I choose', 'I want', 'I am ambitious', 'It is my fierce determination'). This could also be interpreted as part of a broader strategy of framing herself as a metaphorical hero: a passionate fighter for her country's better future. Notably, in terms of social action representation, all of these claims are about her internal mental processes and therefore cannot be easily countered or proven wrong.

Presenting the 'out-group' in a negative light

When people think that they face a common adversary or enemy, it can boost their feelings of in-group loyalty (Druckman, 1994; Riek et al., 2006; Stephan et al., 2008). This is why the discursive construction of national identity often involves putting emphasis on international differences, drawing implicit and explicit comparisons with 'the others' and using negatively connotated attributions and personified toponyms (e.g. 'Brussels') – all of which taken together may be called "strategies of dissimilation" (Wodak et al., 2009, p. 33). Political elites in several member states have framed the EU as an external threat to their country's domestic affairs because this allows them to cast themselves as safeguards against this threat (Schlipphak & Treib, 2017). Moreover, it is possible that "citizens who are persuaded that 'the EU is more influential and performing worse than I thought' may, in a next step, unaided by further information, conclude that national politicians are not performing so badly after all" (Kumlin, 2011, p. 579). Therefore it should not come as a surprise that in Brexiteers' text and talk, positive presentation of the in-group (Britain, 'us') is sometimes combined with more or less subtle negative presentation of the European Union as an out-group.

Example 6: 'not in Luxembourg'

In Theresa May's statement on triggering the Brexit process, the positive self-presentation of the UK is reinforced by casting the EU as a negative out-group that limits the sovereignty of the UK and its government. Speaking of the positive outlook for Britain outside of the EU, May said:

> (10) Leaving the European Union will mean that our laws will be made in Westminster, Edinburgh, Cardiff and Belfast. And those laws will be interpreted by judges not in Luxembourg, but in courts across this country (May, 2017).

In terms of argumentation, these sentences could be seen as evidence (premises) that May provides in support of the standpoint that leaving the EU is good for Britain. It is necessary to explicate the unstated warrants, i.e. presumably commonsensical conclusion rules that link the stated premises with the conclusion (see Reisigl, 2014). Here, the warrant that May relies on could be restated as follows: 'If the laws of a country cannot be made and interpreted exclusively within that country, then this is bad and should be changed'. In the first sentence, May expects her audience to regard it as common knowledge that as long as the UK is a member of the EU the laws enforced in Britain cannot be made in Britain. In the second sentence, 'Luxembourg' stands metonymically for the European Court of Justice, the highest court in matters of EU law, and May presumes that her audience believes that as long as the UK is a member of the EU the laws enforced in Britain can only be interpreted by the European Court of Justice. In sum, the EU is cast as having complete control over a member state's legislation and courts – notwithstanding that EU law is designed to be subsidiary to comprehensive rules in each member state, and that the representatives of each member state, including the UK, are actually active participants in shaping EU legislation. It could be said that May is exploiting any limited (or distorted) understanding that her audience may have of the complicated multilevel governance system of the EU as well as the well-documented tendency of many EU citizens to blame 'Europe' for their woes (Hobolt & Tilley, 2014).

Example 7: 'there is no demos'

Similar assumptions are reflected in the Foreign Secretary Boris Johnson's 'Uniting for a Great Brexit' speech that he delivered on 14 February 2018. He claimed that Brexit 'is the expression of a legitimate and natural desire for self-government' and said:

> (11) If we are going to accept laws, then we need to know who is making them, and with what motives, and we need to be able to interrogate them in our own language, and we must know how they came to be in authority over us and how we can remove them. And the trouble with the EU is that for all its idealism, which I acknowledge, and for all

> the good intentions of those who run the EU institutions, there is no demos – or at least we have never felt part of such a demos – however others in the EU may feel (Johnson, 2018).

In the first sentence, Johnson lists what might be called the epistemic preconditions of democracy: the kinds of knowledge that are supposedly required by the British people ('we') to accept laws enforced in their country. In the following sentence, he implies that the EU does not possess any of these democratic qualities: that is, the EU is undemocratic. He somewhat obscures and softens this rather harsh evaluation – probably so as to avoid offending his colleagues in the EU – by using the term 'demos' (the populace of a democracy) rather than 'democracy', and by attributing some positive characteristics ('idealism', 'good intentions') to the EU. By insisting that 'we have never felt part of such a demos – however others in the EU may feel', Johnson exploits discursive group polarisation between Britain ('we') and the EU ('others') to suggest that the British people are, and have always been, united in their rejection of the 'undemocratic' European political system. His argument of the missing 'demos' rests on an unstated warrant that nation states are the only legitimate form of government – an understanding that is probably not shared by the millions who voted Remain (McCabe, 2018).

Example 8: 'we can't be blackmailed'

On 1 September 2017, a leading pro-Brexit cabinet minister, the International Trade Secretary Liam Fox, gave an interview on the progress of the first part of the exit negotiations over the departure settlement with the EU. Asked by ITV News whether it was time for the UK government to agree on the financial settlement to speed up the talks, Fox said:

> (12) We can't be blackmailed into paying a price on the first part. We think we should begin discussions on the final settlement because that's good for business, and it's good for the prosperity both of the British people and of the rest of the people of the European Union (quoted in Dinnen, 2017).

Here, the verb 'blackmail' functions as an important framing device. Its use evokes the image of the European Union as a metaphorical villain who is threatening the UK. By extension, this implies that the UK and its government ('we') should be seen as victims. Thereby, in addition to attributing negative intentions to the EU, the government assumes a role that by definition excludes deserving blame for any harm or loss caused in the Brexit process.

Fox's use of the language of extortion precipitated much critical response in Britain (Blitz, 2017; Deng, 2017; Wearmouth, 2017). So this example also serves as a useful reminder that officeholders' rhetorical attempts at shifting blame may sometimes backfire.

Dealing with charges of inconsistency

Lack of consistency in politicians' actions – including between their earlier and current statements – is generally seen as negative. Therefore, when accused of inconsistency, they may try to change the topic to avoid addressing the criticism, claim that there has been a misunderstanding, deny the inconsistency, cast it in a positive light or retract the earlier standpoint to maintain the current one (Andone, 2013). As mentioned above, some Conservative cabinet members had delivered pro-Remain statements before the referendum but apparently changed their stance after Leave won. Moreover, in 2016, some ministers had made optimistic forecasts and promises about the Brexit process that, after the beginning of the exit negotiations in 2017, they did not stand by any more. I bring two examples of how Brexiteers tried to deal with charges related to such inconsistencies.

Example 9: 'I don't answer hypothetical questions'

On 25 April 2016, less than two months before the Brexit referendum, the then Home Secretary Theresa May gave a speech on the opportunities and risks of the UK's membership of the EU. She stuck to the government line and concluded: 'I believe it is clearly in our national interest to remain a member of the European Union' (May, 2016). However, when she became the leader of the Conservative party and formed a new Cabinet in the aftermath of the referendum, she promised to 'deliver the Brexit people voted for'. Therefore, she was seen by many as leading the UK in a direction that only a few months earlier she advocated was not in the country's best interests.

The inconsistency between May's pre- and post-referendum standpoints came into sharp focus during the Prime Minister's radio appearance on LBC on 10 October 2017, when the interviewer Iain Dale asked her whether she would vote for Brexit if there was another EU referendum. Here is an excerpt from the transcript of that interview:

(13)	Interviewer:	If there was a Brexit vote now, would you vote Brexit? [. . .]
	May:	I don't answer hypothetical questions [. . .] I voted Remain. Circumstances move on. I think we should all be focused on delivering Brexit. You're asking me to say how would I vote now against a different background (quoted in Swinford, 2017).

In this example, the interviewer asks a closed question but the Prime Minister does not give a straight 'yes' or 'no' answer. First, May tries to opt out by making a metacommunicative observation about the type of the first question ('hypothetical') and indicating that answering that would violate a norm that supposedly governs her communicative choices ('I don't answer hypothetical questions').

By sidestepping the question, May probably attempts to avoid upsetting both sides of the Brexit debate, knowing that Leave voters would get angry if she expressed doubts about her commitment to Brexit while Remain voters would increasingly blame her for hypocrisy if she completely backtracked from her pre-referendum pro-Europe stance. She then confirms her pre-referendum standpoint ('I voted Remain') as well as her post-referendum commitment to 'delivering Brexit'. She suggests that the question of possible inconsistency between these standpoints is irrelevant because the international and economic circumstances have changed.

Example 10: 'that was then, this is now'

In July 2016, two days before becoming Secretary of State for Brexit, David Davis published an article on the ConservativeHome blog where he claimed that leaving the EU would give the UK much better opportunities for negotiating free trade deals. He wrote:

> (14) We can do deals with our trading partners [. . .] quickly. I would expect the new Prime Minister [. . .] to immediately trigger a large round of global trade deals with all our most favoured trade partners. I would expect [. . .] most of them to be concluded within between 12 and 24 months (Davis, 2016).

Some 17 months later, in January 2018, Davis admitted at the House of Commons Special Committee hearing that the UK is actually not allowed to start negotiating any deals until the 29 March 2019 departure date. When pressed by the committee chair to admit that his claims about quick deals were wrong, Davis said, laughing:

> (15) What date was that [written]? I think that was before I was a minister. [. . .] Right, so that was then, this is now! (Quoted in Pasha-Robinson, 2018)

Here, Davis tries to dissociate himself from the earlier statement: he juxtaposes temporal references ('then' vs 'now'), thereby foregrounding the idea that his earlier standpoint belongs to the past and should not be compared to the current one. From the perspective of argumentation, Davis' claim rests on a presumably shared understanding that the inconsistency at hand is irrelevant because (a) people's standpoints inevitably change over time, (b) anyone who is not a cabinet minister should not be expected to provide adequate information about policy processes and (c) a cabinet minister should not be held to account for what they have said before taking up their current post. While (a) could be regarded as a plausible warrant, the other two seem more problematic. From a normative point of view, which demands sincere and truthful communication from anyone who is deliberating the serious matters of public life, all politicians, disregarding the institutional position they hold at any given time, should be held to account for saying things that are evidently false.

Conclusion: avoiding blame for a highly contested policy?

In this chapter, I have explicated some of the ways in which top officeholders who planned and executed Brexit – a divisive and highly contested policy – tried to 'get away with it' by using language strategically. The discursive moves identified here – modifying the perception of agency and loss, appealing to in-group loyalty and brushing off criticism – could be typical of times of political conflict, when people in leadership positions struggle to hold on to power.

Admittedly, not every instance of discursive blame avoidance behaviour in government should be regarded as essentially negative. Understandably, officeholders try to present themselves in a positive light and make a positive case for their policies. It seems clear that Theresa May and the members of her Cabinet needed to choose their words rather carefully as they tried to avoid irritating the hard-line Leavers as well as those who wholeheartedly opposed Brexit, including Remainers within their own Conservative party. However, certain strategic uses of language for the purpose of self-preservation at any cost could be seen as manipulative and possibly detrimental to democratic debate over public issues. For instance, talking of Brexit as if it were a consensual policy could be regarded as misleading because the results of the referendum do not affirm that. Downplaying the legislative and executive powers of the national government and casting the EU as an omnipotent external actor in control of how the UK is governed seems equally misleading. Systematic ridiculing of the critics of potentially harmful policies could result in silencing certain disaffected groups and excluding them from public discussions. And the extensive use of emotional appeals to the audience's feelings of nationalism ('great union [. . .] with a proud history and a bright future') could easily derail a rational debate over the merits or shortcomings of specific courses of action. It is therefore necessary for the critical analysts of political (linguistic) behaviour to try to improve public understanding of the discursive strategies used by officeholders to deflect blame and evade accountability for loss-inducing policies.

Notes

1 The 'victims of Brexit' label has been used, for example, in relation to the UK's universities (Morrison, 2016), women (Norris, 2018), and British people living in the EU (O'Carroll, 2018). Both the results of the Brexit referendum and subsequent public opinion surveys portray a deeply divided country (Hobolt, 2016; Vasilopoulou & Talving, 2018). Critical scholars have described Brexit in terms of a broader crisis of the British state (Jessop, 2017; Jennings & Lodge, 2018) and noted that it has given rise to "fears that Britain may become less open, less diverse, and less liberal" (Gamble, 2018, p. 1229).

2 On the ways in which various identities are constructed through the ambiguous uses of the personal pronoun 'we', see Petersoo (2007) and Dori-Hacohen (2014). On the ways in which Brexit is used to perform identities, see Adler-Nissen et al. (2017).

References

Adler-Nissen, R., Galpin, C., & Rosamond, B. (2017). Performing Brexit: How a post-Brexit world is imagined outside the United Kingdom. *British Journal of Politics and International Relations, 19*(3), 573–591. https://doi.org/10.1177/1369148117711092

Andone, C. (2013). *Argumentation in political interviews: Analyzing and evaluating responses to accusations of inconsistency*. Amsterdam: Benjamins.

Blitz, J. (2017, 1 September). Liam Fox's cry of 'blackmail' over Brexit. *Financial Times*. Available (subscription) at www.ft.com/content/60c66d4e-8f09-11e7-a352-e46f43c5825d, accessed 16 August 2018.

Bulmer, S., & Qualiga, L. (2018). The politics and economics of Brexit. *Journal of European Public Policy, 25*(8), 1089–1098. https://doi.org/10.1080/13501763.2018.1467957

Davis, D. (2016, 14 July). David Davis: Trade deals. Tax cuts. And taking time before triggering Article 50. A Brexit economic strategy for Britain. Available at www.conservativehome.com/platform/2016/07/david-davis-trade-deals-tax-cuts-and-taking-time-before-triggering-article-50-a-brexit-economic-strategy-for-britain.html, accessed 16 August 2018.

Deng, B. (2017, 1 September). Brexit: David Davis declines to back Liam Fox's Brussels blackmail claim. *The Times*. Available at www.thetimes.co.uk/article/davis-declines-to-back-foxs-brussels-blackmail-claim-tgs530f7g, accessed 16 August 2018.

Dinnen, C. (2017, 1 September). Brexit: Liam Fox accuses EU of trying to 'blackmail' UK over divorce bill. *ITV News*. Available at www.itv.com/news/2017-09-01/liam-fox-eu-blackmailing-uk-into-agreeing-brexit-bill, accessed 16 August 2018.

Dori-Hacohen, G. (2014). Establishing social groups in Hebrew: 'We' in political radio phone-in programs. In T.-S. Pavlidou (Ed.), *Constructing collectivity: 'We' across languages and contexts* (pp. 187–206). Amsterdam: Benjamins.

Druckman, D. (1994). Nationalism, patriotism, and group loyalty: A social psychological perspective. *Mershon International Studies Review, 38*(1), 43–68. https://doi.org/10.2307/222610

Gamble, A. (2018). Taking back control: The political implications of Brexit. *Journal of European Public Policy, 25*(8), 1215–1232. https://doi.org/10.1080/13501763.2018.1467952

Graham, J., Haidt, J., & Nosek, B. A. (2009). Liberals and conservatives rely on different sets of moral foundations. *Journal of Personality and Social Psychology, 96*, 1029–1046. https://doi.org/10.1037/a0015141

Hansson, S. (2015). Discursive strategies of blame avoidance in government: A framework for analysis. *Discourse & Society, 26*(3), 297–322. https://doi.org/10.1177/0957926514564736

Hansson, S. (2017). Anticipative strategies of blame avoidance in government: The case of communication guidelines. *Journal of Language and Politics, 16*(2), 219–241. https://doi.org/10.1075/jlp.15019.han

Hansson, S. (2018a). Defensive semiotic strategies in government: A multimodal study of blame avoidance. *Social Semiotics, 28*(4), 472–493. https://doi.org/10.1080/10350330.2017.1334358

Hansson, S. (2018b). Analysing opposition-government blame games: Argument models and strategic maneuvering. *Critical Discourse Studies, 15*(3), 228–246. https://doi.org/10.1080/17405904.2017.1405051

Hansson, S. (2018c). The discursive micro-politics of blame avoidance: Unpacking the language of government blame games. *Policy Sciences, 51*(4), 545–564. https://doi:10.1007/s11077-018-9335-3

Hinterleitner, M. (2017). Reconciling perspectives on blame avoidance behaviour. *Political Studies Review, 15*(2), 243–254. https://doi.org/10.1111/1478-9302.12099

Hinterleitner, M., & Sager, F. (2017). Anticipatory and reactive forms of blame avoidance: Of foxes and lions. *European Political Science Review, 9*(4), 587–606. https://doi.org/10.1017/S1755773916000126

Hobolt, S. B. (2016). The Brexit vote: A divided nation, a divided continent. *Journal of European Public Policy, 23*(9), 1259–1277. https://doi.org/10.1080/13501763.2016.1225785

Hobolt, S. B., & Tilley, J. (2014). *Blaming Europe? Responsibility without accountability in the European Union*. Oxford: Oxford University Press.

Hood, C. (2011). *The blame game: Spin, bureaucracy and self-preservation in government*. Princeton, NJ: Princeton University Press.

Hood, C., Jennings, W., & Copeland, P. (2016). Blame avoidance in comparative perspective: Reactivity, staged retreat and efficacy. *Public Administration, 94*(2), 542–562. https://doi.org/10.1111/padm.12235

Jennings, W., & Lodge, M. (2018). Brexit, the tides and Canute: The fracturing politics of the British state. *Journal of European Public Policy*. Advance online publication. https://doi.org/10.1080/13501763.2018.1478876

Jessop, B. (2017). The organic crisis of the British state: Putting Brexit in its place. *Globalizations, 14*(1), 133–141. https://doi.org/10.1080/14747731.2016.1228783

Johnson, B. (2017, 15 September). My vision for a bold, thriving Britain enabled by Brexit. *Telegraph*. Available at www.telegraph.co.uk/politics/2017/09/15/boris-johnson-vision-bold-thriving-britain-enabled-brexit, accessed 16 August 2018.

Johnson, B. (2018, 14 February). Uniting for a Great Brexit: Foreign Secretary's speech. Available at www.gov.uk/government/speeches/foreign-secretary-speech-uniting-for-a-great-brexit, accessed 16 August 2018. Contains public sector information licensed under the Open Government Licence v3.0.

Kumlin, S. (2011). Claiming blame and giving credit? Unintended effects of how government and opposition frame the Europeanization of welfare. *European Union Politics, 12*(4), 575–595. https://doi.org/10.1177/1465116511417296

Lakoff, G. (2008). *The political mind: Why you can't understand 21st-century American politics with an 18th-century brain*. New York: Penguin.

Leech, G. (2014). *The pragmatics of politeness*. Oxford: Oxford University Press.

Leong, C., & Howlett, M. (2017). On credit and blame: Disentangling the motivations of public policy decision-making behaviour. *Policy Sciences, 50*(4), 599–618. https://doi.org/10.1007/s1107701792904

Malle, B. F., Guglielmo, S., & Monroe, A. E. (2014). A theory of blame. *Psychological Inquiry, 25*(2), 147–186. https://doi.org/10.1080/1047840X.2014.877340

May, T. (2016, 25 April). Home Secretary's speech on the UK, EU and our place in the world. Available at www.gov.uk/government/speeches/home-secretarys-speech-on-the-uk-eu-and-our-place-in-the-world, accessed 16 August 2018. Contains public sector information licensed under the Open Government Licence v3.0.

May, T. (2017, 29 March). Prime Minister's Commons statement on triggering Article 50. Available at www.gov.uk/government/speeches/prime-ministers-commons-statement-on-triggering-article-50, accessed 16 August 2018. Contains public sector information licensed under the Open Government Licence v3.0.

McCabe, H. (2018, 21 February). Does Brexit really realise the ideals of JS Mill? Available at www.psa.ac.uk/insight-plus/blog/does-brexit-really-realise-ideals-js-mill, accessed 16 August 2018.

Morrison, N. (2016, 27 June). Brexit's first victims are already feeling the pain. *Forbes*. Available at www.forbes.com/sites/nickmorrison/2016/06/27/brexits-first-victims-are-already-feeling-the-pain, accessed 16 August 2018.

Mortensen, P. B. (2012). 'It's the central government's fault': Elected regional officials' use of blame-shifting rhetoric. *Governance, 25*(3), 439–461. https://doi.org/10.1111/j.1468-0491.2012.01585.x

Mortensen, P. B. (2016). Agencification and blame shifting: Evaluating a neglected side of public sector reforms. *Public Administration, 94*(3), 630–646. https://doi.org/10.1111/padm.12243

Moynihan, D. P. (2012). Extra-network organizational reputation and blame avoidance in networks: The Hurricane Katrina example. *Governance, 25*(4), 567–588. https://doi.org/10.1111/j.1468-0491.2012.01593.x

Norris, S. (2018, 28 March). Women: The unmentioned victims of Brexit. *Politics.co.uk*. Available at www.politics.co.uk/comment-analysis/2018/03/28/women-the-unmentioned-victims-of-brexit, accessed 16 August 2018.

O'Carroll, L. (2018, 6 June). Britons living in EU tell MPs they are forgotten victims of Brexit. *Guardian*. Available at www.theguardian.com/politics/2018/jun/06/britons-living-eu-tell-mps-forgotten-victims-brexit, accessed 16 August 2018.

Pal, L. A., & Weaver, R. K. (Eds). (2003). *The Government taketh away: The politics of pain in the United States and Canada*. Washington, DC: Georgetown University Press.

Pasha-Robinson, L. (2018, 25 January). David Davis ridiculed over Brexit exchange: 'He backtracked more times than a mountaineer with no map'. *Independent*. Available at www.independent.co.uk/news/uk/politics/brexit-david-davis-video-questioning-select-committee-mocked-a8177881.html, accessed 16 August 2018.

Petersoo, P. (2007). What does 'we' mean? National deixis in the media. *Journal of Language and Politics, 6*(3), 419–438. https://doi.org/10.1075/jlp.6.3.08pet

Propp, V. (1968 [1928]). *Morphology of the folktale*, 2nd ed. (L. Scott, Trans.). Austin, TX: University of Texas Press.

Reisigl, M. (2014). Argumentation analysis and the discourse-historical approach: A methodological framework. In C. Hart & P. Cap (Eds), *Contemporary critical discourse studies* (pp. 67–96). London: Bloomsbury.

Reisigl, M., & Wodak, R. (2001). *Discourse and discrimination*. London: Routledge.

Reisigl, M., & Wodak, R. (2015). The discourse-historical approach. In R. Wodak & M. Meyer (Eds), *Methods of critical discourse studies*, 3rd ed. (pp. 23–61). London: Sage.

Riek, B. M., Mania, E. W., & Gaertner, S. L. (2006). Intergroup threat and outgroup attitudes: A meta-analytic review. *Personality and Social Psychology Review, 10*(4), 336–353. https://doi.org/10.1207/s15327957pspr1004_4

Schlipphak, B., & Treib, O. (2017). Playing the blame game on Brussels: The domestic political effects of EU interventions against democratic backsliding. *Journal of European Public Policy, 24*(3), 352–365. https://doi.org/10.1080/13501763.2016.1229359

Smith, M. (2018, 4 July). 69% of Brits think Brexit is going badly: Who do they think is to blame? Available at https://yougov.co.uk/news/2018/07/04/whos-blame-brexit-going-badly, accessed 16 August 2018.

Stephan, W. G., Renfro, L. C., & Davis, M. D. (2008). The role of threat in intergroup relations. In U. Wagner, L. R. Tropp, G. Finchilescu, & C. Tredoux (Eds), *Improving intergroup relations: Building on the legacy of Thomas F. Pettigrew* (pp. 55–72). Malden, MA: Blackwell.

Sulitzeanu-Kenan, R. (2006). If they get it right: An experimental test of the effects of the appointment and reports of UK public inquiries. *Public Administration, 84*(3), 623–653. https://doi.org/10.1111/j.1467-9299.2006.00605.x

Swinford, S. (2017, 11 October). Theresa May refuses to say whether she would vote leave if Brexit referendum were held again. *Telegraph*. Available at www.telegraph.co.uk/

news/2017/10/10/theresa-may-refuses-say-would-vote-leave-brexit-referendum-held/, accessed 16 August 2018.

van Dijk, T. A. (1992). Discourse and the denial of racism. *Discourse & Society*, *3*(1), 87–118. https://doi.org/10.1177/0957926592003001005

van Dijk, T. A. (2006). Discourse and manipulation. *Discourse & Society*, *17*(3), 359–383. https://doi.org/10.1177/0957926506060250

van Leeuwen, T. (2007). Legitimation in discourse and communication. *Discourse & Communication*, *1*(1), 91–112. https://doi.org/10.1177/1750481307071986

van Leeuwen, T. (2008). *Discourse and practice: New tools for critical discourse analysis*. New York: Oxford University Press.

Vasilopoulou, S., & Talving, L. (2018). British public opinion on Brexit: Controversies and contradictions. *European Political Science*. https://doi.org/10.1057/s4130401801569

Vis, B. (2016). Taking stock of the comparative literature on the role of blame avoidance strategies in social policy reform. *Journal of Comparative Policy Analysis: Research and Practice*, *18*(2), 122–137. https://doi.org/10.1080/13876988.2015.1005955

Wearmouth, R. (2017, 1 September). Liam Fox told to 'get a grip' as he accuses EU of 'blackmailing' Brits. *Huffington Post*. Available at www.huffingtonpost.co.uk/entry/fox-brits-blackmail_uk_59a90619e4b0b5e530fd91cf, accessed 16 August 2018.

Weaver, R. K. (1986). The politics of blame avoidance. *Journal of Public Policy*, *6*(4), 371–398. https://doi.org/10.1017/S0143814X00004219

Wodak, R. (2011). *The discourse of politics in action: Politics as usual*, 2nd ed. Basingstoke: Palgrave Macmillan.

Wodak, R. (2017). The 'establishment', the 'élites', and the 'people': Who's who? *Journal of Language and Politics*, *16*(4), 551–565. https://doi.org/10.1075/jlp.17030.wod

Wodak, R., De Cillia, R., Reisigl, M., & Liebhart, K. (2009). *The discursive construction of national identity*, 2nd ed. Edinburgh: Edinburgh University Press.

13

BREXIT AS 'HAVING YOUR CAKE AND EATING IT'

The discourse career of a proverb

Andreas Musolff

Introduction: a proverb proven wrong?

In his book *Proverbs Are Never Out of Season*, Wolfgang Mieder, a pioneer of contemporary proverb studies ('paremiology'), includes the statement 'One can't have his cake and eat it' among the core group of proverbs ('paremiological minimum') in Anglo-American English usage (Mieder, 1993, p. 52). It is still included, in the slightly differing versions 'You cannot have your cake and eat it' and 'You cannot eat your cake and have it', in present-day proverb and idiom dictionaries, which also give an impressive history of its continuous usage dating back to the mid sixteenth century (*Brewer's Dictionary of Phrase & Fable*, 1999, p. 189; Wilkinson, 2008, p. 47; Ayto, 2010, p. 53; Speake, 2015, pp. 147–148). The 'have' of this construction means 'holding' or 'keeping possession' (*Shorter Oxford English Dictionary*, 2002, p. 1206), which contradicts the eating/consuming action schema concerning the same object. This contradiction is reflected in the proverb's meaning explanations, which converge on paraphrases such as "You cannot consume or spend something, and still keep possession of it" (Speake, 2015, p. 147).

In the non-canonical asserted version ('You are having your cake and eating it'), this combination of mutually excluding types of action may be viewed as a paradox (Abrams, 1971, pp. 119–120). Ascribing the intention for such an action to others expresses a sarcastic denunciation of their plans as absurd. It is not surprising then that the political scientist Matthew Goodwin, writing in the magazine *Politico*, employed it to criticise the British public's position on Brexit as being contradictory:

(1) Britain's 'have cake and eat it' stance on Brexit. [. . .] a clear majority of Brits (59 per cent) say that Britain should not be bound by [European courts'] judgments [. . .] At the same time, a clear majority (51 per cent) want to stay part of the European Economic Area [. . .] these are incompatible positions (Goodwin, 2017).

In another *Politico* article from the same year, the Prime Minister of Luxembourg, Xavier Bettel, was quoted with a hyperbolically enriched and, hence, even more sarcastic application of the proverb to Brexit:

(2) They want to have their cake, eat it, and get a smile from the baker. (Dallison, 2017).[1]

Uses of the proverb such as those in examples (1) and (2) are in line with its prototypical, ironic meaning as indicated above. However, the summer of 2017 also saw statements such as the following:

(3) [W]hen the Press Association asked [Jacob Rees-Mogg, Conservative MP and ardent Brexit supporter] whether the UK will be able to 'have its cake and eat it' when it leaves the European Union, [he] replied: "I like cake, I like eating it, I like having it and I like baking bigger cakes, which was Margaret Thatcher's great saying" (Hannan, 2017).
(4) The UK was already having its cake and eating it in the EU [. . .] Brexit negotiations have now stalled as the UK seeks to retain the economic benefits of EU membership from outside the union. As Britain is forced to realise that it cannot have its cake and eat it, it may yet recall that it was already doing so (Eaton, 2017).
(5) The deep relationship with the EU that Mrs May urges to be 'creatively' constructed – a continuation of the cake-and-eat-it approach Britain has sought and partly achieved as an EU member – cannot be done outside it (Hutton, 2017).

Here the seemingly absurd 'having-and-eating' combination is treated as eminently desirable and indeed as a well-established practice (example 3) or as having been fully or partly achieved as a previous position of the UK within the EU, which, from the commentators' viewpoint is, alas, no longer feasible, on account of the current Conservative government's Brexit policy (examples 4 and 5). Such an earnest endorsement of the proverb is not fully compatible with its traditional meaning. If Rees-Mogg's reply can perhaps still be explained as a facetious response to an already ironically loaded critical question, Eaton and Hutton's argumentation seems to imply that having the cake and eating it was in fact possible once – but that this previous beneficial state of affairs is now jeopardised by Brexit.

The variation in the pragmatic force of the proverb indicated by the above examples – ranging as it does from sarcastic criticism (based on the canonical version) to bold assertions of the non-canonical version (example 3) and complex differentiation of scenarios (having and eating the cake as possible before but not after Brexit) – calls for a discourse-historical analysis (Wodak, 2009) that triangulates linguistic, sociocultural and political datasets to explain the emergence of key discourse traditions. This chapter charts the discourse history of the

Brexit-related uses of the 'having-the-cake-and-eating-it' phrase (from here on, '*cake* phrase'),[2] and sets out to explain how it gained prominence in British public discourse, how its polemical exploitations made it a key metaphor to frame Brexit as a bold, promising enterprise 'against all odds' and how counter-discourses have tried to recapture its critical argumentative function.

From proverb to joke to allusion: how to have one's cake, eat it and still lose the plot

In April 2009, an almost adulatory article appeared in the conservative-leaning newspaper, the *Daily Telegraph*, about the incumbent Tory Mayor of London, Boris Johnson, who had by then been in office for less than a year. The author, Andrew Gimson, who had already published a biography of Johnson (Gimson, 2006), affectionately described him as representative of "a generous conservatism in which cakes and ale are never willingly sacrificed on the altar of some desiccated doctrine" (Gimson, 2009). Expanding on the motif of 'cakes', Gimson then recalled occasions when Johnson had been "accused of trying to have his cake and eat it" and cited him with as follows:

(6) Well, I still am [. . .] My policy on cake is still pro having it and pro eating it (Gimson 2009).

The quoted joke was not supposed to make Johnson look ridiculous in the eyes of *Telegraph* readers, who since the mid-1990s had come to appreciate his characteristically hyperbolic (and strongly Eurosceptic) articles (Gimson, 2006, pp. 90–102; Purnell 2011, pp. 106–126). On the contrary, his self-ironic use of the proverb was meant to make fun of his political ambitions, which were clearly visible but moderated by a sense of humour.

Johnson's joke was given a completely new pragmatic meaning when it was repeated in the 2016 campaign for the EU referendum, once its author had decided to become a leading figure in the Vote Leave campaign. Johnson declared himself emphatically in favour of Leave in his column in the *Daily Telegraph* (21 February 2016) while he was still in office as London Mayor. The *cake* phrase did not appear in that article but was immediately associated with him. The very next day, the *Guardian*'s former political editor, Michael White, highlighted and at the same time denounced it as an expression of the politician's wishful thinking:

(7) [He] thinks he can have his Brexit cake and eat it, that Angela Merkel [German Federal Chancellor] will say "just kidding, here's the deal I know you really want". It is cloud cuckoo land in a Europe which is slipping dangerously close to fragmentation as opportunistic rascals less charming than Boris copy his example (White, 2016).

It was, however, in the aftermath of the referendum, which took place on 23 June 2016, and in the following power struggle in the Conservative Party (which after an abortive leadership bid landed Johnson the post of Foreign Secretary) that the *cake* phrase truly became a catchphrase. Some remaining anti-Brexit voices (who were by now dubbed 'Bremoaners' or 'Remoaners' by the victorious 'Brexiteer' side; see Lalić-Krstin & Silaški, Chapter 14 this volume) reiterated White's warnings:

(8) [I]f the Brexiteers were to be proved right in their blithe promises that Britain can have all the economic advantages of EU membership with none of the disadvantages [. . .] then their French, Dutch and Danish counterparts will surely cry: "I want what they are having." After all, who would not like to have their cake and eat it? (Garton Ash, 2016).

(9) The hard task will be telling Britons who voted to Leave that the free having and eating of cake is not an option (*The Economist*, 2016).

On the other hand, Johnson and his allies recited and elaborated the *cake phrase* as a rousing slogan by playfully extending its food-related source concepts and leaving its precise political target meaning wide open, as in the following excerpt from an interview with the *Sun* in September 2016:

(10) Mr Johnson told the *Sun*: "Our policy is having our cake and eating it. We are Pro-secco but by no means anti-pasto" (*The Sun*, 2016).

By the autumn of 2016, Johnson's phrase was so widely known that foreign EU leaders picked it up and criticised it. EU Council president Donald Tusk, for instance, ironically promoted it to a 'philosophy' while debunking it at the same time at both its source and target levels:

(11) Without naming Johnson, notorious in Brussels for his jokey phrase that Britain could have its cake and eat it, Tusk criticised "the proponents of the cake philosophy" who argued the UK could be part of the EU single market without bearing any of the costs. "That was pure illusion, that one can have the EU cake and eat it too. To all who believe in it, I propose a simple experiment. Buy a cake, eat it and see if it is still there on the plate" (Rankin & Stewart, 2016).[3]

However, the final political breakthrough for the *cake* phrase as a quasi-officially endorsed strategy statement came in November 2016 when Julia Dockerill, an aide to Tory party vice chairman Mark Field who was closely involved in the government's Brexit preparations, was photographed carrying policy planning documents into the Prime Minister's Office at 10 Downing Street that contained the handwritten note:

(12) What's the model? Have cake and eat it (Bloom, 2016).

The press, which had been kept in the dark about the government's negotiation strategy by Prime Minister May's repeated 'Brexit means Brexit' assertions (Coates, 2016; Rankin & Stewart, 2016), pounced on the find, despite the government's attempts at downplaying it as "not reflect[ing] Downing Street conversations" (Elgot & Rankin, 2016). The *Daily Telegraph*'s commentator Kelly (2016) asked rhetorically, "Why shouldn't we try to have our Brexit cake and eat it too?", only to then sarcastically denounce its (non-)originality: "Brilliant! I'm surprised nobody thought of this before". The conservative-leaning *Sunday Times* admitted that the *cake* phrase had undermined the government's "attempts to give 'no running commentary'" (Coates, 2016). In the government-critical left-leaning press, the disapproval was more outspoken, bordering on derision: The tabloid *Daily Mirror* saw in the photo that "Tory 'have cake and eat it' Brexit strategy explained in all its humiliating glory" (Bloom, 2016), while the broadsheet the *Guardian* cited the Liberal Democrat Leader Tim Farron's verdict – "If this is a strategy, it is incoherent" – as well as the Scottish National party spokesman Stephen Gethin's mock-translation of the *cake* phrase into the contrasting idiom, "to cut off their nose to spite their face" (Elgot & Rankin, 2016).[4]

The *cake* phrase was by now so well established in the public arena as an expression of the pro-'hard Brexit' groups' (mainly right-wing Conservatives but also the UK Independence Party) preference that its party-political index function (i.e. as a proudly asserted slogan on their side) seemed unchangeable. The one remaining uncertainty was about its target reference. One type of interpretation focused on the government's contradictory goals of limiting immigration but retaining access to the EU single market (which presupposed freedom of movement; see e.g. Bloom, 2016); others claimed that there was an option of the UK negotiating trade deals with individual countries while it was still an EU member state (although EU member states are not entitled to conduct such independent negotiations; see Elgot & Rankin, 2016; Kelly, 2016).

Over the course of the following months, which saw the UK government formally triggering Article 50 of the Lisbon Treaty (i.e. announcing officially its intention to leave) and a national election, the *cake* phrase remained a "floating signifier" (Lévi-Strauss, 1987, pp. 63–64) in terms of its precise target reference. As a political strategy, it seemed to lose some of its significance, with several papers reporting that May's government started to recognise the infeasibility of combining all or most of the benefits of EU membership without incurring any obligations, which motivated headlines such as "Cake Off the Menu" or "'Cake and Eat It' Brexit Turns Stale" (Henley, 2017; Khan, 2017; Roberts, 2017). Perhaps British journalists felt encouraged to engage in such punning on the *cake* phrase by the Chancellor of the Exchequer, Philip Hammond, who had provided a model for mocking it when, in a speech in Germany on 27 June 2017, he quoted the German economist and politician Ludwig Erhard, who once said that "compromise [was] the art of dividing a cake in a such a way that everyone believes he has the biggest piece". Hammond then added:

(13) Wise words with some applicability to the Brexit negotiations although I try to discourage talk of cake amongst my colleagues (quoted in Ferguson, 2017).

He continued the analogy by urging his audience to work with Britain to get the best possible Brexit deal that would ensure that the UK and the EU together could '"maximise the size of the cake and each enjoy a bigger piece"' (quoted in Ferguson, 2017). This ironic *cake*-phrase application, complete with the reverential quoting of Erhard, popularly known as the 'father' of West Germany's post-war 'economic miracle', was quickly interpreted in the press as a 'dig' or 'swipe' at Boris Johnson and as setting out a 'soft' Brexit vision (Ferguson, 2017; Watts, 2018). Hammond had gone on record earlier in contradicting Johnson by asserting that Britain could not really "have its cake and eat it" (Hunt, 2017; Mason & Asthana, 2017). Now, by late June 2017, Hammond might have intended to bury Johnson's catchphrase once and for all by exposing its incommensurability with Erhard's 'wise words'. If so, he had probably not reckoned with some leading members of the oppositional Labour Party starting just then to articulate their own views on Brexit by reviving the *cake* phrase. In mid-June 2017, Lord Andrew Adonis, a Labour peer who opposed Brexit, appeared to adopt Johnson's phrase, albeit from a pessimistic perspective:

(14) If we can't have our cake and eat it then we face a serious relative decline in our living standards compared with France and Germany and I don't believe the British people will put up with that. So we would, in that event, I believe face a crisis (quoted in Zatat & Cowburn, 2017).

Following Adonis' line of thought, it could be argued that vis-à-vis the 'bad' alternative of decline and crisis as a result of Brexit (especially in its 'hard' version of maximum distance to the EU, which would equal 'neither having the cake nor eating it'), the 'good' alternative (to be pursued by Labour) would be a solution that would still allow the nation to 'have its cake and eat it,' presumably by remaining as close as possible to pre-Brexit status (along similar lines as those in examples 3 and 4 above). Two days later, Rebecca Long-Bailey, Labour's shadow business secretary, described her party's position in a BBC interview as follows:

(15) We want to have our cake and eat it, as do most parties in Westminster (quoted in Walker, 2017).

When asked by the BBC interviewer if that did not put her in the same position as that of Boris Johnson, she tried to get out of the conundrum by asserting:

(16) We need to be flexible. We've got to not cut our nose off to spite our face (quoted in Walker, 2017).

Long-Bailey's two interview statements are a non sequitur, if not a contradiction (see Gethin's criticism that used the same phrases as opposites, cited above). Accordingly, they were quickly seized upon by opponents as revealing a confused or duplicitous stance of Labour on Brexit. The Liberal Democrat spokesman, Tom Brake, gave a damning verdict that Labour's Brexit position was

(17) so indistinguishable from the Conservatives that they have started parroting Boris Johnson (quoted in Merrick, 2017).

Using mock-psychotherapy terminology, the conservative-leaning magazine the *Spectator* gleefully portrayed Long-Bailey as "channel[ing] her inner Boris Johnson" and pointed out the contrast between her stance and Labour's derision of his use of the phrase, thus making her appear hypocritical:

(18) If her words sound familiar it may be because this is what Boris Johnson once said his position on Brexit was. At the time, the Foreign Secretary's comments were the subject of mockery from the opposition (*Spectator*, 2017).

Subsequently, the *cake* phrase became a battle cry for Labour-internal divisions. When, for instance, in the late autumn of 2017, their Shadow Chancellor, John McDonnell, attempted to square his party's circle on Brexit policy again by suggesting that, if returned to power, they would abide by the Brexit referendum result, i.e. leave the single market, but also strive for a UK–EU "negotiated relationship", he was accused by the former Labour leader Tony Blair and his allies of caving in to the Tories' 'having-cake-and-eating-it' stance (Murphy, 2017; *New European*, 2017; Maidment, 2018; Walker, 2018).

For a while in autumn/winter 2017/18, the *cake* phrase seemed to be applicable to any form of Brexit strategy, irrespective of its party-political origins or europolitical effects. In addition to Labour's internal confusion, the Tory government's stance was acknowledged as shifting away from the wish of 'having the cake and eating it' (Roberts & Boffey, 2017; Wilson, 2017) but was at the same time also criticised as still pursuing what was now pejoratively dubbed 'cakeism' (Lis, 2017, 2018). Prime Minister May's pleas for a 'bespoke Brexit deal' earned her a sardonic comment from an unnamed German official, who was quoted in the ardent pro-Brexit tabloid the *Daily Express*, deriding the idea as

(19) the latest episode in the cake and eat it sitcom series (Hall, 2018).

The *Daily Express* pro-(hard) Brexit ally and tabloid competitor, the *Sun*, made the confusion perfect by claiming that it was now the

(20) EU [who wanted] to have their cake and eat it – so we must prepare for 'no deal' exit (*The Sun*, 2017).

The *cake* phrase, which the *Sun* had so triumphantly adopted from Boris Johnson (example 10), was in this case meant to refer to the EU Commission negotiator, Michel Barnier's, supposedly 'overreaching' intention to have "all his demands met on citizens' rights, [. . .] the Irish border question [. . .] and a monstrous exit bung" (*The Sun*, 2017). In this version, 'to have one's cake and eat it' is reinterpreted as merely 'getting maximum benefits', i.e. *not* the Johnsonian feat of consuming all the benefits and still keeping possession of them.[5] On the other hand, the *Daily Telegraph*, which was pro-Brexit but also concerned about the government's confused Brexit objectives, published articles advocating realism, i.e. the realisation that:

(21) The having cake and eating it Brexit fantasy is over. Time to recognise reality over our future trade with the EU (Warner, 2018).

Thus, by early 2018, after almost two years of prominent usage, changes of reference and party-political indexicality, and ironic and/or sarcastic re-evaluations, the proverb seemed to have lost its status as a generally accepted "short sentence of wisdom" (Mieder, 1993, p. 18) and to have instead become a slogan that changed its colours and pragmatic import with every politician's and journalist's particular polemic.

Analysis: interplay of metaphor, quotation and irony

Proverbially characterising some action as a form of 'having the cake and eating it (too)' can be analysed as a metaphorical mapping (Lakoff & Johnson, 1980, 1999) that carries with it a strong evaluative bias, i.e. that of criticising the referent as an impossible accomplishment. The *cake* phrase includes an experientially based metaphor, insofar as it can be linked to the everyday experience of food consumption. It has a potentially hyperbolic aspect on account of its combination of logically incompatible action schemas. When applied to a target referent that is not, strictly speaking, impossible, the criticism is exaggerated, i.e. the metaphorical proverb serves to denounce hyperbolically something that is perhaps only difficult or improbable as being impossible or absurd. It is this highly negative evaluative function that is recorded in the dictionary definitions quoted above and that informs many quotations in the present sample, i.e. all those that criticise the alleged wishful thinking of Brexit proponents (see examples 2, 7, 8, 11 and, by way of implicit contrast, 13).

We also have to take into account, however, that the great majority of the examples, i.e. 80 out of 103 (78 per cent) are in fact explicit quotations of politicians' statements, with many of the remaining 22 per cent containing implicit allusions, especially to Boris Johnson's invocation of his jokey catchphrase. In particular, his wordplay version "We are Pro-secco but by no means anti-pasto" (example 10), became so notorious that by spring 2017 a *New Statesman* article parodied its laboured Anglo-Italian wordplay and mockingly begged:

(22) Stop it, Boris! This recycling is pasta joke. If you carry on, Liam Fox will want a pizza the action. Or you'll be moved to the Minestrone of Defence [*Please, please stop – Ed.*] (*New Statesman*, 2017).

Regardless of whether they have such ostentatious parodying function or not, all quotations of, and allusions to, another speaker's application of the *cake* phrase represent second-order, meta-representational (Wilson, 2000) language uses. Thus, in their own utterance, the current speaker A (typically a journalist) quotes or alludes to a preceding speaker B's (typically a politician) use of the *cake* phrase, which can, in turn, allude to a further preceding speaker's (C) usage. Examples (11) and (13) fall into this category, with Donald Tusk and Philip Hammond (B) being quoted in the press (A) as mocking Johnson's catchphrase (C). Other instances of such meta-meta-representation are (17) and (18), where a Labour politician is quoted and accused by a commentator of naively (or hypocritically) 'parroting' Johnson. In many of these meta-representations the respective current speaker A goes to some length to explain to his or her audience the 'pedigree' of the *cake* phrase, going back to Boris Johnson's 2016 use as well as the argumentative and/or polemical purpose of the first-order representation.

A further group of meta-representations in the data, however, give no such explanation and assume readers' familiarity with the catchphrase and its history, so that the latter is only alluded to, as in examples (19) and (21) or in the neologism 'cakeism',[6] which suggests a comparison of the government's policy with terms for political and/or philosophical systems such as communism, liberalism etc. In these uses, the authors tacitly assume that readers are familiar with, or at least vaguely aware of, a 'track record' of the proverb template. This identifiability concerns not just the general history of the proverb; after all, proverbs are commonly assumed to have been passed on through many generations (Mieder, 1993, p. 23). Yet to understand the reference in new coinings such as 'cakeism' or the 'cake and eat it sitcom series', readers must be aware of the topical micro-history that has developed during the Brexit debate; only when this discourse tradition has been meta-represented can they process the evaluative stance taken by the current speaker (A), i.e. an ironic denunciation.

Besides quotations and allusions, however, we also find throughout the corpus prima facie cases that are not meta-representational, such as (1), (9) and (20), which apply the proverb as a sarcastic denunciation, without alluding to any preceding speaker (B or C). Nonetheless, it could be argued that the high density of usage of the proverb and its quoted instances in the public debate over a relatively short space of time (two to three years) have created a heightened intertextual awareness on the part of the reading audience, so that every new use provides a vague echo of its previous uses, even if there are no explicit or inferable allusions to them. For attentive press readers in particular, even apparently non-allusive examples may thus have weak ironic implicatures.

This latter aspect may provide a solution for the initially puzzling stance in examples (4), (5) and also (14). Here we have leftist-leaning and Brexit-critical voices (i.e. Eaton, Hutton, Lord Adonis) referring to a past or future possibility of Britain 'having its cake and eat it' in EU politics. In (4) and (5) the favourable 'have-and-eat' condition is predicated on Britain's pre-Brexit position; in (14), the UK's previous position is hinted at implicitly as the opposite of a Brexit-caused 'serious relative decline in our living standards', which the British people will not 'put up with'. As the author of (14) still holds out some hope of preventing such a disaster, he must implicate the possibility of maintaining at least part of the favourable condition, presumably as an optimistic perspective for a future Labour government. In all three cases, the 'having-one's-cake-and-eat-it' condition is not asserted as a description of a state of affairs but rather its mention hints at a chance that has either been lost or is difficult to regain.

On the other hand, there are two cases where the 'have-and-eat' condition appears to be simply asserted as describing a speaker's own present position or future preference, as in examples (12) and (15), i.e. the photographed Brexit memo and Long-Bailey's interview statement. Unlike the hyperbolic assertions such as those made by Boris Johnson and Jacob Rees-Mogg (examples 3, 6 and 10), this small group of utterances includes no meta-representational referencing. The speakers seem to be unaware of the proverb's canonical, negated version and employ it instead as an expression for getting maximum benefit out of negotiations. The conceptual range of proverb applications to Brexit thus ranges from canonical negation and counter-canonical assertion to meta-representational uses (quotations, allusions) and to reductive reinterpretations as in (12) and (15).

Conclusions: conceptual variation and pragmatic drift

Summarising the above findings we can identify four main types of applying the proverb 'You can't have your cake and eat it' to Brexit:

(a) Boris Johnson's initially self-ironic, deliberately hyperbolic and counter-proverbial claim that he could 'have the cake and eat it' as regards his political ambitions; this was later repeated and provocatively re-asserted as an expression of defiance against Brexit opponents during the Leave campaign.

(b) A responding denunciation of Johnson and other Brexiteers' professed optimism by Brexit opponents who highlighted an alleged impossibility of leaving the EU and still enjoying (most of) its economic benefits. The respective speakers apply the proverb in its canonical negated form as a (negative) prediction about the outcome of such a strategy ('you cannot have . . . '), implying that Brexit would be a disaster.

(c) Meta-representational quotations of, and allusions to, the proverb as applied to Brexit with the purpose of ironically or sarcastically referencing a preceding speaker (or group of speakers) as ridiculously naïve or over-optimistic.

(d) Reductive re-interpretations of the proverb in terms of a non-paradoxical expression of the intention to maximise benefits as a straightforward desirable or favourable condition, i.e. as having more than one available benefit.

Quantitatively, the critical usage types (b) and (c) provide the bulk of the sample (103 texts = 100 per cent) with 42 and 46 instances each, totalling 88 (85 per cent) of all instances, whereas type (a), i.e. unequivocal endorsements of the notion that the UK 'could have its cake and eat it' in Johnson's pro-Brexit sense account for only 13 (13 per cent) occurrences,[7] and type (d) for the remainder with just two occurrences in the sample (2 per cent). The types appear to exist side by side and build a micro-tradition of public discourse within the Brexit debate that derives its coherence from explicit and implicit intertextual referencing. The ratio of about 1:9 between assertive and critical uses indicates that the *cake* phrase was predominantly (and increasingly) being used to deride a maximally optimistic Brexit planning, i.e. ironically confirming the proverb's canonical implicature.

The high amount of metarepresentational and often ironic uses within the sample indicates a humorous, entertaining effect of the proverb's application to the Brexit conundrum. Journalists and politicians on all political sides made a special effort in construing new versions, puns and intertextual links (e.g. in examples 2 and 13) in order to achieve a "change of context, change of focus and change of perspective" (Bublitz, 2015, p. 4). They thus can negotiate a "metastance" (Vandergriff, 2012) that adds further rhetorical value to their contribution to the public debate, exploiting as they do both the primary stance of the proverb in its canonical form (i.e. that it is impossible to have the cake and eat it) and also that of Johnson's non-canonical reformulation (example 6).

The functioning of this intertextual echo-system is based on the well-known proverb as a shared conceptual platform. It acts as the basis for a figurative 'scenario' with experiential grounding and a narrative-evaluative content that provides default conceptual input for framing political topics (Musolff, 2016, pp. 25–53). When used prominently (e.g. on account of a specific speaker, a specific situation or a salient reformulation as in Johnson's 2016 use) in a controversial and/or competitive context such as the Brexit debate, applications of a figurative idiom can become quotable targets for repetition, interpretive variation and elaboration. After a short starting phase, a pragmatic drift sets in: while the semantic core of the idiom or proverb's default meaning remains stable, its pragmatic applications become (a) conceptually more varied and (b) often characterised by meta-representational and often also meta-communicative, i.e. explicitly commenting, usage. The template scenario is thus transformed from a routine application of the idiom or proverb into an intertextual point of reference that signals party-political allegiances and serves to show the speaker's proficiency in creating common ground with his or her hearers/readers through sharing allusions, echoic irony and metastance. The pragmatic drift observed for the *cake* phrase, i.e. away from the striking, hyperbolic formulations towards critical and ironic uses of the *cake* phrase that highlight its absurdity, throws a light on the discursive development of the whole Brexit debate, indicating as it does a growing disillusionment about the chances of bringing about an optimally 'favourable condition' for Britain vis-à-vis the EU as its result. As in the case of other Brexit promises, the hope of 'having the cake and eating it' looks almost certain to be disappointed.

Notes

1 Dallison freely re-translates the French equivalent of the English proverb, which already contains the hyperbolic third element of the baker's smile: *avoir le beurre, et l'argent et le sourire de la crémière.*

2 The database for the discourse-historical overview is a 87,363 token-size corpus of 103 British press texts from the period 2015–2018, which contain the *cake* phrase or recognisable allusions to it and that is complemented by two smaller samples of French- and German-speaking press texts (each just over 10,000 word tokens) that reported on the British Brexit debate. This database is part of a larger research corpus of figurative language use in British and German debates about European Union politics, EUROMETA (Musolff, 2016, pp. 14–15). The sample of press media that include the *cake* phrase ranges across a wide political spectrum in Britain; it is drawn from print and online versions of the *Daily Express, Daily Mail, Daily Mirror, Financial Times, Marxism Today, New Statesman, New European, Daily Telegraph, The Economist, The Times, Sunday Times, The National, The Scotsman, The Spectator, The Street, The Guardian, Independent, Observer, Sun* and the *Yorkshire Post.* The French texts, which are sourced from French, Belgian and Luxembourgish media all use the French proverb *avoir le beurre et l'argent*; some also quote Bettel's version (see example 2) *avoir le beurre, et l'argent et le sourire de la crémière.* The German sources either translate it literally as a specifically English proverb or refer to it as *Rosinenpickerei* ('cherry picking', literally: 'raisin picking') or as an 'à la carte' approach, both of which have been well-established metaphors in EU debates since the 1990s (Musolff, 2000, pp. 112–114).

3 Other EU leaders who condemned or ridiculed the *cake* phrase as Brexit strategy included the EU Commission President Juncker, the former French President Hollande, Luxembourg's Prime Minister (see example 2) and the Maltese Prime Minister Joseph Muscat (Brössler, 2016; Oliphant, 2016).

4 Ayto (2010, p. 244) explains 'cut off your nose to spite your face' as "disadvantag[ing] yourself in the course of trying to disadvantage another" and traces its use back to medieval Latin and French, from where it was borrowed as a loan translation into early modern English.

5 The *Sun* was not the first to try and apply the proverb to denounce the EU's position. As early as April 2017, the *Daily Express* complained, "EU wants to have its cake and eat it! Brussels plot to dodge tariffs but STILL charge UK", referring, as it did, to alleged EU plans for an early agreement on trade tariffs while deliberately delaying one on financial services, so that Britain could be "held to ransom" (Culbertson, 2017).

6 See e.g. Greer (2017): "What is now known as 'cakeism' – the idea that the UK can have everything it wants merely because it wants it – is becoming, like climate-change denial, the subject of rational discussion." See also Lis (2017, 2018).

7 Of these Brexit-endorsing uses, 11 group into the period September 2016–September 2017, with two outliers in December 2017.

References

Abrams, M. H. (1971). *A glossary of literary terms.* New York: Holt, Rinehart & Winston.

Ayto, J. (Ed.). (2010). *Oxford dictionary of English idioms.* Oxford: Oxford University Press.

Bloom, D. (2016, 29 November). That Tory 'have cake and eat it' Brexit strategy explained in all its humiliating glory. *Daily Mirror.*

Brewer's dictionary of phrase & fable (1999). 16th ed. Ed. A. Room. London: Cassell.

Brössler, D. (2016, 10 October). Ende mit Schrecken [A horror ending]. *Süddeutsche Zeitung.*

Bublitz, W. (2015). Introducing quoting as a ubiquitous meta-communicative Act. In J. Arendholz, W. Bublitz, & M. Kirner (Eds), *The pragmatics of quoting now and then* (pp. 1–26). Berlin: de Gruyter.

Coates, S. (2016). 'Have cake and eat it': Aide reveals Brexit tactic. *Sunday Times*, 29 November 2016.

Culbertson, A. (2017, 3 April). EU wants to have its cake and eat it! Brussels plot to dodge tariffs but STILL charge UK. *Daily Express.*

Dallison, P. (2017, 31 August). A brief history of having cake and eating it. *Politico.*

Eaton, G. (2017, 14 September). The UK was already having its cake and eating it in the EU. *New Statesman.*

Economist, The (2016, 25 June). A tragic split.

Elgot, J., & Rankin, J. (2016, 29 November). Minister dismisses 'have cake and eat it' Brexit notes. *Daily Mirror.*

Ferguson, K. (2017, 27 June). Hammond mocks Boris for 'cake and eat' it Brexit plan in fresh sign of Cabinet splits as he appeals for Germans not to let 'petty politics' damage trade after the UK exits the EU. *Daily Mail.*

Garton Ash, T. (2016, 2 June). As an English European, this is the biggest defeat of my political life. *Guardian.*

Gimson, A. (2006). *Boris: The rise of Boris Johnson.* London: Simon & Schuster.

Gimson, A. (2009, 10 April). Has Boris Johnson left the buffoon behind? *Daily Telegraph.*

Goodwin, M. (2017, 27 September). Britain's 'have cake and eat it' stance on Brexit. *Politico.*

Greer, B. (2017, 15 September). The delusions of cakeism. *New European.*

Hall, M. (2018, 10 January). 'It takes two to tango!' Hammond tells EU business chiefs to protect UK from EU punishment. *Daily Express.*

Hannan, M. (2017, 10 July). Jacob Rees-Mogg on Brexit: 'I like cake and I like eating it'. *The National.*

Henley, J. (2017, 4 July). Brexit weekly briefing: cake off the menu as hard choices loom. *Guardian.*

Hunt, T. (2017, 30 March). 'Believe in Britain' Johnson hails Brexit & claims UK will have the 'best of both worlds'. *Daily Express.*

Hutton, W. (2017, 24 September). Mrs May's falsehoods and fantasies are designed only to keep her party together. *Observer.*

Kelly, S. (2016, 29 November). Why shouldn't we try to have our Brexit cake and eat it too? *Daily Telegraph.*

Khan, S. (2017, 2 July). Brexit: Britain drops 'have cake and eat it' strategy as officials resigned to single market trade-off. *Independent.*

Lakoff, G., & Johnson, M. (1980). *Metaphors we live by.* Chicago, IL: University of Chicago Press.

Lakoff, G., & Johnson, M. (1999). *Philosophy in the flesh: The embodied mind and its challenge to Western thought.* New York: Basic Books.

Lévi-Strauss, C. (1987). *Introduction to Marcel Mauss.* London: Routledge.

Lis, J. (2017, 29 November). Face it: Brexit means choosing – not having our cake and eating it. *Guardian.*

Lis, J. (2018, 10 January). David Davis's petulant leaked letter is the latest slice of Brexit cakeism. *Guardian.*

Maidment, J. (2018, 4 January). Tony Blair attacks Jeremy Corbyn's 'cake and eat it' approach to Brexit. *Daily Telegraph.*

Mason, R., & Asthana, A. (2017, 29 March). Philip Hammond on leaving EU: 'We can't have our cake and eat it'. *Guardian.*

Merrick, R. (2017, 16 July). Key Corbyn ally steals Boris Johnson's infamous 'have cake and eat it' line on Brexit. *Independent.*

Mieder, W. (1993). *Proverbs are never out of season: Popular wisdom in the modern age.* Oxford: Oxford University Press.

Murphy, N. (2017, 27 November). John McDonnell had a chance to shine with the budget, but he blew it. *Guardian.*

Musolff, A. (2000). *Mirror images of Europe: Metaphors in the public debate about Europe in Britain and Germany*. Munich: iudicium.

Musolff, A. (2016). *Political metaphor analysis: Discourse and scenarios*. London: Bloomsbury.

New European (2017, 11 December). Now McDonnell says Labour would try to stay in 'reformed single market'.

New Statesman (2017, 6 April). The A to Z of Brexit.

Oliphant, V. (2016, October 5). Britain can't 'have its cake and eat it': Brussels will gang up on UK over Brexit talks. *Daily Express*.

Purnell, S. (2011). *Just Boris: Boris Johnson: The irresistible rise of a political celebrity*. London: Aurum Press.

Rankin, J., & Stewart, H. (2016, 14 October). EU council president: it's hard Brexit or no Brexit at all. *Guardian*.

Roberts, D. (2017, 3 July). Brexit: British officials drop 'cake and eat it' approach to negotiations. *Guardian*.

Roberts, D., & Boffey, D. (2017, 26 September). Donald Tusk: UK is dropping cake-and-eat-it approach to Brexit. *Guardian*.

Shorter Oxford English dictionary (2002). Vol. I. Eds. W. R. Trumble & A. Stevenson. Oxford: Oxford University Press.

Speake, J. (Ed.) (2015). *Oxford dictionary of proverbs*. Oxford: Oxford University Press.

The Spectator (2017, 16 July). 'Steerpike'. Watch: Rebecca Long-Bailey channels her inner Boris Johnson.

The Sun (2016, 30 September). 'WE'LL HAVE OUR CAKE AND EAT IT' [Interview with Boris Johnson].

The Sun (2017, 21 November). THE SUN SAYS: EU want to have their cake and eat it – so we must prepare for 'no deal' exit.

Vandergriff, I. (2012). Taking a stance on stance: Metastancing as legitimation. *Critical Approaches to Discourse Analysis Across Disciplines*, *6*(1), 53–75.

Walker, P. (2017, 16 July). Labour's Long-Bailey: 'We want to have our cake and eat it' on Brexit. *Observer*.

Warner, J. (2018, 9 February). The having cake and eating it Brexit fantasy is over. Time to recognise reality over our future trade with the EU. *Daily Telegraph*.

Watts, J. (2018, 4 January). Tony Blair: Timid Labour risks becoming handmaiden of Brexit. *Independent*.

White, M. (2016, 22 February). No Boris, you can't have your Brexit cake and eat it too. *Guardian*.

Wilkinson, P. R. (2008). *The concise thesaurus of traditional English metaphors*. London: Routledge.

Wilson, D. (2000). Metarepresentation in linguistic communication. In D. Sperber (Ed.). *Metaprepresentations: A multidisciplinary perspective* (pp. 411–448). Oxford: Oxford University Press.

Wilson, P. (2017, 27 September). Donald Tusk: 'UK abandons having Brexit cake and eating it'. *The Scotsman*.

Wodak, R. (2009). The discourse-historical approach. In R. Wodak & M. Meyer (Eds). *Methods of critical discourse analysis*. 2nd ed. (pp. 63–94). London: Sage.

Zatat, N., & Cowburn, A. (2017, 14 July). Brexit compared to appeasing the Nazis by Labour peer Lord Andrew Adonis. *Independent*.

14

'DON'T GO BREXIN' MY HEART'

The ludic aspects of Brexit-induced neologisms

Gordana Lalić-Krstin and Nadežda Silaški

Introduction

The UK's decision to leave the European Union (popularly referred to as 'Brexit') has had an interesting impact on the English language. This impact has mainly manifested itself in the coinage of neologisms, which have appeared at an amazing speed during the 2016 UK referendum campaign and immediately following the Leave vote. Modelled after 'Brexit' (itself already a blend), using 'Brexit' as a source word, or being inspired by this now household word in the English language,[1] the majority of these neologisms have a common denominator: they exhibit a notable degree of linguistic creativity and ludicity (e.g. 'bremorse', 'regrexit' or 'brexhausted'). Such wordplay seems to have functions other than merely providing short-termed comic relief and showcasing the coiner's creativity. By playing with language, the speakers seem to ridicule and satirise the whole event, while at the same time expressing their political attitude. The goal of this chapter is to explore (a) the reasons why such a serious social, political and economic event as Brexit has provoked language users to be so very playful when coining new words; (b) creative linguistic mechanisms applied in the formation and use of Brexit-induced neologisms; and (c) any pragmatic functions this ludicity may be fulfilling.

The discussion will be based on material that was compiled in the period from June to November 2016 (i.e. closely preceding and following the 23 June referendum) from various types of sources: news media (broadcast and online), social media such as Facebook and Twitter, blogs and internet forums. Available photographs and videos taken during some of the pro-Brexit and pro-EU protests held in the UK around the time of the referendum were also examined in search of any new Brexit-related words. While most words come from British media, the sources were not limited geographically and include non-British texts as well. The process of compiling the list of new words was not systematic but is rather a result of extensive reading and following media coverage on the topic. A number of neologisms which have appeared during the post-referendum period will also be taken into account, with the most recent example dating from February 2018. The list includes 228 words and although it is not exhaustive and more neologisms may be expected in the future as new Brexit-driven political and economic developments continue to unfold, it allows us to analyse these neologisms as a mechanism that public discourse participants deploy in order to express their attitude towards, and involvement in, a major political event.

The linguistic story of 'Brexit' begins with the 2012 crisis in Greece, when 'Grexit 'was coined to denote "the possibility of Greece leaving the Eurozone" (Maxwell, 2016). The Greek crisis sparked the formation of other witty neologisms, such as 'drachmageddon', 'Grexodus', 'Acropalypse' or 'Acropolis Now',[2] referring to various aspects of the economic and political turmoil in that country. As the crisis threatened to spread across the EU, names for similar hypothetical or possible scenarios in other countries quickly sprang: 'Spanic', 'Spexit', 'Spailout' and 'Spaindemonium' for Spain, 'Itexit' and 'Italexit' for Italy, 'Portexit' and 'Portuxit' for Portugal, as well as a general word for the demise of the euro as the common EU currency, 'eurogeddon'.[3] Later in 2012 'Brexit' was coined (see Lutzky & Kehoe, Chapter 7 this volume), and after its relatively short co-existence with 'Brixit', another new word coined to refer to the same event, 'Brexit' soon established itself as a household word in the English lexicon and was added to the Oxford English Dictionary in March 2017. However, this was just the beginning of a true explosion of Brexit-related neologisms (or would that be a 'Brexplosion'/'Brinvasion' of the 'Brexicon'?), many of which feature ludicity and humour.

The chapter is structured in the following way: in the next section we address the issue of the recent informalisation of political discourse, especially as triggered by the appearance of digital media, stressing the fact that the process of coining new words (particularly through the process of blending) may be considered one of the characteristics of such a changed public discourse. The section after that deals with the main reasons why Brexit has provoked unprecedented linguistic creativity and triggered a myriad of novel forms. The fourth section is an account of the main features of Brexit-induced blends which make them playful and ludic. The focus of the subsequent section is possible pragmatic functions that may be fulfilled by playing with language via the coinage of Brexit-induced neologisms, in addition to providing short-term comic relief and showcasing the coiner's creativity. Finally, we offer some concluding remarks.

Informalisation of political discourse and neologisms

A trend towards the informalisation, democratisation or conversationalisation[4] (Fairclough, 1994) of public discourse (of which political discourse, both primary and secondary[5] is an integral part) has long been recognised as one of the major developments in media discourse (e.g. Leech, 1966; Fairclough, 1992, 1995;

Bell, 1995; Talbot, 2007). This trend is characterised by an increased level of informality in the media (Breeze, 2015), which is manifested in the blurring of the boundary between the public and private spheres of social life (Fairclough, 1992), in intertextuality (ibid.) and in the "deployment of a distinct style of communication" (Talbot, 2007, p. 25), often referred to as a "public colloquial" language (Leech, 1966; Fairclough, 1995).

It is now common knowledge that the emergence of the Internet has had a profound effect on public discourse (both written and oral) in that it enabled ordinary users of language to have their voices heard and reach out to an unprecedentedly large audience, at the same time preserving their anonymity (the importance of the Internet in this regard has been discussed, among others, in Hacker and van Dijk, 2000, who call this development "digital democracy"; see also Hill & Hughes, 1998; Kellner, 1999; Papacharissi, 2004; Janssen & Kies, 2005). As Goodman (1996, p. 146) points out, the informalisation of public discourse implies "that there is a requirement for English speakers generally not only to deal with, and respond to, this increasingly [. . .] informal English, but also to become involved in the process". This is particularly true when it comes to events of great political, economic and social importance, of which Brexit is a prime example. Both ordinary English speakers actively taking part in the Leave or Remain campaigns or being simply observers of events, as well as newspaper reporters and journalists, reacted promptly and "readily embraced the chance to manifest their linguistic creativity" (Lalić-Krstin & Silaški, 2018, p. 6), sometimes even making a lasting contribution to the English lexicon with newly coined words.

The main markers of informal English as increasingly used in the media are the following: modified terms of address, contraction of negatives or auxiliary verbs, increased use of colloquialisms and slang, common use of active instead of passive voice, situationally adapted intonation (Goodman, 1996) and a changed use of personal pronouns (e.g. Breeze, 2015), with some more recent markers triggered by the emergence of social media, such as more variation in grammar and spelling (Lee, 2011) and the use of emoticons and emojis (Spina, 2016, p. 280). To this list, which is by no means exhaustive, we can add the process of new word coinage, particularly blending as the word formation process "in which different ideas are brought together into a new, integrated concept by simply fusing the corresponding words into a single lexical item" (Kemmer, 2003, p. 69). We are witnessing, almost on a daily basis, the emergence of new blends in English, many of which are one-off, nonce word forms, where speakers and hearers need to expend a great deal of effort in recognising the source words. These blends "are coined by speakers online to fit a specific communicative purpose, and may or may not become part of the shared lexicon of the linguistic community" (Benczes, 2009, p. 49). Therefore, from the perspective of word formation, the participation of "ordinary people" in public discourse on the Internet is of particular importance, since it facilitates the fast dissemination of newly coined words that in the pre-Internet era would have probably remained idiosyncratic one-off forms, unlikely to produce any noticeable or lasting impact on the English language. In this ongoing process of using "colloquial language and informal register" (Breeze, 2015, p. 8) in public/political discourse, of which the use of neologisms is the paradigmatic example, digital media have played a major role. This especially refers to social media, such as Facebook or Twitter, which have largely contributed to a changing landscape of public discourse nowadays. Social media, therefore, have provided a convenient channel through which neologisms are disseminated all over the virtual world, which increases the likelihood that they will be conventionalised, lexicalised and institutionalised in the English language.

The flood of new coinages inspired by Brexit and the speed with which they are still (and probably will be) multiplying is fascinating. The next section discusses what may account for such unprecedented speed and playfulness in reacting linguistically to a political event, and why the speakers of English have so readily manifested their ludicity in wordplay.

Why has Brexit triggered such a myriad of neologisms?

There are linguistic and extra-linguistic factors that led to an explosion of blends surrounding Brexit immediately before and after the UK referendum, i.e. the reasons why such a serious social, political and economic event has provoked language users to be so very playful when coining new words.

Linguistic factors

In his account of the reasons why Brexit triggered so many new words, Kelly (2016) offers the phonological suitability of the blend itself as one of the possible explanations for the proliferation of Brexit-induced neologisms, together with the fact that the word 'Brexit' welcomed prefixes and suffixes due to the familiarity of the blend's lexical load. In our data two tendencies are observable in relation to the word formation behaviour of 'Brexit': it is being used both as a constituent in the formation of other blends and as a base in the process of affixation, both quite atypical of novel blends. Blends are not usually used to form other blends, probably because it would greatly impede interpretation due to low transparency. However, 'Brexit' seems to be an exception: 'bremain', 'breverse', 'Brexiversary', 'Brexile', 'brextard', 'brexciting', 'Brextrovert', 'Brintrovert', etc. Likewise, newly formed blends do not usually attract affixes, with 'Brexit' again being atypical in this respect: 'Brexitesque', 'Brexity', 'Brexitish', 'brexiter', 'brexiteer', 'brexiteering', 'Brexitism', 'Brexitness', 'Brexitdom', 'Brexitana', 'Brexitly' (see also Lutzky & Kehoe, Chapter 7 this volume); with agentive affixes also being added to blends that contain 'Brexit' as a constituent: 'bregretter', 'bremainer', 'bremoaner', 'Brexshiteer'.

Compactness, closely related to language economy, is another linguistic factor that provoked a myriad of Brexit neologisms allowing the speaker "to minimise the surface complexity of the utterance while at the same time aim[ing] to maximise the information that is communicated to the hearer" (Benczes, 2010, p. 221).[6]

In other words, blends, similarly to compounds, "are able to express complex ideas in a compact, wordlike form (as opposed to expressing the same idea with a longer phrase)" (Benczes, 2009, p. 53). Compactness results in vividness, since, for example, 'regrexit' evokes a much more vivid image than its longer explication as 'regretting the decision to vote for Britain leaving the EU', as this new word suggestion is defined in the *Collins Dictionary*.[7]

As for analogy as another influencing factor regarding the proliferation of Brexit-induced neologisms, a close analysis confirms that "[t]he analogical principle can account for much of the ability of people to interpret and form new combinations; they simply make appropriate substitutions in previously learned combinations used as exemplars" (Lamb, 1998, p. 265, quoted in Benczes, 2009, p. 60). This is attested by some of the examples in our corpus such as 'Gerxit' [Germany + exit], 'Frexit' [France + exit], 'Texit' [Texas + exit] (a hypothetical scenario of Texas leaving the United States), etc., which have been readily formed in analogy with 'Brexit'.[8]

Extra-linguistic factors

Some extra-linguistic factors also affected the emergence and proliferation of Brexit-induced neologisms. At the most general level, there is a social incentive in that "other speakers and writers create similar forms by analogy simply because it is fashionable to do so; they want to show that they, too, are trendy, creative, and cool" (Lehrer, 2007, p. 116). Immediate social context played a crucial role in the formation of neologism deriving from 'Brexit' as well. As already convincingly shown in the literature, the political and social context frequently induces the coinage of new words in a language (for English, see e.g. Bauer, 1983; Benczes, 2009, 2010; Fontaine, 2017; for Serbian, Lalić-Krstin, 2014b). Therefore, linguistic creativity is not "simply an act of mind; it is also a contextual act", as Carter (2007, p. 598) points out, or, in Fontaine's (2017, p. 1) words, "[a]ny newly-formed word is formed for a purpose and therefore it is reasonable to assume that the word will bear some meaning that is related to its context of use". According to Bauer (1983, p. 42), "[w]hen a word first appears in a language [. . .] it appears that speakers are aware of its newness, that is they are aware that they are exploiting the productivity of the language system". Brexit as a major political event in British history seems to be a prime example of a context that has provided a very fertile ground for the formation of new words. By the time the UK referendum took place, "[m]any in politics, media, and, of course, the UK and Europe were long familiar with the 4-year-old Brexit" (Kelly, 2016).

Finally, following the referendum results, people turned to social media in order to process the surprising Leave victory (see also Bouko & Garcia, Chapter 11 this volume), leaning on "humor to understand, cope with, celebrate, or try to articulate such a dramatic and chaotic experience. *Brexit* wordplay was a way to participate in and make sense of this historic moment in real time" (Kelly, 2016). While trying to cope with the referendum results, unforeseen or unforeseeable by many, people resorted to humour and political satire, which "entails the use of ridicule, irony or sarcasm to lampoon someone or something, and is designed to generate laughter" (Botha, 2014, p. 364). This will be further discussed in the next two sections.

Aspects of ludicity in Brexit-induced neologisms

As noted by Lalić-Krstin & Silaški (2018), many of the Brexit-induced neologisms are lexical blends. Lexical blends, or portmanteaus as they are sometimes called, are words that are formed by combining at least two bases and that feature either (a) truncation of at least one of the bases (e.g. 'Brotland' [Br(exit) + (Sc)otland]), (b) overlap of the bases (e.g. 'Euthanasia' [*EU* + *eu*thanasia]), or (c) both truncation and overlap (e.g. 'bredictable' [B*re*(xit) + (p)*re*dictable]) (Cannon, 2000; López Rúa, 2004; Ronneberger-Sibold, 2006; Lehrer, 2007; Brdar-Szabó & Brdar, 2008; Renner & Lalić-Krstin, 2011; Renner, 2015).[9] On the whole, they tend to be informal and are generally considered to be playful, ludic formations (Bugarski, 2001; Bagasheva & Stamenov, 2013; Cacchiani, 2016; Lalić-Krstin, 2018). In his paper on blends as forms of wordplay, Renner (2015, p. 121) ranks blends very high on the ludicity continuum, saying that "blending can be claimed to be the most complex form of wordplay in word-formation".

But what is it that makes blends playful? First of all, they defy morphological rules. Unlike some of the other word-formation processes such as derivation or compounding, they are non-rule governed in that the output of the word-formation process is not fully predictable (Mattiello, 2013). As such, they are often treated as extra-grammatical phenomena (Dressler & Merlini Barbaresi, 1994; Bat-El, 2000; Dressler, 2000; Fradin, 2000; Mattiello, 2013) or as instances of what Zwicky and Pullum (1987) call "expressive morphology". As illustrated by Renner (2015, pp. 126–127), this structural transgression can occur in various aspects of blend structure: phonological, syntactic or semantic. By not complying with the rule-governed principles of morphological processes, blends are "associated with an expressive, playful, poetic, or simply ostentatious effect of some kind" (Zwicky & Pullum, 1987, p. 335). This playfulness is further enhanced by the fact that blends are frequently analogy-driven (as shown by Mattiello, 2016, 2017). Thus, for example, 'Brentry' was coined by analogy with 'Brexit' to refer retrospectively to Britain becoming a member of the EEC in 1973 and it is only through this analogy with 'Brexit' that the pragmatic effect of 'Brentry' can be appreciated.

Focusing more closely on the type of analogy that is at work here, the 'Brexit-Brentry' pair would represent a case of a surface analogy, which, according to Mattiello (2017, p. 64), is a "word-formation process whereby a new word is coined that is clearly modelled on an actual model word", i.e. 'exit' is replaced with its antonym, 'entry'. According to Arndt-Lappe (2015, quoted in Mattiello, 2017, p. 64), this type of analogy is characterised by limited productivity, producing sometimes only one analogous new word, as is the case here. In other cases, however, a whole series of neologisms are modelled upon a single word, as has happened with the words that denote hypothetical scenarios of other countries leaving the EU. Besides 'Brexit', there are: 'Auxit' [Austria], 'Oexit' [Österreich/Austria], 'Bexit' [Belgium], 'Chexit' [the Czech Republic], 'Cyprexit' [Cyprus], 'Dexit' [Denmark], 'Daxit' [Danmark/Denmark], 'Dexit' [Deutschland/Germany], 'Germexit' or 'Gerxit' [Germany], 'Fixit' [Finland], 'Frexit' [France], 'Irelexit' or 'Irexit' [Ireland], 'Italexit' or 'Itexit' [Italy], 'Luxembexit' [Luxembourg], 'Maltexit' [Malta], 'Nexit' [the Netherlands], 'Pexit, 'Portexit', 'Portugexit' or 'Portuxit' [Portugal], 'Polexit' [Poland], 'Spexit' [Spain], 'Swexit' [Sweden] and possibly others.[10] They are all clearly modelled upon the original 'Grexit', and have been created in two waves, the first started by the Greek crisis and the second by the Brexit referendum. What we have here is not a single word that is modelled on another one but the extension of a model to establish a word formation pattern, or a schema (Mattiello, 2017, p. 68), i.e. in this instance both a series of words sharing the same formation (the name of the country + 'exit') and a group of words sharing the same base ('exit').

Interestingly, the extension does not end here. Whereas all the above examples refer to the possibility of member states leaving the EU or the eurozone, a number of new words have been recorded where this meaning is extended to mean 'a country or state leaving any political union', e.g. 'Calexit' (California leaving the US), 'Catalexit' (Catalonia leaving Spain), 'Scexit' or 'Scoxit' (Scotland leaving the UK) and 'Texit' (Texas leaving the US). It has also been used to refer not to countries but other entities leaving a place or a position: 'Elsexit' (the end of subscriptions to Elsevier academic services), 'Mexit' (Lionel Messi's retirement from international football), 'Rexit' (Raghuram Rajan's stepping down from the Royal Bank of India), 'Trexit' (exit from the US on account of Donald Trump) and 'Zumxit' (the resignation of South Africa's President Jacob Zuma). Using a somewhat different word-formation pattern, this extended meaning is also found in 'BrexPitt', a humorous coinage for the divorce of the Hollywood actors Brad Pitt and Angelina Jolie. As Lalić-Krstin and Silaški (2018, p. 5) point out, the word 'Brexit' itself has also occasionally been used to mean 'any exit related to Britain', as in a headline from the *Los Angeles Times* about Andy Murray, a British tennis player: "No 'Brexit' for Andy Murray, who wins second Wimbledon title in 4 years" (Farmer, 2016), or to refer to England being ousted by Iceland in the 2016 UEFA European Championship, days after the referendum.[11] As a result, in a relatively short time, we have witnessed the rise of a new morphemised splinter, '-(e)xit', being very similar in its morphological behaviour to other such elements in English, such as '-aholic', '-licious' or '-mercial'.[12]

Two different, already existing schemata for formations with '-geddon' and '-pocalypse' have also been used: 'Borisgeddon',[13] 'Brexageddon', 'Brexigeddon', 'Brexitageddon', 'Brexitgeddon', 'Labourgeddon', 'Torygeddon', etc.; 'Brexitpocalypse', 'europocalypse', 'Torypocalypse', etc. They are both well established (Lalić-Krstin, 2014a, 2016) and refer to apocalyptic scenarios or, more often than not, not truly apocalyptic ones but presented as such for reasons of expressivity. These formations exhibit a relatively high degree of variability of form, which is one of the features of expressive morphology, according to Zwicky and Pullum (1987). If they were rule-governed, only one output would be possible that would result from the application of the grammatical rule. However, this is not the case here and with some there are several attested forms, albeit not all of the same frequency, e.g. 'Brexageddon', 'Brexigeddon', 'Brexitageddon' or 'Brexitgeddon'; 'Pexit', 'Portexit', 'Portugexit' or 'Portuxit'; 'Germexit' or 'Gerxit'; 'Brexitversary' or 'Brexiversary'.

A different type of analogy is applied in the formation of words such as 'Byegium', 'Caleavefornia', 'Czechout', 'Italeave', 'Oustria', 'Remainia', 'Retireland', 'Slovakout', 'Texodus'. They draw on an already established practice of using a blend to refer to a country or state leaving a union. Examples like these would be instances of what Mattiello (2017, pp. 65–66) calls surface analogy with no invariable parts, where the target words exhibit similarity with the model at the morphotactic and/or semantic level (Mattiello, 2017, pp. 65–66). All these examples are blends, just like 'Brexit', and are semantically similar in that they have to do with a country leaving a union.

Second, according to Renner (2015), another aspect of blend structure that makes the neologisms ludic is their formal complexity. Of course, not all structurally complex words are ludic. Blending is special in this sense because it features some phenomena not commonly encountered in grammatical morphology: disregard for morpheme boundaries (e.g. 'Caleavefornia'), segmental overlap (e.g. 'Texodus', 'brexpert') and originally non-morphemic constituents (e.g. 'Brexittastic'). It is for this reason that blends have been called "lexical puzzles" (Bugarski, 2001). Their reduced morphotactic transparency correlates with an increase in lexical playfulness (Cacchiani, 2016, p. 307) and as such, they require the reader to pause in order to solve the puzzle, which, as Lehrer (2003) claims, creates a sense of amusement and accomplishment in the reader and increases memorability.

Third, there is also graphic play (Renner, 2015). Although it is not as frequent in our data as the other mechanisms, perhaps because it typically works only in the written medium, it is nevertheless found in several examples: '€urogeddon', 'AdiEU', 'EUge (mistake)', 'EUnity', 'EUthanasia', 'Hard BreXXXit',[14] 'Oh **UK!', 'Iron MAYden'. Some exploit the paronymy between 'EU' and 'you' and frequently rely on intertextuality in order to achieve an effect, as shown by the following, all recorded on placards of anti-Brexit protesters: 'See EU later', 'All EU need is love', 'We love EU', 'Never gonna give EU up/Never gonna let EU down/Never gonna run around and desert EU', 'Want EU back for good', 'EU are my sunshine', 'Nothing compares to €U'.

One final aspect of the playfulness of blends as proposed by Renner (2015) is their functional ludicity. Renner (2015, pp. 129–130) relates the three functions of word formation – naming, information condensation and ludic functions (cf. Kastovsky, 1982) – with the degree of playfulness of lexical blends and finds that ludicity is foregrounded when the primary function of word formation is ludic, which is chiefly motivated by the possibility of maximising segmental overlap. Except perhaps for 'Brexit' itself, with the majority of words in our data the function of naming is not primary and even where information condensation is prominent, the ludic function seems to be at the fore, as shown by: 'bredictable', 'bremorse', 'bregret', 'Brexpats', 'Brexodus', 'brexpert', 'brexpectations', 'Brexshit', 'brexcellent', 'brexciting', 'brextremist', 'brextremely', 'bregret', 'regrexit', 'brepeat', etc.

Pragmatic functions of ludicity in Brexit-induced neologisms

It is not always possible to ascertain whether the communicative intention of the coiner of a ludic word is to satirise or merely to show off their linguistic creativity. Blends are often used in journalistic texts as attention-seeking devices (see Ayto, 2003 for the influence of newspapers on creating and spreading neologisms) and although a number of ludic formations in our data are clearly formed with this purpose in mind, it is still indicative that the majority of them ridicule the EU referendum and its results as well as the proponents of Brexit rather than its opponents.

Humour can have different functions in political discourse. It is often used as a means of social protest, to mock and ridicule political opponents and thus undermine their authority but also to maintain the political status quo (see for example Branagan, 2007; 't Hart, 2007 [and other papers in that issue of *International Review of Social History*]; Bal et al., 2009; Tsakona & Popa, 2011; Botha, 2014; Schock, 2015; Sombatpoonsiri, 2015). Humour can help create or strengthen the collective identity of Us vs Them, or opponents versus supporters, and create a strong sense of unity ('t Hart, 2007). As 't Hart (2007, pp. 9–10) says, "collective identities also include and refer to the style of protest, repertoires of action, forms of organization, degree of moderation or radicalism, strategies and claims, and the use of certain terms". Humour can differentiate the humourist and their sympathisers (Basu, 2007, p. 98). As Tsakona and Popa (2011, p. 4) point out, it

> contributes to social bonding between interlocutors who agree on the content and targets of humour (the so-called inclusive function of humour), and to enhancing the gap between speakers who do not adopt the same stance towards humorous themes and targets (the exclusive function of humour).

Disparagement humour in particular has been shown to enhance the solidarity of the in-group (Martineau, 1972 quoted in Ferguson & Ford, 2008, pp. 298–299).

In the case of ludic Brexit-related neologisms, the strategy of using lexical wordplay as forms of expressing disparagement seems to be more frequently directed at the winners, i.e. proponents and beliefs of the Leave camp, as evidenced by many of the above examples but also by: 'brainxit', 'Braccident', 'breverse', 'Brexshit', 'Brex(sh)iteers', 'Ukipania' (integrating the acronym for the UK Independence Party), 'Borisgeddon', 'Borisology', 'Volderage' [Voldemort + Farage], 'brextard', 'Brexwits', 'Homo Brexitus', '(Great) Brexitannia', 'Brexodus', 'Brexile', etc. The Remain camp, on the other hand, has not been mocked as much: although there are some ludic coinages that make fun of anti-Brexiters or promote the Leave vote, they are not as numerous: 'bremoaner', 'Brexmoaner', 'beleave'. This seems to be in accordance with social identity theories of humour, which see disparagement humour as a response to an identity threat by means of which positive distinctiveness is restored (Ferguson & Ford, 2008, p. 298). The results of the British referendum came as a surprise to many, especially those that voted to remain, and humour and ludicity came to the rescue, providing not only comic relief but also a means of coping with fear of an uncertain future outside of the EU.

Conclusion

In this chapter an attempt was made to explore linguistic mechanisms used for the creation of neologisms (mainly blends) that appeared immediately before and after the 2016 EU referendum, to account for possible reasons for their proliferation and explain why a major political event sparked such an explosion of new coinages as well as to shed light on any pragmatic functions of the ludicity showcased in them. Analogy, structural transgression, formal complexity, semantic extension, graphic play and functional ludicity are some of the mechanisms exploited in lexical blends to achieve wordplay. This ludicity seems to have clear pragmatic functions of ridiculing both political, ideological and personal Brexit-related targets.

Acknowledgement

The second author acknowledges funding received by the project of the Ministry of Education, Science and Technological Development of the Republic of Serbia no. 178002 *Languages and Cultures in Time and Space.*

Notes

1 For an account of the predominant word formation patterns see Lalić-Krstin & Silaški (2018).

2 Some lesser known words that have been used in relation to the Greek crisis include: 'Grimbo' [Greek + limbo], 'Gredge' [Greece + edge], 'Greekend' [Greek + weekend], 'Graccident' [Greek + accident], 'Grexident' [Grexit + accident], 'Grexhaustion' [Greece/Grexit + exhaustion], 'Grextension' [Greece + extension], 'Grelection' [Greek + election] etc. (see Liberman, 2015).

3 'Eurogeddon' can also refer to the global economic crisis of 2007–2008 and has moreover been used to refer to the English football team's poor performance at the 2012 UEFA European Championship.

4 Fairclough (1994, p. 260) defines conversationalisation as "the modeling of public discourse upon the discursive practices of ordinary life", which "involves a restructuring of the boundary between public and private order of discourse".

5 Primary political discourse is understood here as the language of traditional political genres in a variety of contexts within institutionalised politics (e.g. the language of political speeches, press releases, press statements of politicians, individual or institutional profiles on social media such as Facebook or Twitter, etc.) whereas secondary political discourse refers to the reactions of readers to primary political discourse, e.g. the language of editorials and political commentaries, whose immediate creators are not politicians but political analysts, newspaper reporters and journalists or readers/followers themselves (Silaški et al., 2009).

6 For a somewhat different view see the section on aspects of ludicity.
7 www.collinsdictionary.com/submission/17506/regrexit.
8 See the section on aspects of ludicity for a more detailed account of the role of analogy in achieving pragmatic effects of blends.
9 Not all authors agree on these as necessary and sufficient criteria for blends. For different views, see for example Kubozono (1990), Bauer and Huddleston (2002), Plag (2003), Bauer (2006, 2012), Arcodia and Montermini (2012), Bat-El and Cohen (2012), Gries (2012).
10 Note the additional ludic aspect achieved by homophony in 'Fixit', 'Chexit' and 'Gerxit'.
11 We thank one of the reviewers for pointing out this second usage.
12 Elements like these have been treated as splinters, combining forms, affixoids, libfixes and bases (see Stein, 1977; Warren, 1990; Prćić, 2005, 2008; Kastovsky, 2009; Panić-Kavgić & Kavgić, 2009; Zwicky, 2010; Mattiello, 2013; Hamans, 2017).
13 [Boris + armageddon], an allusion to a hypothetical catastrophic scenario caused by Boris Johnson's support for the Leave camp.
14 "The kinky movie dubbed 'Hard Brexxxit' shows a leggy model called 'Teaser May Not' in some raunchy scenes with a floppy-haired 'Tronald Dump'" (*Daily Star*, 16 July 2017).

References

Arcodia, G. F., & Montermini, F. (2012). Are reduced compounds compounds? Morphological and prosodic properties of reduced compounds in Russian and Mandarin Chinese. In V. Renner, F. Mazier, & P. J. L. Arnaud (Eds), *Cross-disciplinary perspectives on lexical blending* (pp. 93–113). Berlin: de Gruyter.

Arndt-Lappe, S. (2015). Word-formation and analogy. In P. O. Müller, I. Ohnheiser, S. Olsen, & F. Rainer (Eds), *Word-formation: An international handbook of the languages of Europe* (vol. 2, pp. 822–841). Berlin: de Gruyter.

Ayto, J. (2003). Newspapers and neologisms. In J. Aitchison & D. M. Lewis (Eds), *New media language* (pp. 182–186). London: Routledge.

Bagasheva, A., & Stamenov, C. (2013). The ludic aspect of lexical inventiveness. *Quaderns de Filologia: Estudis Lingüístics, 18*, 71–82.

Bal, A. S., Pitt, L., Berthon, P., & DesAutels, P. (2009). Caricatures, cartoons, spoofs and satires: Political brands as butts. *Journal of Public Affairs, 9*(4), 229–237. https://doi.org/10.1002/pa.334

Basu, S. (2007). 'A little discourse *pro & con*': Levelling laughter and its Puritan criticism. *International Review of Social History, 52*(S15), 95–113. https://doi.org/10.1017/S0020859007003148

Bat-El, O. (2000). The grammaticality of extragrammatical morphology. In U. Doleschal & A. M. Thornton (Eds), *Extragrammatical and marginal morphology* (pp. 61–84). Munich: Lincom Europa.

Bat-El, O., & Cohen, E.-G. (2012). Stress in English blends: A constraint-based approach. In V. Renner, F. Maniez, & P. J. L. Arnaud (Eds), *Cross-disciplinary perspectives on lexical blending* (pp. 193–211). Berlin: de Gruyter.

Bauer, L. (1983). *English word-formation*. Cambridge: Cambridge University Press.

Bauer, L. (2006). Compounds and minor word-formation types. In B. Aarts & A. McMahon (Eds), *The handbook of English linguistics* (pp. 483–506). Malden, MA: Blackwell.

Bauer, L. (2012). Blends: Core and periphery. In V. Renner, F. Maniez, & P. J. L. Arnaud (Eds), *Cross-disciplinary perspectives on lexical blending* (pp. 11–22). Berlin: de Gruyter.

Bauer, L., & Huddleston, R. (2002). Lexical word-formation. In R. Huddleston & G. K. Pullum (Eds), *The Cambridge grammar of the English language* (pp. 1621–1721). Cambridge: Cambridge University Press.

Bell, A. (1995). Language and the media. *Annual Review of Applied Linguistics, 15*, 23–41. https://doi.org/10.1017/S0267190500002592

Benczes, R. (2009). What motivates the production and use of metaphorical and metonymical compounds? In M. Brdar, M. Omazić, & V. Pavičić Takač (Eds), *Cognitive approaches to English: Fundamental, methodological, interdisciplinary and applied aspects* (pp. 49–67). Newcastle-upon-Tyne: Cambridge Scholars Publishing.

Benczes, R. (2010). Setting limits on creativity in the production and use of metaphorical and metonymical compounds. In A. Onysko & S. Michel (Eds), *Cognitive perspectives on word formation* (pp. 219–242). Berlin: de Gruyter.

Botha, E. (2014). A means to an end: Using political satire to go viral. *Public Relations Review, 40*(2), 363–374. http://dx.doi.org/10.1016/j.pubrev.2013.11.023

Branagan, M. (2007). The last laugh: Humour in community activism. *Community Development Journal, 42*(4), 470–481. https://doi.org/10.1093/cdj/bsm037

Brdar-Szabó, R., & Brdar, M. (2008). On the marginality of lexical blending. *Jezikoslovlje, 9*(1–2), 171–194.

Breeze, R. (2015). Or so the government would have you believe: Uses of 'you' in *Guardian* editorials. *Discourse, Context and Media, 10*, 36–44. https://doi.org/10.1016/j.dcm.2015.07.003

Bugarski, R. (2001). Dve reči u jednoj: Leksičke skrivalice [Two words in one: Lexical puzzles]. *Jezik danas, 13*, 1–5.

Cacchiani, S. (2016). On Italian lexical blends: Borrowings, hybridity, adaptations, and native word formations. In S. Knospe, A. Onysko, & M. Goth (Eds), *Crossing languages to play with words: Multidisciplinary perspectives* (pp. 305–336). Berlin: de Gruyter.

Cannon, G. (2000). Blending. In G. Booij, C. Lehmann, & J. Mugdan (Eds), *Morphologie: Ein internationales Handbuch zur Flexion und Wortbildung* [*Morphology: An international handbook on inflection and word formation*] (pp. 952–956). Berlin: de Gruyter.

Carter, R. (2007). Response to special issue of Applied Linguistics devoted to language creativity in everyday contexts. *Applied Linguistics, 28*(4), 597–608. https://doi.org/10.1093/applin/amm046

Dressler, W. U. (2000). Extragrammatical vs. marginal morphology. In U. Doleschal & A. M. Thornton (Eds), *Extragrammatical and marginal morphology* (pp. 1–10). Munich: Lincom Europa.

Dressler, W. U., & Merlini Barbaresi, L. (1994). *Morphopragmatics: Diminutives and intensifiers in Italian, German, and other languages*. Berlin: de Gruyter.

Fairclough, N. (1992). *Discourse and social change*. Cambridge: Polity Press.

Fairclough, N. (1994). Conversationalization of public discourse and the authority of the consumer. In R. Kent, N. Whiteley, & N. Abercrombie (Eds), *The authority of the consumer* (pp. 253–268). London: Routledge.

Fairclough, N. (1995). *Critical discourse analysis*. London: Longman.

Farmer, S. (2016, 10 July). No 'Brexit' for Andy Murray, who wins second Wimbledon title in 4 years. *Los Angeles Times*. Available [not in all European countries] at www.latimes.com/sports/lasp-wimbledon-mens-final-20160710-snap-story.html.

Ferguson, M. A., & Ford, T. E. (2008). Disparagement humor: A theoretical and empirical review of psychoanalytic, superiority, and social identity theories. *Humor, 21*(3), 283–312. https://doi.org/10.1515/HUMOR.2008.014

Fontaine, L. (2017). The early semantics of the neologism BREXIT: A lexicogrammatical approach. *Functional Linguistics, 4*(6). https://doi.org/10.1186/s40554-017-0040-x

Fradin, B. (2000). Combining forms, blends and related phenomena. In U. Doleschal & A. M. Thornton (Eds), *Extragrammatical and marginal morphology* (pp. 11–59). Munich: Lincom Europa.

Goodman, S. (1996). Market forces speak English. In S. Goodman & D. Graddol (Eds), *Redesigning English: New texts, new identities* (pp. 141–163). London: Routledge.

Gries, S. Th. (2012). Quantitative corpus data on blend formation: Psycho- and cognitive-linguistic perspectives. In V. Renner, F. Mazier, & P. J. L. Arnaud (Eds), *Cross-disciplinary perspectives on lexical blending* (pp. 145–167). Berlin: de Gruyter.

Hacker, K. L., & van Dijk, J. (2000). *Digital democracy: Issues in theory and practice*. London: Sage.

Hamans, C. (2017). Language change and morphological processes. *Yearbook of Poznań Linguistic Meeting*, *3*(1), 1–23. doi:0.1515/yplm-2017-0001

Hill, K., & Hughes, J. E. (1998). *Cyberpolitics: Citizen activism in the age of the internet*. Lanham, MD: Rowman & Littlefield.

Janssen, D., & Kies, R. (2005). Online forums and deliberative democracy. *Acta Politica*, *40*(3), 317–335. https://doi.org/10.1057/palgrave.ap.5500115

Kastovsky, D. (1982). Word-formation: A functional view. *Folia Linguistica*, *16*(1–4), 181–198. https://doi.org/10.1515/flin.1982.16.1-4.181

Kastovsky, D. (2009). *Astronaut, astrology, astrophysics*: About combining forms, classical compounds and affixoids. In R. W. McConchie, A. Honkapohja, & J. Tyrkkö (Eds), *Selected proceedings of the 2008 Symposium on New Approaches in English Historical Lexis* (pp. 1–13). Somerville, MA: Cascadilla Proceedings Project.

Kellner, D. (1999). New technologies, the welfare state, and the prospects for democratization. In A. Calabrese & J.-C. Burgelman (Eds), *Communication, citizenship, and social policy* (pp. 239–256). Lanham, MD: Rowman & Littlefield.

Kelly, J. (2016, 4 July). Branger. Debression. Oexit. Zumxit: Why did Brexit trigger a Brexplosion of wordplay? Available at http://leximania.gr/branger-debression-oexit-zumxit-why-did-brexit-trigger-a-brexplosion-of-wordplay, accessed 20 August 2018.

Kemmer, S. (2003). Schemas and lexical blends. In H. Cuyckens, T. Berg, R. Dirven, & K.-U. Panther (Eds), *Motivation in language: Studies in honor of Günter Radden* (pp. 69–97). Amsterdam: Benjamins.

Kubozono, H. (1990). Phonological constraints on blending in English as a case for phonology-morphology interface. *Yearbook of Morphology*, *3*, 1–20.

Lalić-Krstin, G. (2014a). Forms and meanings of the source word *armageddon* in English lexical blends. In T. Prćić & M. Marković (Eds), *Zbornik u čast Draginji Pervaz: Engleski jezik i anglofone književnosti u teoriji i praksi* [*Festschrift in honour of Draginja Pervaz: English language and anglophone literatures in theory and practice*] (pp. 257–273). Novi Sad: Filozofski fakultet.

Lalić-Krstin, G. (2014b). Upotreba slivenica u srpskom političkom diskursu [The use of blends in Serbian political discourse]. In S. Gudurić & M. Stefanović (Eds), *Jezici i kulture u vremenu i prostoru IV* [*Languages and cultures in time and space 4*] (vol. 2, pp. 355–366). Novi Sad: Filozofski fakultet.

Lalić-Krstin, G. (2016). *Morfemizacija krnjih leksičkih osnova u savremenom engleskom jeziku: Leksikološki i leksikografski aspekti* [*Morphemisation of truncated lexical bases in present-day English: Lexicological and lexicographic aspects*]. Unpublished PhD thesis. Novi Sad: University of Novi Sad.

Lalić-Krstin, G. (2018). Translating English wordplay into Serbian: Evidence from three dystopian novels. *BELLS: Belgrade English Language & Literature Studies*, *10*, 327–348.

Lalić-Krstin, G., & Silaški, N. (2018). From *Brexit* to *Bregret*: An account of some Brexit-induced neologisms in English. *English Today*, *34*(2), 3–8. https://doi.org/10.1017/S0266078417000530

Lamb, S. M. (1998). *Pathways of the brain: The neurocognitive basis of language*. Amsterdam: Benjamins.

Lee, C. K. M. (2011). Micro-blogging and status updates on Facebook: Texts and practices. In C. Thurlow & K. Mroczek (Eds), *Digital discourse: Language in the media* (pp. 111–128). New York: Oxford University Press.

Leech, G. N. (1966). *English in advertising: A linguistic study of advertising in Great Britain*. London: Longman.

Lehrer, A. (2003). Understanding trendy neologisms. *Italian Journal of Linguistics, 15*(2), 369–382.

Lehrer, A. (2007). Blendalicious. In J. Munat (Ed.), *Lexical creativity, texts and contexts* (pp. 115–133). Amsterdam: Benjamins.

Liberman, M. (2015). Grexicography. Available at http://languagelog.ldc.upenn.edu/nll/?p=19609, accessed 20 August 2018.

López Rúa, P. (2004). The categorial continuum of English blends. *English Studies, 85*(1), 63–76. https://doi.org/10.1076/enst.85.1.63.29107

Martineau, W. H. (1972). A model of social functions of humor. In J. H. Goldstein & P. E. McGhee (Eds), *The psychology of humor* (pp. 101–125). New York: Academic Press.

Mattiello, E. (2013). *Extra-grammatical morphology in English: Abbreviations, blends, reduplicatives and related phenomena*. Berlin: de Gruyter.

Mattiello, E. (2016). Analogical neologisms in English. *Italian Journal of Linguistics, 28*(2), 103–142.

Mattiello, E. (2017). *Analogy in word-formation: A study of English neologisms and occasionalisms*. Berlin: de Gruyter.

Maxwell, K. (2016). BuzzWord: *Brexit*. Available at www.macmillandictionary.com/buzzword/entries/brexit.html, accessed 20 August 2018.

Panić-Kavgić, O., & Kavgić, A. (2009). Morfeme *-burger, -furter, -holic, -scape* i *-gate* u engleskom jeziku: Reinterpretirani sufiksoidi? [Morphemes *-burger, -furter, -holic, -scape* and *-gate* in the English language: Re-combined final combining forms?]. *Godišnjak Filozofskog fakulteta u Novom Sadu, XXXIV*, 135–148.

Papacharissi, Z. (2004). Democracy online: Civility, politeness, and the democratic potential of online political discussion groups. *New Media & Society, 6*(2), 259–283. doi:10.1177/1461444804041444

Plag, I. (2003). *Word-formation in English*. Cambridge: Cambridge University Press.

Prćić, T. (2005). Prefixes vs initial combining forms in English: A lexicographic perspective. *International Journal of Lexicography, 18*(3), 313–334. https://doi.org/10.1093/ijl/eci026

Prćić, T. (2008). Suffixes vs final combining forms in English: A lexicographic perspective. *International Journal of Lexicography, 21*(1), 1–22. https://doi.org/10.1093/ijl/ecm038

Renner, V. (2015). Lexical blending as wordplay. In A. Zirker & E. Winter-Froemel (Eds), *Wordplay and metalinguistic/metadiscursive reflection* (pp. 119–133). Berlin: de Gruyter.

Renner, V., & Lalić-Krstin, G. (2011). Predicting stress assignment in lexical blends: The case of English and Serbian. In N. Tomović & J. Vujić (Eds), *Proceedings of the International Conference to Mark the 80th Anniversary of the English Department, Faculty of Philology, University of Belgrade: English Language and Literature Studies: Image, identity, reality* (vol. 1, pp. 265–273). Belgrade: Faculty of Philology.

Ronneberger-Sibold, E. (2006). Lexical blends: Functionally tuning the transparency of complex words. *Folia Linguistica, 40*(1–2), 155–181. https://doi.org/10.1515/flin.40.1-2.155

Schock, K. (Ed.) (2015). *Civil resistance: Comparative perspectives on nonviolent struggle*. Minneapolis, MN: University of Minnesota Press.

Silaški, N., Đurović, T., & Radić-Bojanić, B. (2009). *Javni diskurs Srbije: Kognitivističko-kritička studija* [*Serbian public discourse: A cognitive critical study*]. Belgrade: Centar za izdavačku delatnost Ekonomskog fakulteta u Beogradu.

Sombatpoonsiri, J. (2015). *Humor and nonviolent struggle in Serbia*. Syracuse, NY: Syracuse University Press.

Spina, S. (2016). Twitter as a source of change in political discourse. In M. Degani, P. Frassi, & M. I. Lorenzetti (Eds), *The languages of politics/La politique et ses langages* (vol. 2, pp. 259–283). Newcastle-upon-Tyne: Cambridge Scholars Publishing.

Stein, G. (1977). English combining forms. *Linguistica: Acta et Commentationes Universitatis Tartuensis Tartu, 9*, 140–147.

’t Hart, M. (2007). Humour and social protest: An introduction. *International Review of Social History, 52*(S15), 1–20. https://doi.org/10.1017/S0020859007003094

Talbot, M. (2007). *Media discourse: Representation and interaction*. Edinburgh: Edinburgh University Press.

Tsakona, V., & Popa, D. E. (2011). Humour in politics and the politics of humour. In V. Tsakona & D. E. Popa (Eds), *Studies in political humour: In between political critique and public entertainment* (pp. 1–30). Amsterdam: Benjamins.

Warren, B. (1990). The importance of combining forms. In W. U. Dressler, H. C. Luschützky, & O. E. Pfeiffer (Eds), *Contemporary morphology* (pp. 111–132). Berlin: de Gruyter.

Zwicky, A. (2010). Libfixes. Available at https://arnoldzwicky.org/2010/01/23/libfixes, accessed 20 August 2018.

Zwicky, A. M., & Pullum, G. K. (1987). Plain morphology and expressive morphology. In J. Aske (Ed.), *Proceedings of the thirteenth annual meeting of the Berkeley Linguistics Society* (pp. 330–340). Berkeley, CA: Berkeley Linguistic Society.

15

BREXIT AND DISCOURSE STUDIES

Reflections and outlook

Gerlinde Mautner

Introduction

Writing a final 'outlook' chapter for an edited volume comes with a significant privilege. It combines the luxury of meta-level reflection with freedom from onerous empirical work. While the contributors have shouldered the burden of focusing their microscopes on linguistic detail, the author of the final chapter can indulge in a bird's-eye view.

However, there are strings attached – and temptations to be resisted. For one thing, a large collection of separate pieces on an issue as complex as Brexit is bound to raise more questions than it can possibly answer, and will inevitably leave quite a few loose ends. In fact, one might argue that 'loose ends' are the whole point of a scholarly endeavour such as this, and are indeed the very antithesis of the populist approaches that the present volume critiques. An attempt to 'wrap things up', as concluding chapters are traditionally expected to do, may therefore be counter-productive. Yet there is another tension. The author of a final chapter, unlike a reviewer for example, is both inside the volume, as a contributor, and outside it, as a commentator; he or she joins in *constructing* the broader argument and at the same time fulfils a role in *deconstructing* it. In what follows, I will attempt to embrace both these dilemmas.

Plus ça change, plus c'est la même chose

Rereading, some 20 years on, my own work about British media discourse on Europe (Hardt-Mautner, 1995; Mautner, 2000), I am torn between conflicting emotions. Like so many who believe that Brexit is a huge mistake, I am dismayed that the Eurosceptic views that were so strong and widespread in the 1980s and 1990s still hold sway and have now led to such a concrete political outcome.

On the other hand, I cannot help being quite pleased – though rather guiltily so – that studies published so long ago continue to be relevant. So, on two very different levels, it is both an unpleasant surprise and a vindication to note that in British 'Euro' discourse, nothing much seems to have changed.

To this day, Britain's relationship with Europe (and I am using 'Europe' advisedly here, rather than talking about 'the EU') remains fundamentally uneasy – more fundamentally, it appears, than in many other European countries. Revisiting my own findings from the last quarter of the twentieth century, I was reminded how visceral anti-European discourses could be and that xenophobic 'Us vs Them' distinctions were always involved (although, at the time, and before immigration became a major issue, it was anti-German and anti-French sentiment that came to the fore). Perhaps most importantly, it was also clear back then that Euroscepticism had strong historical roots reaching into deep layers of national identity – witness the imaginary of the 'island nation', for example, a powerful and widely used topos then as it is now (Mautner, 2000, pp. 181–185; Wodak, 2016; Cap, Chapter 5 this volume).

Discourse and ideology

Brexit has all the ingredients that scholars in critical discourse studies (CDS) thrive on: large-scale political relevance, social rifts and power differentials, and a massive media fallout. There is the added benefit of a clear timeline with easily identifiable milestones, such as the referendum, the day Article 50 was triggered and so on. Yet clear milestones can be deceptive. Handy though they are for planning research designs, they may also obscure a vast hinterland, a difficult terrain in which historical, cultural, social and political factors interact, shaping both social and discursive behaviour. To capture these more diffuse linkages, it is necessary to look beyond the immediate impact of a particular critical incident, and ground the analysis firmly in its context, broadly conceived. That is why diachronic studies (such as Lutzky & Kehoe, Chapter 7 this volume) are so important. Hence, too, the significance of teasing out more general principles from the data – be it the "ludic" nature of language (Lalić-Krstin & Silaški, Chapter 14 this volume); intertextuality evident in the "discourse career" of a proverb (Musolff, Chapter 13 this volume); the significance of censure and ridicule in conveying value judgements (Zappavigna, Chapter 4 this volume); the binary logic of political argumentation (Bennett, Chapter 2 this volume); and of course the impact of new media on public debate (Bouko & Garcia, Chapter 11 this volume; Kopf, Chapter 10 this volume). In addressing such broader issues, this book provides insights that will be valuable beyond Brexit, both in terms of content and methodology.

One of the general issues raised by this volume is the possibility, or otherwise, of establishing clear links between ideology and discourse; or more precisely, between particular ideologies and particular linguistic manifestations. The editors see the victory of the Brexit camp (slender though it was) as a case of mostly right-wing populism being on the rise; and they view the discourses of Brexit as recontextualisations of such discourses. I would agree that these are plausible hypotheses. At the same time, I would argue that an equally compelling case can be made for seeing specifically right-wing populism as merely one of several interwoven ideological strands that together make up a complex tapestry of values, attitudes and behaviour defying straightforward – and conceptually limiting – categorisation. There is ample evidence – some of it flagged up in this volume – that in the UK, Eurosceptic beliefs and discourses have cut across party lines for a long time. In the early 1990s, George argued that "both Conservative and Labour leaders [. . .] would have faced tremendous problems within their own parties had they embraced European integration too warmly" (George, 1991, p. 82, quoted in Mautner, 2000, p. 116). By the same token, Edwards (1993, p. 210) noted that "reluctance, negativism or simple discomfort were [. . .] only too apparent from the beginning of Britain's membership". The roots of the Brexit vote thus reach far back in time, deeply into the national psyche, and widely across the political spectrum. In that context, the findings by Wenzl (Chapter 3 this volume) seem particularly relevant. Far from promoting a truly pro-European British identity, the Remain camp can be seen to have deployed an argumentative repertoire remarkably similar to the one used by Leave supporters. "Remain arguments", too, Wenzl concludes, "are laced with latent Euroscepticism" (ibid.). No wonder, then, that they weren't a real match for the Brexit campaign.

Reflections on impact

Since critical discourse analysis evolved in the 1990s – and long before the word *impact* had been appropriated by the utilitarian values of research assessment – it has been keen to make a difference in practical as well as theoretical terms. In an early programmatic paper, van Dijk (1993, p. 253) refers to critical discourse analysis (CDA) as "unabashedly normative" and being sustained by "an applied ethics". In that tradition, the present volume not only pursues analytical goals related to how discourse works, but also points towards a potential impact in the social and political arena. The present volume addresses its discourse-analytical aims in remarkable breadth and depth. But how great is its wider impact likely to be?

Ultimately, only time can tell. For the moment, though, it might be worth looking back on the past – not just in relation to Brexit, but more generally in terms of reappraising CDA's position vis-à-vis the 'real' social world. Naturally, it would be naïve to claim that CDA could ever be powerful enough to 'change the world' – eradicate racism, create gender equality, end poverty and so on and so on, all in one fell swoop. On the other hand, is crying over spilt milk really all we can do? How good are we, as a scholarly community, at contributing insights and ideas that prevent the milk from being spilled in the first place? That is, how good are we (and publishers, for that matter) at picking up weak signals *before* an issue has turned into a problem, and a problem into a crisis? If we worked harder on our timing, and improved the strength of our public voice, we would ultimately also increase the political clout of those that our critical discourse analyses profess to support.

References

Edwards, G. (1993). Britain and Europe. In J. Story (Ed.), *The new Europe: Politics, government and economy since 1945* (pp. 207–227). Oxford: Blackwell.

George, S. (1991). *Britain and European integration since 1945*. Oxford: Blackwell.

Hardt-Mautner, G. (1995). 'How does one become a good European?' The British press and European integration. *Discourse & Society*, *6*(2), 177–205. https://doi.org/10.1177/0957926595006002003

Mautner, G. (2000). *Der britische Europa-Diskurs: Methodenreflexion und Fallstudien zur Berichterstattung in der Tagespresse* [*British discourse on Europe: Reflections on methodology and case studies in daily newspapers' reporting*]. Vienna: Passagen Verlag.

van Dijk, T. A. (1993). Principles of critical discourse analysis. *Discourse & Society*, *4*(2), 249–283. https://doi.org/10.1177/0957926593004002006

Wodak, R. (2016). 'We have the character of an island nation': A discourse-historical analysis of David Cameron's 'Bloomberg speech' on the European Union. European University Institute working paper series RSCAS 2016/36. Available at http://cadmus.eui.eu/bitstream/handle/1814/42804/RSCAS_2016_36.pdf?sequence=1&isAllowed=y accessed 6 December 2018.

INDEX